THE MODERN THEATRE
Volume Three

Eric Bentley's most recent book is THE DRAMATIC EVENT, published by Horizon Press, New York.

THE
MODERN THEATRE

Volume Three
Edited by

ERIC BENTLEY

Five Plays

GAMBLERS

AN ITALIAN STRAW HAT

ONE DAY MORE

JUDITH

THIEVES' CARNIVAL

Doubleday Anchor Books 1955

DOUBLEDAY & COMPANY, INC., GARDEN CITY, N.Y.

Cover Design, Antonio Frasconi. Typography, Diana Klemin.

CONTENTS

THE MODERN THEATRE
Volume Three

GAMBLERS

A Comedy in One Act
by

NIKOLAI GOGOL

English version by
ERIC BENTLEY

Why call him a scoundrel? These days, we don't have scoundrels; we have nice people, well-meaning people. As for doing anything that might lead to your getting your face slapped in public, who among us would risk such a scandal? Well, maybe there are a few who would, two or three perhaps—but even they are busy talking virtue. Not a scoundrel, then; at worst, let us call him acquisitive; for it is acquisition that is the root of evil.

NIKOLAI GOGOL, *Dead Souls.*

ACT ONE

The home of FADINARD. *An octagonal parlor. Upstage center, double-winged doors opening into the room. A door in each diagonal wall. Two doors in the downstage side walls. At left, against the wall, a table covered with a runner, on which rests a tray with a pitcher, glass, sugar bowl. Chairs.*

SCENE 1

VIRGINIE, FÉLIX.

VIRGINIE, *to* FÉLIX, *who is trying to kiss her.* Let me go, Monsieur Félix! I haven't got time to play.

FÉLIX. Just one little kiss?

VIRGINIE. I'm not interested!

FÉLIX. But I'm a fellow townsman! I'm from Rambouillet.

VIRGINIE. Oh, well, if I had to kiss everyone from Rambouillet!

FÉLIX. The population is only 4000.

VIRGINIE. That's not the point. Your employer, Monsieur Fadinard, is getting married today. You asked me over to look at the presents. I'm dying to see them.

FÉLIX. We've lots of time. My master went to his father-in-law's last night to sign the marriage contract. He'll be back at eleven o'clock—to go to the marriage bureau with the wedding party.

VIRGINIE. Is the bride pretty?

FÉLIX. Pooh! A bit simple for my taste, but she comes from a good family. Her father is a horticulturist in Charenton-neau—old man Nonancourt.

VIRGINIE. By the way, Monsieur Félix, if you happen to hear that she's looking for a maid, let me know.

FÉLIX. You're thinking of leaving your employer, Monsieur Beauperthuis?

VIRGINIE. Don't even mention him! He's a first class grumbling old sourpuss—cross, sneaky, jealous! And his wife! Not that I believe in criticizing my employers——

FÉLIX. Oh, no!

VIRGINIE. An affected prude, no better than anyone else.

FÉLIX. My word!

VIRGINIE. As soon as my master leaves the house—bang! off she goes by herself, and where? She never tells me, never!

FÉLIX. Oh, you can't stay in a house like that.

VIRGINIE, *lowering her eyes.* And anyway, it would be such a pleasure to work with someone from Rambouillet.

FÉLIX, *kissing her.* County Seine-and-Oise.

SCENE 2

VIRGINIE, FÉLIX, VÉZINET

VÉZINET, *entering through the upstage double door; he is carrying a woman's hat-box.* Dont let me disturb you; it's only me, Uncle Vézinet. Is the wedding party here yet?

FÉLIX, *amiably.* Not yet, you venerable antique.

VIRGINIE, *in a low voice.* What's the matter with you?

FÉLIX. He's deaf as a post. You'll see.

To VÉZINET.

So we're going to the wedding, my fine young man? So we're going to cut a caper? Isn't he pitiful?

Offers him a chair.

Time to go to bed!

VÉZINET. Thank you, my friend, thank you. At first I thought

Characters

IHAREV
GAVROOSHKA, *his valet*
ALEXEY, *a servant at the inn*
KRUGEL
SHONEV
OOTESH
GLOV
GLOV JUNIOR
A CLERK

THE TIME: *Before 1840*

THE PLACE: *A room in an inn in provincial Russia*

Enter IHAREV, *accompanied by* ALEXEY *and* GAVROOSHKA.

ALEXEY. Please come in, sir. Nice little room, sir. Quiet. No noise at all, sir.

IHAREV. That's fine. How about the imperial cavalry?

Pointing to the bed.

ALEXEY. Fleas, sir? If you're bitten by fleas, we take the whole responsibility, sir.

IHAREV, *to* GAVROOSHKA. Bring my things from the carriage, Gavrooshka.

Exit GAVROOSHKA. *To* ALEXEY.

What's your name, my good man?

ALEXEY. Alexey, sir.

IHAREV. I'm Mr. Iharev. Who's staying here right now?

ALEXEY. Oh, a lot of people, sir.

IHAREV. Such as?

ALEXEY. Such as Mr. Ootesh, Mr. Shonev, and Colonel Krugel, sir.

IHAREV. They play cards?

ALEXEY. They've been playing for six nights running, sir.

IHAREV. Here's a couple of rubles!

Thrusts them into his hand.

ALEXEY, *bowing.* Much obliged, I'm sure, sir.

IHAREV. There's more where that came from.

ALEXEY. Glad to hear it, sir.

IHAREV. They play—among themselves?

ALEXEY. No, no, sir. First they played with Lieutenant Artunovsky—but he lost all his money, sir. Then they won thirty-six thousand from Prince Shenkin . . .

IHAREV. Here's another ten rubles. Did *you* buy the cards?

ALEXEY. No, they did, sir.

IHAREV. Where?

ALEXEY. From the local store, sir.

IHAREV. That's a lie, my good man.

ALEXEY. No, really, sir! Oh, no!

IHAREV. Okay. I'll see you again later.

GAVROOSHKA *brings in a box.*

Stand it up here, Gavrooshka! Now—shaving water and towel—quick!

Exeunt both servants.

IHAREV *opens the box, which is filled with decks of cards.* How lovely they are to look at! Every deck worth its weight in gold! Every deck earned in the sweat of my brow! My eyes! I'm still seeing stars from studying those damn markings. But what a sound investment! What a dowry for my daughters! What a start in life for my sons! Look at this deck. I should call it the pearl of great price. No, it's more . . . human than that . . . I shall call it . . . Adelaide. Adelaide, darling, be faithful to me, won't you? Like your little sister here,

Taking another deck.

that won me a cool eighty thousand? Only be faithful, Adelaide, and when we get home, I'll have a monument built in your honor—real Moscow marble!

Hearing a sound, he hurriedly closes the box.
Enter ALEXEY *and* GAVROOSHKA, *bringing a basin, a jug of water, and a towel.*

IHAREV. Where *are* those gentlemen? Are they in?

ALEXEY. Yes, they're in the lounge, sir.

IHAREV. I'll go look 'em over.

Exit.

ALEXEY. You come far?

GAVROOSHKA. No, we're from Smolensk Province.

ALEXEY, Smolensk Province. Nice place to live, huh?

GAVROOSHKA. I wouldn't know.

ALEXEY. Huh?

GAVROOSHKA. He just owns it, he don't live there.

ALEXEY. An estate, huh?

GAVROOSHKA. Two estates. One in Smolensk, one in Kaluga
Province.

ALEXEY. Hm. Quite a set-up.

GAVROOSHKA. Sure. Owns a hundred and eighty serfs. In the
Smolensk house there's Ignaty the butler, Pavlooshka who
used to travel with the master, Gerasim the footman, Ivan
another footman, Ivan the kennel-boy, another Ivan who
plays in the band, the cook Grigory, the cook Semyon,
Baruch the gardener, Dementy the coachman—

Enter KRUGEL *and* SHONEV, *cautiously.*

KRUGEL. You don't think he'll notice.

SHONEV. Of course not. Ootesh will keep him busy.

To ALEXEY.

Run along, boy, they're calling you!

Exit ALEXEY.

SHONEV *goes rapidly up to* GAVROOSHKA.

Where does your master come from, my man?

GAVROOSHKA. Right now—from Ryazan, sir.

SHONEV. He's a landowner?

GAVROOSHKA. Yes, sir.

SHONEV. Does he play cards?

GAVROOSHKA. Yes, sir.

SHONEV. Here's a little something.

Gives him paper money.

Now tell all!

GAVROOSHKA. You won't tell him I told you?

SHONEV. No, no!

KRUGEL. Never!

SHONEV. How is he doing?

KRUGEL. Has he been winning?

GAVROOSHKA. Why? You know Colonel Chebotarov?

SHONEV. No.

KRUGEL. Why?

GAVROOSHKA. We cleaned him out three weeks ago, sir. Eighty thousand rubles, a Warsaw carriage, a box, a rug, gold epaulets, . . . the gold alone was worth six hundred rubles.

SHONEV *looks significantly at* KRUGEL. Eighty thousand?

KRUGEL *shakes his head.*

Sounds fishy, huh? Well, we'll soon find out.

To GAVROOSHKA.

Tell me, when your master stays home, what does he do?

GAVROOSHKA. What does he do? Why, he's a gentleman, he does nothing.

SHONEV. You're lying. I bet you he plays cards the whole damn time.

GAVROOSHKA. Well, I've only been travelling with him two weeks. He always took Pavlooshka. There's Gerasim the footman, Ivan another footman, Ivan the kennel-boy, another Ivan who plays in the band . . .

SHONEV, *to* KRUGEL. Think he's a professional?

KRUGEL. Most likely.

SHONEV. We can only give it a try.

KRUGEL *and* SHONEV *slip out.*

GAVROOSHKA. Pretty tricky, aren't they? Still, this money's gonna come in handy. Enough to buy a bonnet for Masha, some candy for the kids . . . Hey, I like this travel stuff! For one thing, every time he sends you on an errand, you can keep some of the change. A gentleman's life for me! Go where you like when you like! You're tired of Smolensk, so, what the hell? you go to Ryazan. You're tired of Ryazan, so you go to Kazan, you're tired of Kazan, so . . . got it? Now: which is more deestangay—Kazan or Ryazan? Huh? Whadja say? Kazan? Sure, I guess Kazan'd be more deestangay 'cause . . .

Enter IHAREV.

IHAREV. There's nothing special about them, I think. And yet . . . how I should love to clean them out! Jumping Jesus, how I should love it!

Takes brush and soap, sits down before the mirror and begins to shave.

My hand keeps shaking, I can't shave properly.

ALEXEY *enters.* Shall I bring your worship something to eat?

IHAREV. Yes, lunch for four. Caviare, smoked salmon, and four bottles of wine. And feed him.

Points to GAVROOSHKA.

ALEXEY, *to* GAVROOSHKA. Go into the kitchen, it's all ready.

Exit GAVROOSHKA.

IHAREV *goes on shaving.* How much did they slip you?

ALEXEY. Who, sir?

IHAREV. Oh, come on.

ALEXEY. They did slip me something, sir.

IHAREV. Fifty rubles?

ALEXEY. Yes, sir, fifty rubles.

IHAREV. On that table is a hundred ruble bill. Take it. Go on. What are you afraid of? It won't bite you! I ask nothing in return—except honesty—I want you to be honest with me —understand? Whether the cards come from the local store is none of my business. Here's a packet of one dozen.

Gives him a sealed packet.

We understand each other?

ALEXEY. Oh yes, sir! Yes, sir!

IHAREV. Then put those cards out of sight, hm?

Lays down the brush and soap and rubs his face with the towel.

Exit ALEXEY.

I'll show them!

Enter SHONEV, KRUGEL, *and* OOTESH, *bowing.*

IHAREV *goes to meet them, bowing.* You must excuse me. Nothing but four chairs. The room is simple . . .

OOTESH. A warm welcome from the host is better than the finest luxury, Mr. Iharev.

ᴀREV, *to himself.* Your blood will boil, all right, but not for that reason.

Aloud.

Well, gentlemen, while we're discussing our moral obligations, how about a little game of Bank?*

During their conversation, ALEXEY *has come and gone. The table is now laid: caviare, smoked salmon, four bottles of wine.*

ᴏTESH. By all means! Provided, of course, that it's not for high stakes.

ᴋRUGEL. I am never against a little innocent merriment.

ᴤHAREV. What about the cards? I assume we can get some on the premises?

ᴤHONEV. You've only to ask for them, Mr. Iharev!

IHAREV *claps his hands.* Cards!

ALEXEY *arranges the card-table.*

And meanwhile, gentlemen, may I offer you . . . ?
Points to the table and goes to it.

The smoked salmon's nothing special but the caviare's not bad.

SHONEV, *sampling the smoked salmon.* Why, the smoked salmon's rather good!

KRUGEL, *sampling the caviare.* The caviare's not half bad!

SHONEV, *to* KRUGEL. Remember the splendid cheese we had at Pyotr Alexandrovitch Alexandrov's?

KRUGEL. I shall never forget the splendid cheese we had at Pyotr Alexandrovitch Alexandrov's.

IHAREV. Very well, gentlemen, the cards are on the table!

*According to a Gogol expert, Professor Leon Stilman, the game called in Russian *banchik* or *banchók* denoted different games at different times but is here, as in Pushkin's *Queen of Spades,* a variant of Faro. As the word Faro says very little to a modern American audience, I have preferred to let the game be called Bank, not just because that is its name in Russian, but because of the importance of banks in this play. E.B.

SHONEV. It's never the room that matters but the [...]
Mr. Iharev.

OOTESH. I agree! Without company I can't exist!

To KRUGEL.

Remember how I came here, Krugel, all alone [...]
know a soul. The landlady an old woman; on th[...]
a chambermaid with a face like a turnip; I see an [...]
officer trailing her, thankful for small mercies . . . [...]
But then, fate brought Colonel Krugel along! A[...]
Shonev! Was I pleased! I can't exist without compa[...]
for a day, not for an hour. I have to open my h[...]
everyone I meet.

KRUGEL. That's bad.

OOTESH. Bad?

KRUGEL. All excess is bad. Besides, don't you often get p[...]
for a sucker?

OOTESH. Always! Invariably! But I just can't help mysel[...]

KRUGEL. That's beyond me—being open with *ever[...]
Friends, of course, are a different matter.

OOTESH. But man belongs to society.

KRUGEL. Not the whole of him?

OOTESH. The whole of him.

KRUGEL. Not the whole of him, Ootesh!

OOTESH. Yes, the whole of him, Krugel!!

KRUGEL. No, no, not the whole of him, Ootesh!!

OOTESH. Yes, yes, the whole of him, Krugel!!!

SHONEV, *to* OOTESH. Don't argue when you're wrong, Ootesh.

OOTESH, *hotly*. I'll prove it, Shonev. Why, it's a duty! It[...]
moral . . . it's a moral obligation! It's . . .

SHONEV. He's off again! Amazing how worked up he gets: [...]
can make sense of the first three words, but after that[...]

OOTESH. I can't help myself! When it's a question of prin[...]
I don't know what I'm saying. I have to warn peop[...]
anything of the sort is discussed," I have to say, "y[...]
excuse me, but my feelings will run away with [...]
blood will boil!"

the master's own tables. Next evening—when the game is done—Arkady Dergunov is left without a kopeck.

Pause.

IHAREV. Pretty smart! Some people would have a name for that. We know, well, there's something fine about it: as you say, it's a higher mystery.

OOTESH. It's a discipline, and no respecter of persons! It's a duty, it imposes harsh responsibilities! Why, if I sat down to play with my own father, you know what I'd have to do? Cheat him. Cheat my own father! Gambling is the great leveller. All men are equal—at cards.

IHAREV. Very true. People won't understand that a gambler may be the noblest of men. I know one—oh, a very clever fellow with the cards—but would that stop him giving his last ruble to a beggar? Of course not. It's just that if he had two buddies, and, well, the fourth player *isn't* a buddy, why, he'd have to be loyal to his buddies, that's all, even if number four was his grandmother. Like in a civil war, huh? Father against son, son against granny, but all in a great cause. Correct?

OOTESH. Correct.

Pause.

IHAREV. Okay, gentlemen, yes, I'll show you a little trick by all means. But first, tell me: do you know what a made-up deck is?

OOTESH. It's when you can guess any card at a distance.

IHAREV. I have my own system. Nearly six months' work. Couldn't bear the sunlight for a week afterwards. The doctor said I had inflammation of the eyes.

Takes a deck out of his box.

Here she is! You may think it foolish, but this deck has a name. She's human.

OOTESH. A name?

SHONEV. Human?

IHAREV. She's called Adelaide.

OOTESH, *laughing*. Hear that, everybody? This deck's called Adelaide!

SHONEV. Well!

KRUGEL. Glad to meet you, Adelaide!

OOTESH, *examining the cards*. This is something! Can you really identify any card at a distance?

IHAREV. Try me. I'll stand five paces away and name every card. Two thousand rubles if I fail.

OOTESH. Okay, what card is this?

IHAREV. A seven.

OOTESH. Right. And this one?

IHAREV. A knave.

OOTESH. Good God! And this one?

IHAREV. A three.

OOTESH. Incredible!

KRUGEL. Incredible!

SHONEV. Absolutely *incroyable*!

OOTESH. Let me take another look.

Examines the deck.

Adelaide! Well, it deserves a name! Though, of course, she's rather hard to make use of. You'd have to slip her on to the table yourself.

IHAREV. I do it in the heat of the game when the stakes are so high that even the most hardened veteran is all worked up. When a man's been playing for two days and two nights on end—well, he plays himself silly, and in the heat of the game I change the cards. It's all a matter of keeping cool when the other fellows are steamed up. There are thousands of ways of distracting attention: take issue with another player, say his score's been put down wrong, all eyes turn to him, and . . .

OOTESH. Wonderful! To all your other accomplishments, you add the priceless gift of keeping cool! Association with you will be of value to us, Mr. Iharev! So let us drop all further formality, and declare ourselves—comrades!

IHAREV. Agreed!

IHAREV, *showing him a chair*. Please sit down, Mr. Glov.
GLOV *sits*.

Have you been here long?

OOTESH, SHONEV, *and* KRUGEL *are whispering together*.

GLOV. Ah, Mr. Iharev, how sick I am of the town! I shall be thankful, body and soul, to get out of it as quickly as possible.

IHAREV. You are detained by business, Mr. Glov?

GLOV. Yes, Mr. Iharev. And troublesome business too.

IHAREV. A lawsuit, I presume, Mr. Glov?

GLOV. No, no, it's not quite that bad. I am marrying off my daughter, sir, a girl of eighteen. I've come here to make various purchases, but my principal task is to raise a mortgage on my estate. It would all have been finished, but the bank hasn't paid up yet. I am waiting, Mr. Iharev.

IHAREV. May I ask for what sum are you mortgaging your estate, Mr. Glov?

GLOV. Two hundred thousand rubles. They should pay it any day, but it keeps dragging on, and I'm sick of waiting. I left everything at home, you know, expecting to be back at once for the wedding. But delay follows delay . . . so I've decided not to wait any longer.

IHAREV. You won't wait for your money, Mr. Glov?

GLOV. What am I to do? Consider my position: it's a month now since I've seen my wife and children. I don't even get letters; God knows what is going on. I'm leaving the mortgage business to my son, who will stay on here.

Turning to SHONEV *and* KRUGEL.

But I believe I am interrupting you, gentlemen, you are engaged in . . . ?

KRUGEL. Oh, nothing. Just a little game to pass the time.

GLOV. The game of Bank, Colonel Krugel?

SHONEV. Can you call it Bank when you play for one ruble stakes?

GLOV. Ah, my friends, listen to an old man. Of course there is no harm in it, and you can't lose much, but yet . . . ah, gentlemen, I've played myself, and I know from experience, everything in this world begins in a small way, but many, many things end in a big way!

SHONEV, *to* IHAREV. Watch me!

To GLOV.

There, you old folks make a mountain out of a mole hill!

GLOV. I'm not so old, Mr. Shonev, I go by experience.

SHONEV. I'm speaking of old people in general, Mr. Glov. If they burn their fingers, they are sure every one else will too. If a man is bitten by a dog on Main Street, all dogs bite, and we must all keep away from Main Street!

GLOV. True: on the one hand, there is that failing; but, on the other, look at the young folks! They are too reckless! They may break their necks at any minute.

SHONEV. Also true! One never finds a happy medium! When a man is young he is so wild he is insufferable. When he is old he plays the saint and becomes insufferable once again.

OOTESH. As for cards, I agree with Mr. Glov. I used to play, myself. But I'm thankful to say I have given it up—not because I lost money or thought fate was against me. I assure you, that's of no consequence. What is the loss of money to the loss of one's peace of mind? The worry of gambling, the strain, the wear and tear, they take years off a man's life.

GLOV. That is so, Mr. Ootesh! A very wise observation! May I ask an indiscreet question?

OOTESH. Pray do!

GLOV. May I ask, though it's a delicate subject, and I haven't known you very long—how old are you, Mr. Ootesh?

OOTESH. Thirty-nine, Mr. Glov.

GLOV. Thirty-nine! A young, young man! Oh if only we had more men in Russia like you, the golden age would return! So wise, so . . . mature! How thankful I am to have made your acquaintance!

IHAREV. And I agree with him. My children will never *touch* a deck of cards! Of course, with grown-ups, it's a little different. And with *older* grown-ups, poor creatures, they can't dance, they can't . . .

GLOV. True! How true! An old man's round of pleasures is small. But, dear sir, there are other things in life, there are sacred duties to perform. Let me tell you a secret. You are young—you haven't yet known the one true happiness —a father's happiness in a Christian home! How I long for the moment of my homecoming! "Papa, dear papa is home!" my daughter will cry. "Papa, dear papa!" my little boy will echo. Yes, he'll be back from private school, I haven't seen him in six months . . . What bliss, my friends, what balm to the aching heart!

Pause.

After that, can I sink to this?

He indicates the cards on the table.

IHAREV. Paternal feelings are one thing, playing-cards are another: why should they get in each other's way? That's what *I* always ask myself.

Enter ALEXEY.

ALEXEY, *to* GLOV. The horses are ready, sir. Your man's asking about the trunks. Should he take them out?

GLOV. I'll be right with you. Excuse me a moment, gentlemen.

Exit with ALEXEY.

IHAREV. It's no use.

OOTESH. Didn't I tell you? You only have to take one look at him . . .

IHAREV, *a little sulkily.* Still, we could have tried. Why did you have to back him up?

OOTESH. With men like that you've got to be subtle, my dear Iharev!

IHAREV. So you were subtle, and he's leaving.

OOTESH. The end, my friend, is not yet, he laughs best who laughs last, all's well that ends well . . .

Enter GLOV.

See what I mean?

GLOV. I came back to thank you all for the pleasure of your

company. I am sorry not to have made your acquaintance
earlier in life. Maybe God will bring us together again.

SHONEV. It's a small world.

GLOV. True! How true! We may meet next year, next month,
tomorrow afternoon! Goodbye gentlemen, and I thank you.
Above all I thank you, Mr. Ootesh, you broke through the
wall of an old man's solitude!

OOTESH, *sighing.* One does what one can.

GLOV. May I, then . . . ask one little favor, Mr. Ootesh?

OOTESH. We are all at your service, Mr. Glov.

GLOV. No! I shouldn't have suggested it. No!

OOTESH. Yes! Please, I insist. Yes!

GLOV. It's Sasha. My little boy. Not the one in school, the one
here with me. He's twenty-two, poor little thing. He's
finished college and now he wants to join the Hussars. Yes,
the Hussars. I say to him: "Sasha," I say, "Sasha, it's early
days! How do you know you'd like the Hussars? How
about the Civil Service?" But you know how children are:
it's the gold braid, the white uniform, the giant epaulets
. . . so will you help a father in distress? Look after the boy
for me? Shield him from the world and its ways? He has a
little business to attend to for me here . . .

OOTESH. I'll be a second father to him, my dear Mr. Glov.

GLOV. A friend in need!

The two men embrace.

God will reward you, Mr. Ootesh. Goodbye, gentlemen,
and godspeed!

KRUGEL. A pleasant journey to you, Mr. Glov!

SHONEV. May you find all well at home, Mr. Glov!

GLOV. Thank you, thank you!

OOTESH. I'll help you into your carriage, Mr. Glov.

GLOV. Oh, sir, you are too good!

Exeunt GLOV *and* OOTESH.

IHAREV. The bird is flown!

SHONEV. A bird well worth the plucking!

IHAREV. How thrilling those words are: "two hundred thousand"!

KRUGEL. Yes, the mind likes to dwell on words like that.

IHAREV. Doesn't it, though? Just think—for instance—how much waste there is in the world, money thrown down the drain! *Why* should that man have two hundred thousand? What for? He squanders it on fripperies.

SHONEV. On mummery-flummery!

IHAREV. It's economically unsound. Money shouldn't lie rotting in banks, it's the life-blood of the social organism, it must circulate! And why should a single man want all the money in the world? For my part, I'd be happy with that one small amount—that inconsiderable sum—now lying idle in this confounded bank.

SHONEV. Myself, I'd be happy with half of it.

KRUGEL. I'd settle for a quarter.

OOTESH *rushes in, beaming.*

OOTESH. All is well, gentlemen, all is well! The old fool's gone, the son remains behind. And you know what? The poor little thing has power of attorney to collect the money from the bank!

IHAREV. What good does that do us?

OOTESH. What good? Why, man, I'm practically his official guardian. "Mr. Ootesh will take care of everything," the old fool told him. Then again, Mr. Poor Little Thing is dying to be a Hussar . . . I'll show him to you.

He rushes out again.

SHONEV. Three cheers for Ootesh, colleague and friend!

They seize their glasses again.

Hip hip . . .

KRUGEL. Hooray!

SHONEV. Hip hip——

KRUGEL. Hooray!

SHONEV. Hip hip——

KRUGEL. Hooray!

They drink.

IHAREV. So that was why . . .

SHONEV. Sure was.

KRUGEL. He's smart.

SHONEV. A remarkable talent.

KRUGEL. Most likely to succeed.

IHAREV. When the old boy said he was leaving his son
around . . .

SHONEV. You thought of the same thing?

IHAREV. Well, nearly.

KRUGEL. That's the difference. Ootesh thought of it a hundred
per cent.

IHAREV. He's pretty smart.

SHONEV. And you don't know the half of it.

KRUGEL. Not the quarter of it.

Enter OOTESH, *bringing* GLOV JUNIOR.

OOTESH. Gentlemen, I want to introduce Mr. Glov Junior,
elder son of Glov Senior, the best of company, and *my*
friend!

SHONEV. Pleased to meet you.

KRUGEL. Delighted, I'm sure.

IHAREV. Hi, Junior!

GLOV JUNIOR. Gentlemen, I, um . . .

OOTESH. Now don't stand on ceremony. Our motto is liberty——

SHONEV. Equality——

KRUGEL. And what the hell?

SHONEV. Fraternity.

KRUGEL. Thanks, pal.

OOTESH. You agree, of course?

GLOV JUNIOR. What? Oh. Oh, yes.

OOTESH. *We* have all the right opinions, *you* have all the right
opinions. We must celebrate.

Roaring.

Alexey, champagne! And, speaking of Hussars, my friends,
which of us here present would make the best Hussar, the

perfect Hussar, gold braid, white uniform, giant epaulets
. . . Three guesses!

KRUGEL. I guess . . .

Pointing to GLOV JUNIOR.

Him.

OOTESH. Those to the contrary? The motion is carried. Your
father's a pig, we know that. Civil Service? Pah!

He spits.

A fine upstanding sonofagun like you?

He slaps him on the back.

When's your sister's wedding?

GLOV JUNIOR, *furtively.* Know what? I'm sick and tired of her
wedding. Three months in this hole all on *her* account!

OOTESH. How is she, your sister?

KRUGEL. Pretty hot stuff?

SHONEV. Plenty of . . . ?

His hands indicate his idea of an attractive figure.

GLOV JUNIOR, *sniggering.* If she wasn't my sister, I'd . . .

OOTESH. Have a go at her yourself? Gentlemen: a born Hussar!

To GLOV JUNIOR.

Will you help me abduct her?

GLOV JUNIOR, *his jaw falling.* Now?

OOTESH. A Hussar stands always ready! Alexey, champagne!

To the others.

Gentlemen, we have here a real person, warm, human,
humorous, heroic, religious, the whole works, let's embrace
him, let's give him the good old Russian bear hug!

He hugs him.

SHONEV. Dear boy!

Hug.

OOTESH. Dear boy!

Hug.

IHAREV. Dear boy!

Hug.

ALEXEY *has appeared in the doorway during this ceremony with his thumb on the cork of a champagne bottle. At this point, he releases the cork, there is a pop, the cork hits the ceiling, the champagne is poured.*

OOTESH. Gentlemen, I give you our future Ensign of Hussars!

SHONEV. May he be the greatest fighter . . .

KRUGEL. The greatest lover . . .

IHAREV. The biggest drunk . . .

OOTESH. May all his dirtiest dreams come true!

They drink.

Solemnly.

And, now, gentlemen, the rites of initiation!

Quickly.

Mr. Glov, do you play cards?

GLOV JUNIOR. I'd like to. But I have no money.

OOTESH. Oh, come, come, come. My good man, you only need enough to begin with!

GLOV JUNIOR. I don't have enough to begin with.

OOTESH. What?

SHONEV. What??

KRUGEL. What???

OOTESH. Between ourselves, old man, that money in the bank . . .

GLOV JUNIOR. I don't have it.

OOTESH. You will have, though.

GLOV JUNIOR. But I'm not authorized to use it.

OOTESH. You're authorized to collect it.

SHONEV, *brightly.* I have an idea.

OOTESH, *pushing him back.* So have I.

KRUGEL. I wonder what it is?

GLOV JUNIOR. Yes, Mr. Ootesh?

OOTESH. You can give us an I.O.U. Don't worry, we trust you. But, dash it all, I'm talking as if you were going to lose! Ha! ha! ha! You're going to win!

SHONEV. Sure you are!

KRUGEL. Naturally!

GLOV JUNIOR. But, how do you know that, Mr. Ootesh?

OOTESH. What? Ts, ts, ts. Call yourself a Hussar and don't
have faith, hope, and whatever it is? What happens in a
war? You win or you lose. What is the essence of a Christian warrior's life? Risk. Yes, risk. Embracing the Uncertain, caressing the Unknown, and entering into intimate
relations with the higher mysteries! What's wrong, are you
a Jew?

Pause.

GLOV JUNIOR, *as if seeing the light.* Who cares what Father
says? I'll play!

OOTESH. Well done, good and faithful servant. Alexey, the
cards!

*Pours more champagne for GLOV JUNIOR, while ALEXEY
provides him with cards.*

What is the noblest virtue of them all?

KRUGEL. Poverty?

OOTESH, *as if not quite certain.* No.

SHONEV. Chastity?

OOTESH, *musingly.* No-o-o.

IHAREV. Courage! The courage of Mr. Glov Junior!

OOTESH. That's it: very good. I know a poem about it. "O
Courage . . ." or something. Who's holding the bank, me?
Ye-e-es, a nice little bank of twenty-five thousand.

Dealing.

Ensign Glov? How much are *you* putting down, Shonev?
He deals, commenting on the game as it proceeds.

God moves in a mysterious way his wonders to . . . Well,
the knave loses, the nine wins? Dark and inscrutable are
the ways of fate. What? Win with a four? Now, gentlemen,
just watch that Ensign of Hussars, that Lieutenant, that
Captain, that General, how he raises his stakes and the ace
not out yet! Shonev, fill his glass for me, will you? Oh, oh,

here comes the ace, sweeping all before it like a typhoon
in the sea of Marmora.

KRUGEL *has played the ace and is mopping up his win-*
nings.

But General Glov is creeping up on us, he's creeping up,
cree-ee— Bravo! General Glov has won four thousand.

GLOV JUNIOR, *flushed.* Double my stake!

OOTESH, *thoughtfully, as he turns up cards.* Well done, General, well done! The seven leads, the seven . . . oh, oh dear,
the General has lost, too bad, well, my boy, you can't win
every time, once more,
To KRUGEL.

come on, wise guy, stop playing safe, there we are, there
we are, the General wins, I give you Glov, General of
Hussars!
They all drink, then proceed with the game.

They say the Queen of Spades is bad luck.
To SHONEV.

Remember that brunette you called Queen of Spades,
Shonev? Where is she now?
With a catch in his voice.

Where is she now? You're right, General, in the whore-
house downtown, do you have the address?
Suddenly.

Uh, uh! You lose, Krugel. You lose, Shonev. You lose,
Iharev.
To GLOV JUNIOR.

General, I'm amazed, you lose.

GLOV JUNIOR. Oh! Damn it!

OOTESH. Did you hear that, gentlemen? The man's a Hussar:
he swears like a Hussar. Uh, uh! You lose, General.

GLOV JUNIOR, *panting.* How much in the bank?

OOTESH. Fifty thousand, General.

GLOV JUNIOR, *counting out his bid.* Damn it, damn it!

OOTESH. He swears like a man. Like a Hussar.

GLOV JUNIOR *puts his money down.*

Hey, General, that's the whole fifty thousand you have there! Only a very great man would put all that down at once. I don't know if we've anyone as great as that left in the world, I don't know if . . . Uh, uh! He's a national hero. He's lost again.

GLOV JUNIOR. How much in the bank?

OOTESH. A hundred thousand, General.

GLOV JUNIOR, *breathless.* There's my bid.

OOTESH. A hundred thousand, General? Is your real name Napoleon Bonaparte? Look at his eyes, fellows, glowing like hot coals! *De l'audace, de l'audace, et encore de l'audace!* Look! And the king not out yet!! Queen of Diamonds for you, Shonev. A seven for you, Krugel. The primrose path to the everlasting . . . see! General Glov is defeated yet again!

GLOV JUNIOR, *carried away.* Don't stop!!!

OOTESH, *changing his tone.* Just a minute, General! You've lost two hundred thousand. Before you bet again, you must pay up.

GLOV JUNIOR. Pay up? Pay up? But I haven't got it!

OOTESH. It's easy.

KRUGEL. Just give us an I.O.U.

SHONEV. By coincidence, we have pen and paper ready.

GLOV JUNIOR, *acquiescing, sitting down before the paper.* An I.O.U.?

SHONEV. Just a little I.O.U.

OOTESH. And power of attorney to collect!

GLOV JUNIOR. Collect?

KRUGEL. From the bank.

OOTESH. Sign here.

SHONEV. And here.

GLOV JUNIOR *signs.*

GLOV JUNIOR, *brightening*. There. Now let's get back to the game!

OOTESH, *smiling at the others*. "Now let's get back to the game!" Just one thing more. Bring the money.

GLOV JUNIOR. What's the matter? You don't think you'll get paid?

SHONEV. Money on the table!

GLOV JUNIOR. Don't be so mean! I . . .

OOTESH, *coolly*. We're not being mean.

KRUGEL. On the contrary.

SHONEV. We're being magnanimous.

OOTESH. A man who sits down without money can't lose.

KRUGEL. You simply aren't playing the game, old man.

SHONEV. You're not playing the game.

GLOV JUNIOR. Okay. Fix any interest you like. I'll pay double!

OOTESH, *ironically*. Oh, swell! Loan me some cash, and *I'll* pay any interest you like! *I'll* pay double!

GLOV JUNIOR, *pouting*. Will you play or won't you?

SHONEV. We will.

KRUGEL. Oh, we will.

OOTESH. If you bring the money.

GLOV JUNIOR, *taking out a pistol*. Then goodbye! We shall meet in the next world!!

He rushes out.

OOTESH, *alarmed*. I'll take care of this.

He too rushes out.

IHAREV. There'll be hell to pay if the fool kills himself.

SHONEV. It'd be okay if he did it *after* handing the money over.

KRUGEL. But then the fool is a fool . . .

Enter OOTESH, *dragging* GLOV JUNIOR *and his pistol.*

OOTESH. What do you think, gentlemen? He was standing there with this pistol in his handsome mouth!

KRUGEL. Ts, ts, ts!

IHAREV. Really! What next?

SHONEV. A Hussar—killing himself for a mere bagatelle!

IHAREV. Why, at that rate, everyone in Russia could kill himself!

KRUGEL. Which of us hasn't lost at cards?

SHONEV. Which of us isn't going to lose at cards?

GLOV JUNIOR, *miserably*. But I can't stand it!

IHAREV. Never say die! Chin up! Be a good loser!

OOTESH. He who wins loses, he who loses wins, that's in the Bible!

GLOV JUNIOR. But what does it mean?

OOTESH. The loser wins! You for instance. An Ensign that's lost two hundred thousand in one evening? Why, man, the Hussars will carry you on their shoulders!

GLOV JUNIOR, *hopefully*. They will?

OOTESH. Why sure they will!

SHONEV. Sure they will.

KRUGEL. Why, sure.

OOTESH, *handing him a glass*. Here, Ensign Glov.

GLOV JUNIOR, *quaveringly*. Three cheers for the Hussars!

IHAREV. Hip hip——

ALL. Hooray!

SHONEV. Hip hip——

ALL. Hooray!

KRUGEL. Hip hip——

ALL. Hooray!

They drink.

GLOV JUNIOR. I don't give a hoot in hell!

He puts down his glass.

Only, what about Father?

KRUGEL. Father?

SHONEV. Father?

GLOV JUNIOR. What shall I tell him?

OOTESH. Nothing!

IHAREV. Not a thing!

GLOV JUNIOR. But he'll ask—the minute I cross the threshold!

SHONEV. I have an idea.

OOTESH. So have I. Don't cross the threshold.

KRUGEL. Then he won't ask.

OOTESH. Go straight to your regiment! We'll provide the cash.
Ready cash, somebody: the Ensign must enjoy himself!
Where's that girl with the black eyes?

GLOV JUNIOR. You saw her too? Yes, where is she? I want to
storm the fortress!

OOTESH, *to* SHONEV. Two hundred rubles for our Hussar!

IHAREV. Here they are, let *me* pay!

GLOV JUNIOR, *taking a bill from* IHAREV *and waving it.* Alexey,
more champagne!

ALL. Champagne!

   ALEXEY *pours more champagne.*

GLOV JUNIOR. Three cheers for the Hussars! Hip hip—

OOTESH. One moment.

   They put down their glasses.

   I have another idea. Let's toss our friend in a metaphorical
blanket!

   All four seize GLOV JUNIOR *by the arms and legs, toss him,
and sing* For He's a Jolly Good Fellow.

GLOV JUNIOR, *on his feet again and making for the champagne.* Three cheers for the Hussars! Hip hip—

OOTESH. One moment. She's upstairs right now.

GLOV JUNIOR, *stopping in his tracks.* The girl with the black
eyes?

   OOTESH *winks.*

GLOV JUNIOR *pulls himself together. Formally, as if leaving
a party.* Well, gentlemen, I'm afraid I must be leaving.

OOTESH. We'll come with you.

GLOV JUNIOR. No, no, please don't bother.

OOTESH, *winking broadly at the others.* Isn't he a spark? The
gay Lothario? Huh?

GLOV JUNIOR. Goodbye, gentlemen!

SHONEV. Don't forget to give us all details!

Exit GLOV JUNIOR.

OOTESH. We must treat him like Dresden china till we have the cash.

SHONEV. At that, the bank may delay payment.

OOTESH. Leave it to me. Business is business, even in a bank. I shall oil their palms.

A CLERK *in a shabby overcoat peers round the door.*

CLERK. Excuse me. Is Mr. Glov Junior here?

KRUGEL. No.

SHONEV. Mr. Glov Junior has just left.

OOTESH. Why?

CLERK. I've come to see him—on business.

OOTESH. Ah! You're not from the . . . ?

CLERK. I'm from the government bank, sir.

OOTESH. Ah! That's different, of course. Please come in, sir. Please sit down, sir.

The CLERK *sits.*

We do business ourselves, dear sir. In fact we do business with Mr. Glov Junior. In fact it may be possible for you to create in us a fund of gratitude, dear sir.

CLERK. How could I do that, sir?

OOTESH. It's easy. Pay out that money at the earliest possible moment.

CLERK. Oh, it'll take a couple of weeks at the very least.

OOTESH. Oh come, you can't expect much gratitude for that.

CLERK. This is Russia, sir! For that matter, a "couple of weeks" is Russian for a "couple of months."

OOTESH. I can see that might be so . . . for just Russians. We're more than just Russians.

SHONEV. We're friends.

KRUGEL. Of the family, you might say.

OOTESH. What's your name? Fentyfly Perpentitch?

CLERK. Soy Stayhitch.

OOTESH. Same thing. I never forget a name. Or a face. What is more human than a face, Fentyfly Perpentitch?

CLERK. Soy Stayhitch.

OOTESH. Don't change the subject. How's business?

CLERK. Sir, I am a civil servant.

OOTESH. Then, how's tricks?

CLERK. Tricks, sir?

OOTESH. Bribery and corruption.

SHONEV. You know—graft.

KRUGEL. They mean: do you *like* working for the government? Ha! ha! ha!

CLERK. Oh. Oh, well. One has to live, ha! ha! ha!

OOTESH. Hear that, Iharev? One has to live! Ha! ha! ha!

The others join in the laughing which rises to a climax. Then sudden silence as OOTESH *gives the clerk a bribe.*

Okay, Soy Stayhitch, we'll help you to live. Now get going!

CLERK, *picking himself up.* The mills of God grind slowly!

OOTESH. Not when they're oiled with *our* money. Get moving!

CLERK. The mills of God . . .

Exit.

OOTESH. If he's still talking about God, I'd better give him three thousand right off.

He follows the CLERK *off.*

IHAREV. Naturally, we want the money as soon as possible.

SHONEV. Want it? We need it.

KRUGEL, *thoughtfully.* If only we knew how to get round him . . .

IHAREV. Now why are you all in such a hell of a . . .

Enter OOTESH.

OOTESH. He can't do it in less than four days, I could choke!

IHAREV. Three days, four days! What difference does it make?

SHONEV. A lot of difference.

OOTESH. Didn't you know? Why, man, we should be in Nizny

Novgorod right now. The merchants have all sent their
sons to the market there. To do business for them. Well,
you know merchants' sons!

SHONEV. Sissies!

KRUGEL. Suckers!

OOTESH. Quite. We must get there at once!

SHONEV. With a little capital in hand.

KRUGEL. Say two hundred thousand.

IHAREV. At that, I don't see how you can make it.

OOTESH. I have an idea. *You're* not in a hurry, are you?

IHAREV. No.

OOTESH. Then *you* take Glov Junior's I.O.U.

IHAREV. Two hundred thousand rubles—for me?

OOTESH. Take it, take it, my friend!

IHAREV. But——

OOTESH. And let us have your eighty thousand.

IHAREV. What about the other hundred and twenty thousand?

OOTESH. Keep it. Keep it for your trouble.

Pause.

IHAREV. Two hundred thou . . . Okay. Why not?

He goes to his box and takes out a roll of bills.

Here's your eighty thousand.

OOTESH, *waving the I.O.U.* And here's your two hundred
thousand. Now I'll get Glov Junior and we'll regularize the
whole deal. Krugel, take this money to our room. Here's
the key of my cash-box.

Exit KRUGEL.

If only we can get away by tonight!

Exit.

IHAREV. Sure, sure, don't waste time on my account. Two
hundred thou . . .

SHONEV. May I give you a piece of advice, Mr. Iharev? Don't
stay here a moment longer than necessary. Come and join
us. With two hundred thousand rubles you could buy the

whole market . . . One second, I forgot to tell those guys
something . . . I'll be right back.

Exit.

IHAREV, *alone.* Two hundred thou . . . What a day! In the
morning, I have eighty thousand rubles—in the evening,
two hundred thousand. Why, some men would spend a
lifetime putting that amount together, twelve hours a day,
six days a week, their hair turns grey, their teeth drop out,
they get sick and die . . . whereas I . . . in one day! . . . two
hundred thousand rubles!! How could you *earn* such money
in *these* times? Even a country estate wouldn't yield that
much, and who wants to waste a lifetime with yokels and
hicks? A college graduate like me? Well, not a graduate exactly, but you know what I mean: Culture, Self-improve-
ment . . . if I want to go to Petersburg, I can go to Petersburg. I can just see myself strolling down the English
Embankment there—in the Summer Gardens—in front of the
Imperial Palace—going to the theatre in a carriage, *my* carriage . . . I'll go to Moscow too, dine at Yar's, wear the
right clothes, hob-nob with . . . and . . . and, well, in general, do my duty to Tsar and country. And to what do I
owe my success? When they ask me what made me what I
am today, so the little Russians of the future can go and do
likewise, what shall I reply? "Cheating at cards." Of
course, children, that's an oversimplification. It's not cheating really. Not really. There should be another word . . .
maybe there *is* another word . . . a telling phrase . . . "business acumen"? . . . "Success in business, my friends, is the
reward of long years of service, not to mention innate
business acumen . . ." Et cetera. Well, grant that it's
cheating, how can we get along without? Huh? In a sense,
it's merely, what shall I say? the self-preservation instinct.
If I hadn't known how to cheat, *they'd* have cheated *me*,
isn't that true? It was when they saw my . . . business
acumen that they asked my assistance. You have to be
smart. No, dedicated—that's the word. You have to be a
dedicated man. To live foolishly is easy, but to live with
skill, finesse, subtlety, *savoir faire, savoir vivre, je ne sais*

quoi, in other words to cheat and not be cheated, for *that* you have to be a dedicated man.

GLOV JUNIOR *runs in.*

GLOV JUNIOR. Where are they all? Their room's empty.

IHAREV. They stepped out for a minute.

GLOV JUNIOR. Out? With your money?

IHAREV. We made a deal. I stay—on your account.

Enter ALEXEY.

ALEXEY, *to* GLOV JUNIOR. Your worship asked for the gentlemen?

GLOV JUNIOR. Yes.

ALEXEY. They've left.

GLOV JUNIOR. Left?

ALEXEY. Yes. Their horses have been waiting outside for the past half hour.

GLOV JUNIOR, *excited.* Oh, sir, we're ruined!

IHAREV. Speak for yourself, Mr. Glov. With your two hundred thousand, *I* shall be perfectly all right.

GLOV JUNIOR. What? *My* two hundred thousand?

IHAREV. Now calm down, young man. You're the loser. Get used to it.

GLOV JUNIOR, *shouting.* Don't you see you've been cheated?

IHAREV. What?

GLOV JUNIOR. Cheated!

IHAREV. That word! What *are* you talking about, Mr. Glov?

GLOV JUNIOR. What do you think's going on? You think my name is Glov? You think that old man . . . ? My name's not Glov. His name's not Glov. He's not my father. I'm not his son.

IHAREV. You're joking.

GLOV JUNIOR. Joking? Don't you see—I got cheated too!! They didn't give me my cut!!!

IHAREV. You're hysterical. What's all this about cuts and cheating? Do you think *I* am such a fool as . . . What

about the bank? The power of attorney? Why, the clerk
from the bank was here in this room. His name is . . .

GLOV JUNIOR. No, it isn't. He's one of the gang too! His name
is . . .

IHAREV, *appalled at last.* What? What??

Pause.

Then who are you? The devil himself come to plague me?

GLOV JUNIOR. They cleaned me out, sir, they stripped me to
the blast, what could I do? They offered me three thousand
—to pretend to be Glov Junior. Haven't I come clean? I'm
an honorable man, sir.

IHAREV, *grabbing him by the collar.* Honorable? Do you know
what *you* are?

ALEXEY, *aside.* If it's a fight, I blow.

Exit.

IHAREV, *dragging* GLOV JUNIOR *across the room.* You come
with me!

GLOV JUNIOR. Where are you taking me, sir?

IHAREV. Where do you think, you crook? To the police station!

GLOV JUNIOR. Stop! Just for a minute! Please, stop, sir!

IHAREV. Well?

GLOV JUNIOR. Well, sir, I'd say you had no case.

IHAREV, *bellowing.* No case? Why, it's highway robbery in
broad daylight! Wait till I have you in the jail at Ner-
chinsk, I'll show you if I have a case or not! We'll catch the
whole pack of you! I'll teach you to take advantage of
people! I'll have the law on you!

He grabs him again.

GLOV JUNIOR. Yes, sir, that's very good, sir, but how about
your intentions?

IHAREV. Huh?

GLOV JUNIOR. What about those super-special decks of cards,
sir?

IHAREV. The cards? Do you know everything?

*He thinks desperately of something to say, then cries out
plaintively.*

AN ITALIAN STRAW HAT

A Comedy with Songs in Five Acts
by

EUGÈNE LABICHE AND MARC-MICHEL

English version by
LYNN and THEODORE HOFFMAN

Printed by permission of Lynn and Theodore Hoffman.
Copyright ©, 1955, by Lynn and Theodore Hoffman.

Characters

FADINARD, *a landowner*
NONANCOURT, *a horticulturist*
BEAUPERTHUIS
VÉZINET, *who is deaf*
TARDIVEAU, *a bookkeeper*
BOBIN, *nephew of* NONANCOURT
ÉMILE TAVERNIER, *a lieutenant*
FÉLIX, *servant of* FADINARD
ACHILLE DE ROSALBA, *a young dandy*
HÉLÈNE, *daughter of* NONANCOURT
ANAÏS, *wife of* BEAUPERTHUIS
BARONESS DE CHAMPIGNY
CLARA, *a milliner*
VIRGINIE, *chambermaid of* BEAUPERTHUIS
CHAMBERMAID *of the* BARONESS
CORPORAL
SERVANT
GUESTS OF BOTH SEXES
MEMBERS OF THE WEDDING PARTY

The action takes place in Paris.

we were meeting at the marriage bureau, but I found out it was here, so I came here.

FÉLIX. You don't say!

VÉZINET. No, I didn't walk, I took a cab.

Giving his package to VIRGINIE.

Here, put that in the bride's room. It's my wedding present. Look out, it's fragile.

VIRGINIE, *aside.* Here's my chance to see the wedding presents.

Curtseying to VÉZINET.

So long, you deaf old dear.

She exits second door left, with the box.

VÉZINET. Such a sweet young thing. Well, well, it's nice to run into a pretty face.

FÉLIX, *offering him a chair.* Really! At your age! It won't last, you old joker, it won't last!

VÉZINET, *seated left.* Thank you.

Aside.

What a pleasant young man.

SCENE 3

VÉZINET, FADINARD, FÉLIX

FADINARD, *entering upstage, speaking offstage.* Unhitch the carriage.

Onstage.

What a mess! It cost me twenty francs, but I got off cheap. Félix!

FÉLIX. Sir?

FADINARD. Can you imagine . . .

FÉLIX. You're all alone, sir? Where's the wedding party?

FADINARD. It's just starting out from Charentonneau, in eight hired cabs. I came on ahead to see that all was well in the conjugal nest. Are the decorators finished? Are the wedding presents on display?

FÉLIX. Yes, sir, everything is in the room there.

Pointing to the room off the second door left.

FADINARD. Fine! Just imagine, after I left Charentonneau at eight o'clock this morning . . .

VÉZINET, *to himself.* My nephew is certainly keeping us waiting.

FADINARD, *seeing* VÉZINET. Uncle Vézinet!

To FÉLIX.

Go away. I've got a better audience.

FÉLIX *retreats upstage. Begins his speech again.*

Just imagine, after I left . . .

VÉZINET. My nephew, allow me to congratulate you.

He tries to embrace FADINARD.

FADINARD. What on earth? Oh yes!

They embrace each other. Aside.

They're always kissing in my wife's family.

Aloud, reciting again.

After I left Charentonneau at eight o'clock this morning . . .

VÉZINET. Where's the bride?

FADINARD. Oh, she's following after me, in eight cabs.

Trying again.

After I left Charentonneau at eight o'clock this morning . . .

VÉZINET. I've just brought my wedding present.

FADINARD, *pressing his hand.* It's terribly good of you.

Resuming his speech.

I was in my carriage, crossing the Bois de Vincennes, when all of a sudden I discovered I had dropped my whip . . .

VÉZINET. These sentiments do you honor, nephew.

FADINARD. What sentiments? Oh, hell, I keep forgetting he's deaf. Well, what does it matter?

Continuing.

Since it's got a silver handle on it, I stop my horse and get down. A hundred feet off, I see it in a bunch of nettles. I get my fingers pricked.

VÉZINET. I'm glad to hear it.

FADINARD. Thanks! I come back—no more carriage! My carriage had disappeared!

FÉLIX, *coming back downstage.* You lost your carriage, sir?

FADINARD, *to* FÉLIX. Félix, I am talking to my uncle who can't hear a word I say. I beg you not to meddle in these family affairs.

VÉZINET. Furthermore, good husbands make good wives.

FADINARD. Certainly. Diddle diddle diddle. Rum tum tum—— My carriage had disappeared. I ask around, I inquire. Someone tells me it's standing in a corner of the park. I run over and what do I find? My horse, eating away at a bunch of straw decorated with poppies. I go over. Just then I hear a woman's voice in the next path yelling "Heavens! My hat!" The bunch of straw was a hat! She'd hung it on a tree while she was chatting with a soldier.

FÉLIX, *aside.* Ha! Ha! What a laugh!

FADINARD, *to* VÉZINET. If you ask me, I think she's a pretty fast number.

VÉZINET. No, I come from Chaillot. I live in Chaillot.

FADINARD. Diddle diddle diddle. Rum tum tum.

VÉZINET. Next to the fire house.

FADINARD. Yes, naturally! I was just about to apologize and offer to pay the damages when the soldier butted in, a sort of horribly fierce officer from the African corps. He started out by treating me like a baby. Hell, I got hot under the collar and the next thing I knew I called him an army bastard! He started for me; I took a flying leap and landed in my carriage. The jolt set the horse off and here I am! I just had time to toss him a twenty franc piece for the hat—or twenty sous, I'm not sure which. I'll find out this evening when I go over my accounts.

Pulling a fragment of a straw hat adorned with poppies from his pocket.

Here's my change!

VÉZINET, *taking the hat and looking at it.* First class straw!

FADINARD. Yes, but it's not worth the price.

VÉZINET. It's not easy to find a hat like that. I've had some experience.

FÉLIX, *who has come forward and has taken the hat from* VÉZINET. Let's see . . .

FADINARD. Félix, I beg you not to meddle in my family affairs.

FÉLIX. But sir . . .

FADINARD. Silence, knave, as they say in the Comédie Française.

FÉLIX *retreats again.*

VÉZINET. By the way, when do we have to be at the marriage bureau?

FADINARD. At eleven o'clock! Eleven o'clock!

He counts on his fingers.

VÉZINET. We'll be eating late. I think I've time to get some toast and milk. Do you mind?

Goes upstage.

FADINARD. Not a bit. I'd be delighted.

VÉZINET, *returning to kiss him.* Goodbye, nephew.

FADINARD. Goodbye, uncle.

To VÉZINET, *who is trying to kiss him.*

What on earth? Oh yes, it's a family tic.

Letting himself be kissed.

There!

Aside.

Once I'm married, you won't catch me playing that game, no sir!

VÉZINET. What about the other side?

FADINARD. Just what I was saying, what about the other side?

VÉZINET *kisses him on the other cheek.*

There!

TOGETHER.

AIR. *Quand nous sommes si fatigués.* REPRÉSENTANTS EN
VACANCES, *Act I*

FADINARD.

Old fuddy-dud, goodbye to you,
And to your mania as well.
As soon as I have said "I do,"
Your kissing can go straight to hell.

VÉZINET.

My nephew, though I say "adieu,"
This parting causes me no pain,
For long before you've said "I do,"
I hope to kiss you once again.

(VÉZINET *goes out upstage.* FÉLIX *goes out the middle door
left, carrying the fragment of hat.*)

SCENE 4

FADINARD, *alone.* At last! In another hour I'll be married! I
won't have to listen to my father-in-law constantly screaming "My son, it's all off!" Have you ever had dealings
with a porcupine? That's my father-in-law! I met him on
a bus. His first word to me was a kick in the shins. I was
going to reply by taking a poke at him when a look from
his daughter changed my mind, and I passed on his six
big sous to the conductor. After I'd done him this favor,
he lost no time in telling me that he was a horticulturist
at Charentonneau. There's nothing like love to sharpen
your wits. I said to him, "Do you sell carrot seeds, sir?"
He replied, "No, but I have some fine geraniums." This
inspired me. "How much a pot?" "Four francs." "Let's go."
As soon as we got to his house, I picked out four pots—
it happened to be my porter's birthday—and asked if I

could marry his daughter. "Who are you?" "I'm a landlord with an income of twenty-five francs." "Get out!" "A day!" "Oh, please sit down." You've got to admire such baseness of soul! I was immediately asked in for cabbage soup along with Cousin Bobin, a big idiot who has a mania for kissing everybody, especially my wife. Apropos of which I was told, "For goodness' sake, they grew up together," which I don't call sufficient grounds. As soon as I'm married—Married!!!

To the audience.

Do you feel the same way? The word gives me ants in my soul. There's no use denying it, in one hour, I'll be

Excitedly.

—married! I'll have a little wife all to myself, and I'll be able to kiss her without that porcupine yelling at me, "Sir, one must observe the decencies!" Poor little girl!

To the audience.

Well, I've decided to be faithful to her—word of honor! No? Oh, but I will! She's so sweet, my Hélène, under that bridal veil.

AIR: *Serment*

> *In Barcelona did you know,*
> *Did you know,*
> *A gypsy girl with eyes of flame,*
> *Eyes of flame?*
> *This Amazon was dark as crow*
> *And like a tigress she did go;*
> *I'm not to blame,*
> *She had no shame.*
> *Thank God my bride-to-be is not the same,*
> *She's nice and tame,*
> *And never will disgrace my family name.*

A rose, with a crown of orange blossoms, that's the portrait of my Hélène. I've got a delicious little suite fixed up for her. This room's not bad,

Pointing off left.

but that one's absolutely delicious, a rosewood paradise, with chamois drapes. It cost the sky but it looks terrific— real honeymoon décor! If only it was already a quarter to twelve.—Someone's coming up—it's her and the rest of them! Oh, I've got the ants again!—Thousands of them!

SCENE 5

ANAÏS, FADINARD, ÉMILE *in officer's uniform. The door opens; a hatless lady and an officer appear.*

ANAÏS, *to* ÉMILE. Monsieur Émile, I beg of you——

ÉMILE. Don't be afraid, madame. Come in.

They enter.

FADINARD, *aside.* What the hell! The hat lady and her African!

ANAÏS, *upset.* Don't make a scene, Émile!

ÉMILE, Don't worry! I'm at your service.

To FADINARD.

I don't suppose you thought you'd be seeing us so soon, sir?

FADINARD, *with a forced smile.* Not at all. I'm greatly honored by your visit—but I'm afraid that just now . . .

Aside.

What in the world do they want?

ÉMILE, *rudely.* Well, come on, offer Madame a chair!

FADINARD, *pushing an armchair forward.* Oh, excuse me! Will Madame take a seat? I didn't realize——

Aside.

What about my wedding?

ANAÏS *seats herself.*

ÉMILE, *seating himself on the right.* You have a very fast horse, sir.

FADINARD. Not bad. You're too kind. Did you follow on foot?

ÉMILE. Of course not, sir. I had my orderly jump on the back of your carriage.

FADINARD. What a pity! If only I'd known.

Aside.

I had my whip——

ÉMILE, *grimly.* If only you'd known?

FADINARD. I'd have asked him to get inside.

Aside.

Honestly, this brute is getting me sore!

ANAÏS. Émile, we haven't much time. Let's cut our visit short.

FADINARD. I absolutely agree with Madame, let's cut it short.

Aside.

My wedding party's coming.

ÉMILE. Sir, someone ought to teach you a few manners.

FADINARD, *insulted.* Lieutenant!

Émile gets up. Calming down.

I've had lessons.

ÉMILE. You rushed off very rudely in the Bois de Vincennes.

FADINARD. I was in a hurry.

ÉMILE. And you dropped, probably by mistake, this little coin . . .

FADINARD, *taking it.* Twenty sous! Well, so it was twenty sous! Just as I thought.

Fumbling in his pocket.

It was an error. I'm so sorry you went to all that trouble.

Handing him a gold piece.

Here!

ÉMILE, *refusing to take it.* What's that?

FADINARD. Twenty francs, for the hat.

ÉMILE, *angrily.* Sir!

ANAÏS, *getting up.* Émile!

ÉMILE. True enough! I promised Madame to control myself.

FADINARD, *fumbling in his pocket again.* I thought that would take care of it. Do you want three francs more? It's all one to me.

ÉMILE. That's not the point, sir. We didn't come here for money.

FADINARD, *astonished*. No? Well—but—what for, then?

ÉMILE. First of all, sir, for an apology—an apology to Madame.

FADINARD. Me, apologize?

ANAÏS. Never mind, sir, I don't insist.

ÉMILE. Madame, I am at your service.

FADINARD. Let's forget about it, madame, since, to tell the truth, it wasn't me personally who ate your hat. And another thing, madame, are you really convinced that my horse wasn't acting within his rights when he ate up that piece of millinery?

ÉMILE. What's that?

FADINARD. Look here! What does Madame go around hanging her hat on trees for? A tree isn't a hat rack, you know. And what is she wandering around the woods with soldiers for? That's pretty suspicious, madame.

ANAÏS. Sir!

ÉMILE, *angrily*. Just what are you getting at?

ANAÏS. I'll have you know that Monsieur Tavernier——

FADINARD. Tavernier? Who's that?

ÉMILE, *brusquely*. That's me, sir!

ANAÏS. That Monsieur Tavernier is—my cousin. We grew up together.

FADINARD, *aside*. I know all about it! He's her "Bobin."

ANAÏS. And if I agreed to walk arm in arm with him, it was only to discuss his future—his chances for promotion. To give him some advice.

FADINARD. Without a hat?

ÉMILE, *upsetting a chair and stamping on the floor in a rage.*

What the Devil!

ANAÏS. Émile, don't shout!

ÉMILE. If you please, madame——

FADINARD. Well, don't smash up my chairs!

Aside.

I'm going to throw him out on his ear—— No, he might fall on top of my wedding party!

ÉMILE. Let's cut it short, sir.

FADINARD. Just what I was about to say. You took the words right out of my mouth.

ÉMILE. Will you or will you not apologize to Madame?

FADINARD. What do you mean? Why I'd be delighted—I'm in a hurry anyway. Madame, I beg to remain your most humble and devoted servant—and, in addition, well, I'll give Cocotte a good beating.

ÉMILE. That won't do.

FADINARD. It won't? I'll send her to jail for life.

ÉMILE, *pounding a chair with his fist*. Sir!

FADINARD. Look here, you, stop smashing my chairs!

ÉMILE. That's just the beginning!

Voice of NONANCOURT *offstage*. You wait here. We'll be right down.

ANAÏS, *in terror*. Good Heavens! Someone's coming!

FADINARD, *aside*. Damn it! My father-in-law! If he finds there's a woman here, "It's all off!"

ANAÏS, *aside*. Caught at a stranger's! What ever shall I do?

Seeing the small room off right.

Ah!

She goes in.

FADINARD, *rushing over to her*. Madame, allow me!

Rushing over to ÉMILE.

Sir!

ÉMILE, *exiting left, upstage door*. Get those people out of here! We're going to settle this business.

FADINARD, *shutting the door on* ÉMILE *and seeing* NONANCOURT, *who enters from the back*. Just in time!

SCENE 6

FADINARD, NONANCOURT, HÉLÈNE, BOBIN. *They are all dressed up for the wedding.* HÉLÈNE *is wearing her bridal veil and is carrying a bouquet.*

NONANCOURT. My son, it's all off! You've been acting like a boor.

HÉLÈNE. But Papa!

NONANCOURT. Be quiet, my child.

FADINARD. But what have I done?

NONANCOURT. The whole party is waiting downstairs—— Eight cabs!

BOBIN. A terrific sight!

FADINARD. Well?

NONANCOURT. You should have greeted us at the foot of the stairs.

BOBIN. So you could kiss us.

NONANCOURT. Apologize to my daughter.

HÉLÈNE. But, Papa——

NONANCOURT. Be quiet, my child.

To FADINARD.

All right, sir, apologize!

FADINARD, *aside.* It seems that's all I ever get to do.
Aloud, to HÉLÈNE. I beg to remain your most humble and devoted servant . . .

NONANCOURT, *interrupting.* Another thing! Why did you leave Charentonneau this morning without saying goodbye to us?

BOBIN. He didn't kiss anybody!

NONANCOURT. Be quiet, Bobin.

To FADINARD.

Answer me!

FADINARD. For pity's sake, you were asleep!

BOBIN. 'S not true. I was shining my shoes.

NONANCOURT. It's because we're country people, hicks.

BOBIN, *weeping.* Hornyculturists!

NONANCOURT. People like us don't count!

FADINARD, *aside.* My, the porcupine is getting prickly.

NONANCOURT. You're already looking down on your in-laws.

FADINARD. Look here, sir, why don't you take a little walk. It might cool you off.

NONANCOURT. But you're not married yet, sir. We can always call it off.

BOBIN. Call it off, call it off!

NONANCOURT. No one's going to tread on my toes!

Shaking his foot.

Damn!

FADINARD. What's the matter?

NONANCOURT. It's these store bought shoes. They pinch me and they annoy me and they drive me mad!

Shaking his foot.

Damn!

HÉLÈNE. It'll go away when you walk.

She wriggles her shoulders.

FADINARD, *watching her do it, aside.* Funny, what's wrong with her?

NONANCOURT. Has my pot of myrtle arrived?

FADINARD. A pot of myrtle? What for?

NONANCOURT. It's a symbol, sir.

FADINARD. Oh!

NONANCOURT. You're laughing. You're making fun of us, because we're country people, hicks.

BOBIN, *weeping.* Hornyculturists!

FADINARD. All right, all right!

NONANCOURT. But I don't care. I want to put it personally in my daughter's bedroom, so that she will be able to say——

HÉLÈNE, *to her father.* Oh, Papa, you're so good!

She wriggles her shoulders.

FADINARD, *aside.* There she goes again. It must be a tic. I never noticed it before.

HÉLÈNE. Papa?

NONANCOURT. What?

HÉLÈNE. There's a pin sticking me in the back.

FADINARD. I thought there was something.

BOBIN, *excitedly, rolling up his sleeves.* Just a minute, cousin.

FADINARD, *preventing him.* Stay where you are, sir!

NONANCOURT. Look here, they grew up together.

BOBIN. She's my cousin.

FADINARD. I don't care. One must observe the decencies!

NONANCOURT, *pointing to the room where* ÉMILE *is.* Look, go in there.

FADINARD, *aside.* With the African, oh sure!

Blocking the door.

Not in there!

NONANCOURT. Why?

FADINARD. It's full of paper-hangers.

NONANCOURT, *to his daughter.* Well, walk around, give it a shake, that'll make it come out.

Shaking his foot.

Damn, I can't bear it. I'm going to put on my slippers.

He goes toward the room where ANAÏS *is.*

FADINARD, *blocking his way.* Not in there!

NONANCOURT. And why not?

FADINARD. I was just about to tell you. It's full of painters.

NONANCOURT. You seem to employ all the workmen in town. Well, come on, let's not keep ourselves waiting. Bobin, give your cousin your arm. Off to the marriage bureau, my boy!

Shaking his foot.

Damn!

FADINARD, *aside.* And what about those other two?

Aloud.

I'll follow right behind, just as soon as I find my hat and gloves.

ENSEMBLE

AIR: *Cloches, sonnez!* MARIÉE DE POISSY.

NONANCOURT.

Come, my son, do not delay!
Our eight cabs wait for us below.
All over Paris folks will say
They never saw a better show.

FADINARD.

Go, my father, do not stay,
I'm coming down, I won't be slow,
And long before you're on your way,
I promise I'll be set to go.

HÉLÈNE *and* BOBIN.

Come, dear sir, do not delay, etc.

NONANCOURT, HÉLÈNE and BOBIN *exit upstage.*

SCENE 7

FADINARD, ANAÏS, ÉMILE, *then* VIRGINIE.

FADINARD, *running quickly toward the room where the lady is.*

Come out, madame, you can't stay here.

Running to the upstage left door.

Let's get going, sir!

VIRGINIE *enters laughing by the second door left. She is holding the bit of straw which* FÉLIX *has brought in to her, and doesn't notice the other actors. During this time,* FADINARD *goes upstage to listen to* NONANCOURT'S *departing footsteps. He doesn't see* VIRGINIE.

VIRGINIE, *to herself.* Ha! ha! ha! How funny!

ÉMILE, *aside.* Good God! Virginie!

ANAÏS, *opening the door.* My chambermaid! We're lost!

She listens, along with ÉMILE, *in great anxiety.*

VIRGINIE, *to herself.* A woman who goes and gets her hat chewed up in the Bois de Vincennes with a soldier!

FADINARD, *turning around and noticing her; aside.* Where did *she* come from?

He comes downstage left a bit.

VIRGINIE, *to herself.* It looks like Madame's hat. Wouldn't that be a scream?

ÉMILE, *in a low voice.* Get that girl out of here or I'll kill you!

VIRGINIE. I've simply got to find out!

FADINARD, *leaping forward.* Good Lord!

He seizes the fragment of hat from VIRGINIE.

Get out of here!

VIRGINIE, *surprised and frightened by the sight of* FADINARD. Oh, sir!

FADINARD, *pushing her toward the door upstage.* Get out or I'll kill you!

VIRGINIE, *uttering a cry.* Ah!
She disappears.

SCENE 8

ÉMILE, ANAÏS, FADINARD.

FADINARD, *coming back.* Who is that girl? What's going on?
Supporting ANAÏS, *who is staggering in.*

There now, take it easy. She's going to faint!
He seats her at right.

ÉMILE, *going up to her.* Anaïs!

FADINARD. You've got to hurry, madame. I haven't much time.

NONANCOURT'S *voice downstairs.* My son! My son!

FADINARD. Coming! Coming!

ÉMILE. A glass of sugar water, sir, a glass of sugar water!

FADINARD, *losing his head*. Coming! Coming! Lord, what a mess!

He takes what he needs from the table and stirs the glass.

ÉMILE. Darling Anaïs!

To FADINARD, *rudely*.

Good God, get a move on.

FADINARD, *stirring the sugar water*. For goodness' sake, it's dissolving.

To ANAÏS.

Madame, I hate to turn you out, but I'm sure that if you went home . . .

ÉMILE. Unfortunately, sir, that is no longer possible.

FADINARD, *astonished*. Oh, look here! What do you mean?

ANAÏS, *in a shaky voice*. That girl . . .

FADINARD. Well, madame?

ANAÏS. That girl is my chambermaid! She recognized the hat —she'll go tell my husband . . .

FADINARD. A husband? Oh, Lord save us, there's a husband!

ÉMILE. A brute! A monster!

ANAÏS. If I come back without that wretched hat, he'll be worse than a raging bull; he'll imagine . . .

FADINARD, *aside*. Horns!

ANAÏS, *in despair*. I'm lost! Compromised! Oh, I think I'm going to be ill.

FADINARD, *quickly*. Not here, madame! This is a very unhealthy apartment.

Voice of NONANCOURT *downstairs*. My son! My son!

FADINARD. Coming! Coming!

He drinks the sugar water. Coming back to ÉMILE.

What are we going to do?

ÉMILE, *to* ANAÏS. We've got to find a hat just like it. Then you'll be saved!

FADINARD, *enchanted*. Oh, terrific! The African isn't so dumb!

Handing her the fragment of hat.

Here, madame, that's your sample, and when you make the
rounds of the shops . . .

ANAÏS. Me, sir? But I'm at death's door!

ÉMILE. Don't you see that Madame is at death's door? Where's
that sugar water?

FADINARD, *offering her the glass.* Here it is.
Seeing it empty.

Dear me, someone must have drunk it.
Offering the sample to ÉMILE.

What about you, sir? You're not "at death's door."

ÉMILE. Do you expect me to leave Madame in such a state?

Voice of NONANCOURT. My son! My son!

FADINARD. Coming!
Going to put the glass on the table.

But damn it, that hat isn't going to drop onto Madame's
head all by itself.

ÉMILE. Of course not. You'd better hurry up.

FADINARD. Who, me?

ANAÏS, *rising, in a state of agitation.* For the love of God, sir,
hurry!

FADINARD, *protesting.* That's all very well to say, but I'm just
about to get married, madame; allow me to acquaint you
with the ghastly news. My wedding party is waiting for me
downstairs.

ÉMILE, *rudely.* I don't give a damn about your wedding!

FADINARD. Lieutenant!

ANAÏS. Don't forget, sir, to pick out a straw that's exactly the
same. My husband knows the hat.

FADINARD. But madame . . .

ÉMILE. With poppies.

FADINARD. If you please . . .

ÉMILE. We're willing to stay here fifteen days, a month even,
if we have to.

FADINARD. It seems I either have to go chasing after a hat or put my wedding party in a state of vagrancy! How kind of you!

ÉMILE, *seizing a chair.* Are you going or not, sir?

FADINARD, *exasperated, taking the chair.* All right, sir, I'm going. Leave my chairs alone and for pity's sake don't touch anything.

To himself.

I'll go into the first hat shop. But what shall I do with my eight cabs? And the judge who's waiting for us?

Seats himself mechanically on the chair he's been holding.

Voice of NONANCOURT. My son! My son!

FADINARD, *rising and going upstage.* I'm going to explain everything to my father-in-law!

ANAÏS. Heavens, no!

ÉMILE. One word and you're finished!

FADINARD. Wonderful! You really are too kind!

Voice of NONANCOURT, *who knocks at the door.* My son! My son!

ANAÏS and ÉMILE, *running to* FADINARD. Don't open the door!

They stand to right and left of the entrance so that they will be hidden by the two doors when they open.

SCENE 9

FADINARD, ÉMILE and ANAÏS, *hidden;* NONANCOURT *upstage, then* FÉLIX.

NONANCOURT, *appearing at the main entrance and carrying a pot of myrtle.* My son, it's all off!

He tries to come in.

FADINARD, *barring his way.* Yes, let's go!

NONANCOURT, *trying to come in.* Wait till I put down my myrtle.

FADINARD, *pushing him back.* Don't come in, don't come in!

NONANCOURT. Why not?

FADINARD. It's full of plumbers! Come on, come on!

   They both disappear. The door shuts.

ANAÏS, *in tears, throwing herself into* ÉMILE's *arms.* Ah! Émile!

ÉMILE, *whose gestures coincide with those of* ANAÏS. Ah! Anaïs!

FÉLIX, *entering and seeing them.* What's going on here?

ACT TWO

A millinery establishment. At left, a counter parallel to the side wall. Above it, on a shelf, one of those cardboard heads used in hat shops. A lady's hood is displayed on this head. On the counter, a big ledger, ink, pens, etc. A door upstage left. Two doors center and downstage right. The main door is upstage center. Benches on either side of the entrance. Chairs. There are no hats to be seen in the room, except on the cardboard head. It is the reception room of the shop; the work rooms are presumably off to one side, through the right center door. The main entrance opens on to an anti-chamber.

SCENE 1

CLARA, *then* TARDIVEAU.

CLARA, *speaking offstage through the right center door.* Hurry up, girls, my client's in a big rush.

   Onstage.

   Isn't Monsieur Tardiveau here yet? I've never seen such a lazy bookkeeper. He's too old. I'd better get someone young.

TARDIVEAU, *entering by the main door.* Whew! I made it! I'm dripping!

He takes a handkerchief from his hat and mops his forehead.

CLARA. Congratulations, Monsieur Tardiveau. You're so early.

TARDIVEAU. I couldn't help it, mademoiselle. I got up at six o'clock.

Aside.

Lord, I'm hot.

Aloud.

I made the fire, I shaved, I fixed my soup and ate it . . .

CLARA. Your soup! What has your soup got to do with me?

TARDIVEAU. I can't drink coffee; it gives me gas, and since I've got duty with the National Guard——

CLARA. You?

TARDIVEAU. I had to take off my uniform. I couldn't wear it in a hat-shop, you know.

CLARA. Naturally, but Monsieur Tardiveau, you're over fifty-two.

TARDIVEAU. I'm sixty-two, mademoiselle, ready to serve you.

CLARA, *aside.* Thanks.

TARDIVEAU. But the government allowed me to continue my service.

CLARA. My, what devotion!

TARDIVEAU. Oh, it's not that. It's so I could be with Trouille-bert.

CLARA. Who's that?

TARDIVEAU. Trouillebert? A clarinet teacher. We arranged to have guard duty together and we spend the night playing for glasses of sugar water. It's my only vice. Beer gives me gas.

He takes his place behind the counter.

CLARA, *aside.* What an old maniac!

TARDIVEAU, *aside.* Lord, I'm hot. My shirt is soaking.

CLARA. Monsieur Tardiveau, I've an errand for you. You've got to go . . .

TARDIVEAU. Excuse me, I've my little dressing room over there and if you don't mind, I'd like to put on a flannel undershirt first.

CLARA. As soon as you get back, you're to go to Rambuteau Street to the notions shop.

TARDIVEAU. It's just that . . .

CLARA. You're to pick up some tri-colored sashes.

TARDIVEAU. Tri-colored sashes?

CLARA. For that provincial mayor, you know.

TARDIVEAU, *coming out from behind the counter.* It's just that my shirt is soaking.

CLARA. Well, what are you waiting for? Get along.

TARDIVEAU. All right.

Aside.

Lord, I'm hot. I'll change when I get back.

He leaves by the main door.

SCENE 2

CLARA, *then* FADINARD.

CLARA, *alone.* My girls are working away. Everything's fine. Setting myself up in this business was a real brainstorm. Only four months, and already I'm flooded with customers. Oh, well, I'm not just an ordinary milliner. I'm sober, I don't have any lovers—for the moment.

A noise of carriages is heard.

What's all that?

FADINARD, *rushing in.* Madame, I've got to have a straw hat, rush job, quick, hurry up!

CLARA. A straw hat?

Noticing FADINARD.

Good heavens!

FADINARD, *aside*. Horrors! My old flame, Clara—and there's the wedding party just outside!

Aloud, edging toward the door.

You don't think you can do it? That's all right. I'll be back.

CLARA, *stopping him*. So there you are! And where have you been?

FADINARD. Hush! Don't yell! I'll explain everything. I've just come back from Saumur.

CLARA. It took you six months?

FADINARD. Yes, I missed the bus.

Aside.

What a ghastly coincidence!

CLARA. My, you're gallant! So that's how you treat ladies!

FADINARD. Hush! Don't yell! I confess I've been a bit remiss.

CLARA. What do you mean, "a bit remiss"? You say to me, "I'll take you to the Flower Palace." We set off, it starts to rain, and instead of a cab, what do you offer me? A row of awnings along the arcade!

FADINARD, *aside*. True! I was cad enough to do that.

CLARA. After we got there, you said, "Wait, I'm going to fetch an umbrella." So I wait. At the end of six months you pop up again—without an umbrella!

FADINARD. Oh, Clara, that's not quite true! In the first place, it's only been five and a half months. As for the umbrella, I just forgot. I'll go get one.

False exit.

CLARA. Don't be ridiculous! You owe me an explanation!

FADINARD, *aside*. Damn! And there's my wedding marking time at hourly rates—in eight cabs!

Aloud.

Clara, my darling Clara, you know how I love you!

Kisses her.

CLARA. When I think that this creature promised to marry me!

FADINARD, *aside*. What a time to bring that up!

Aloud.

But I still mean to.

CLARA. Just the same, if you married anyone else, I'd make a stink.

FADINARD. Oh my, what a silly! Me, marry some other girl? The proof is that I'm giving you my trade.

Changing his tone.

I've got to have an Italian straw hat, right now, with poppies.

CLARA. Oh sure, for another girl.

FADINARD. Oh my, what a silly! A straw hat for—for a captain of the guards who wants to deceive his colonel.

CLARA. Humph! Not a very good story, but I'll forgive you— on one condition!

FADINARD. Anything you say, but hurry up!

CLARA. That you'll have dinner with me.

FADINARD. My dear!

CLARA. And take me to a show—this evening.

FADINARD. What a marvellous idea! I just happened to be free this evening. I was just saying to myself, "Dear me, what ever am I going to do with my evening?"—Let's look at the hats.

CLARA. This is my reception room. The workroom is over here, but don't you dare flirt with any of my girls.

She exits center right. FADINARD *is about to follow her.* NONANCOURT *enters.*

SCENE 3

FADINARD, NONANCOURT, *then* HÉLÈNE, BOBIN, VÉZINET *and* MEN AND WOMEN OF THE WEDDING PARTY.

NONANCOURT, *entering with a pot of myrtle.* It's all off, my son!

FADINARD, *aside.* Good God, my father-in-law!

NONANCOURT. Where is His Honor?

FADINARD. Just a second. I'm getting him. You wait here.

He runs off quickly second door right. HÉLÈNE, BOBIN, VÉZINET, *and the* WEDDING PARTY *enter in a procession.*

CHORUS.

> AIR: *Ne tardons pas.* MARIÉE DE POISSY.

> *Kith and kin!*
> *Let us joyfully go in,*
> *And wait here,*
> *For His Honor to appear.*
> *In this place,*
> *Two hearts fondly keeping pace,*
> *Will unite*
> *In the solemn marriage rite!*

NONANCOURT. At last, here we are at the marriage bureau. My children, I beseech you, don't make any blunders. Keep your gloves on—those of you who've got any. As for me——

Shaking his foot; aside.

Damn! What a nuisance this myrtle is. If I'd known, I'd have left it in the carriage.

Aloud.

I am extremely moved. What about you, my daughter?

HÉLÈNE. Papa, it's still sticking me in the back.

NONANCOURT. Walk around; that'll make it fall out.

HÉLÈNE *goes upstage.*

BOBIN. Father Nonancourt, why don't you put your myrtle down?

NONANCOURT. I shall part with it only when I part with my daughter!

To HÉLÈNE, *tenderly.*

Hélène!

> AIR: *from the song "L'Amandier"*

> *The very day that you were born*
> *Into a pot this tree did go.*
> *Your windowsill it did adorn*
> *And by your cradle it did grow,*
> *Next to your cradle it did grow.*

> *And when each evening before bed*
> *To suckle you your mother ran,*
> *This little tree I also fed,*
> *By virtue of—my watering can.*
> *Oh yes, each evening before bed,*
> *I fed it with my watering can.*

Interrupting himself and shaking his foot.

Damn!

Giving the myrtle to BOBIN.

Here! Take it. I have a cramp.

VÉZINET. It's very pleasant here.

Pointing to the counter.

There's His Honor's desk.

Pointing to the book.

The civil registry. We're all going to have to sign our names in it.

BOBIN. What if you don't know how?

VÉZINET. You make a cross.

Noting the cardboard head.

Well, well. A statue of Liberty.* But she's different from the ones I've seen before.

BOBIN. The one in the town hall at Charentonneau is better than that.

HÉLÈNE. Papa, what do I have to do?

NONANCOURT. Nothing, my child. You've only got to say "yes" and lower your eyes, and it will be all over.

BOBIN. All over . . . Oh!

Handing the myrtle to VÉZINET.

Take it, I feel like crying.

VÉZINET *is beginning to blow his nose.*

---

*The original refers to the bust of Marianne, symbol of the French Republic, which was a fixture in every municipal office. The translators have rendered it "statue of Liberty" in order to make its meaning more evident to American audiences.

VÉZINET. Gladly.

Aside.

Drat it, just when I wanted to blow my own nose.

Giving the myrtle back to NONANCOURT.

Here, Father Nonancourt.

NONANCOURT. Thanks!

Aside.

If I'd known, I'd have left it in the carriage.

SCENE 4

The same. TARDIVEAU

TARDIVEAU, *coming in all out of breath, goes behind the counter.* Lord, I'm hot!

He puts the tri-colored sashes on the counter.

My shirt is soaking!

NONANCOURT, *seeing* TARDIVEAU *and the sashes.* Ahem! Here's His Honor. Keep your gloves on.

BOBIN, *in a low voice.* Uncle, I've lost one.

NONANCOURT. Put your hand in your pocket.

BOBIN *puts his gloved hand in his pocket.*

Not that one, you idiot.

He puts both hands in. TARDIVEAU *has taken out a flannel undershirt from beneath the counter.*

TARDIVEAU, *aside.* At last I'm going to get a chance to change.

NONANCOURT *takes* HÉLÈNE *by the hand and presents her to* TARDIVEAU. Your Honor, this is the bride.

In a low voice.

Curtsey!

HÉLÈNE *makes several curtseys.*

TARDIVEAU, *quickly hiding his flannel undershirt; aside.* What's all this?

NONANCOURT. She's my daughter.

BOBIN. My cousin.

NONANCOURT. I'm her father.

BOBIN. I'm her cousin.

NONANCOURT. And these are our relatives.

To the others.

Everybody bow!

The members of the wedding bow.

TARDIVEAU *bows back to them right and left; aside.* They're very polite, but they're going to keep me from changing.

NONANCOURT. Do you want to start by taking our names?

He places his myrtle on the counter.

TARDIVEAU. Gladly.

He opens the ledger and says, aside.

It's a country wedding party come to make some purchases.

NONANCOURT. Are you ready?

Dictating.

Antoine, Petit-Pierre.

TARDIVEAU. I don't need the Christian name.

NONANCOURT. Oh!

To the wedding party.

They ask for it at Charentonneau.

TARDIVEAU. Let's hurry, sir. I'm terribly hot.

NONANCOURT. Certainly.

Dictating.

Antoine Voiture, Petit-Pierre, called Nonancourt.

Interrupting himself.

Damn! Forgive my emotion. My shoe is killing me.

Opening his arms to HÉLÈNE.

Oh, my child!

HÉLÈNE. Oh, Papa, it keeps sticking me!

TARDIVEAU. Let's not waste time, sir.

Aside.

I'm sure to catch pneumonia. Your address?

NONANCOURT. Adult citizen.

TARDIVEAU. But where do you live?

NONANCOURT. Horticulturist.

BOBIN. Member of the Syracuse Horticultural Society.

TARDIVEAU. But I don't need that.

NONANCOURT. Born at Grosbois, December 7, 1798.

TARDIVEAU. That's enough, now. I'm not asking for your auto-biography.

NONANCOURT. I'm finished.

Aside.

This judge has a pretty sharp tongue.

To VÉZINET.

You're next.

VÉZINET *doesn't move.*

BOBIN, *pushing him.*

You're next.

VÉZINET *goes majestically up to the counter.* Sir, before ac-cepting the position of witness——

TARDIVEAU. Excuse me?

VÉZINET, *continuing.* I became deeply conscious of the seri-ousness of my duties.

NONANCOURT, *aside.* Where the devil has my son-in-law gone?

VÉZINET. It occurred to me that a witness must combine three qualities.

TARDIVEAU. But sir . . .

VÉZINET. The first . . .

BOBIN, *opening the right center door.* Oh Uncle, come look!

NONANCOURT. What's the matter?

Looking and uttering a cry.

Son of a horticulturist! My son-in-law kissing a woman!

ALL. Oh!

A murmur goes through the crowd.

BOBIN. The brute!

HÉLÈNE. How dreadful!

NONANCOURT. His wedding day!

VÉZINET, *who has heard nothing, to* TARDIVEAU. The second is to be a French citizen—or at least naturalized.

NONANCOURT, *to* TARDIVEAU. Stop! This shall go no further! I'm breaking everything off. Erase everything, sir. Erase!

TARDIVEAU *erases.*

I'm taking back my daughter. Bobin, she's yours!

BOBIN, *joyous.* Oh, Uncle!

SCENE 5

The same. FADINARD

ALL, *seeing* FADINARD *appear.* Ah! There he is!

CHORUS, *together.*

AIR: *C'est vraiment une horreur.* TENTATIONS D'ANTOINETTE, *end of Act II.*

> Truly how perfidious,
> Shameful and insidious,
> Odious,
> Scandalous,
> Terrible and hideous!

FADINARD.

> What is so perfidious,
> Shameful and insidious,
> Odious,
> Scandalous,
> Terrible and hideous?

What's all the commotion? Why didn't you stay in the cabs?

NONANCOURT. My son, it's all off!

FADINARD. Naturally!

NONANCOURT. Your conduct suggests the orgies of the Regency! Fie, sir, fie!

BOBIN *and the* GUESTS. Fie! Fie!

FADINARD. But what have I done now?

ALL. Oh!

NONANCOURT. You're asking me? After catching you with your Columbine? You Harlequin!

FADINARD, *aside*. Damn, he saw me!

Aloud.

Well, I won't deny it.

ALL. Ah!

HÉLÈNE, *weeping*. He admits it!

BOBIN. Poor little cousin.

Kissing HÉLÈNE.

Fie, sir, fie!

FADINARD, *to* BOBIN, *pushing him off*. Take it easy, you! One must observe the decencies!

BOBIN. She's my cousin.

NONANCOURT. There's nothing wrong.

FADINARD. Oh, so there's nothing wrong. Well, the lady I was just kissing is also my cousin.

ALL. Ah!

NONANCOURT. Introduce her to me. I'll invite her to the wedding.

FADINARD, *aside*. That's all I need.

Aloud.

Don't bother. She wouldn't accept. She's in mourning.

NONANCOURT. In a pink dress?

FADINARD. Yes, it's for her husband.

NONANCOURT. Oh.

To TARDIVEAU.

Your Honor, I've decided to go on with it. Bobin, I'm taking her back.

BOBIN, *irritated, aside.* Old Indian giver!

NONANCOURT. We can begin.

> *To the others.*

> Take your places.

> *The whole* WEDDING PARTY *sits down right, facing* TARDI-
> VEAU.

FADINARD, *at the extreme left, near the footlights, aside.*
What the devil are they doing now?

TARDIVEAU, *leaving his ledger and going to get his undershirt
at the end of the counter, aside.* No, I'm not going to stay
this way.

NONANCOURT, *to the* WEDDING PARTY. He's going somewhere
else. It seems this isn't where people get married.

TARDIVEAU, *his flannel undershirt in his hand, aside.* I've absolutely got to change.

> *He leaves the counter, going around by the footlights.*

NONANCOURT, *to the* WEDDING PARTY. Let us follow His Honor.

> *He takes his myrtle from the counter and goes behind the
> counter following* TARDIVEAU. *The whole* WEDDING PARTY
> *follows* NONANCOURT *Indian file;* BOBIN *takes the ledger,*
> VÉZINET *the sash, the others take the inkwell, pen, ruler.*
> TARDIVEAU, *seeing himself followed, doesn't know what to
> make of it, and exits precipitously downstage right.*

CHORUS

> AIR: *Vite! que l'on se rende.* TENTATIONS D'ANTOINETTE.

> *Since this dignitary*
> *Deigns our steps to guide,*
> *Behind him let us hurry*
> *And never leave his side.*

SCENE 6

FADINARD, *then* CLARA.

FADINARD, *alone.* What are they up to? Where are they going?

CLARA, *entering downstage right.* Monsieur Fadinard!

FADINARD. Oh! Clara!

CLARA. Look, here's your sample. I've nothing to match it.

FADINARD. What?

CLARA. It's made of a very fine straw which isn't usually stocked. You won't find it anywhere, believe me!
She gives the fragment of hat to him.

FADINARD, *aside.* Hell! Now I am in a mess.

CLARA. If you're willing to wait fifteen days, I'll order you one from Florence.

FADINARD. Fifteen days! Silly girl!

CLARA. I only know of one like it in Paris.

FADINARD, *excitedly.* I'll buy it!

CLARA. Yes, but it's not for sale. I had it made up eight days ago for the Baroness de Champigny.
CLARA goes over by the counter and begins to tidy the store.

FADINARD, *aside.* A baroness! I can't go up to her and say, "Madame, how much for the hat?" What the hell! Too bad about that gentleman and lady. First I'm going to get married and then . . .

SCENE 7

The same. TARDIVEAU, *the* WEDDING PARTY.

TARDIVEAU, *very upset, enters by the upstage door; he is holding his flannel undershirt.* Lord, I'm hot!
At the same time the whole WEDDING PARTY *pours in behind him.* NONANCOURT *with his myrtle,* BOBIN *carrying the ledger, and* VÉZINET *the sash.* TARDIVEAU, *seeing them, starts out again left, followed by the* WEDDING PARTY.

CHORUS (*same as above*)
Since this dignitary, etc.

CLARA, *stupefied.* What's all that?

She goes out left.

FADINARD. What are they buying in there? Father Nonancourt!

He is about to follow the WEDDING PARTY *when he is stopped by* FÉLIX, *who enters quickly by the main door.*

SCENE 8

FADINARD, FÉLIX, *then* CLARA.

FÉLIX. I've just come from your house, sir.

FADINARD, *excitedly.* What about that soldier?

FÉLIX. He's swearing, grinding his teeth, smashing chairs!

FADINARD. Good God!

FÉLIX. He says you're standing him up, that you ought to have been back in ten minutes, but that he'll get you sooner or later, whenever you come in.

FADINARD. Félix, you're in my employ. I order you to throw him out the window.

FÉLIX. He'd never agree to it.

FADINARD, *excitedly.* And the lady? The lady?

FÉLIX. She's having convulsions, rolling around in fits, crying!

FADINARD. She'll dry up.

FÉLIX. So they sent for a doctor. He made her get in bed and won't leave her side.

FADINARD, *yelling.* In bed? What do you mean, bed? Which bed?

FÉLIX. Yours, sir!

FADINARD, *forcibly.* Sacrilege! I won't have it! My Hélène's bed, that I didn't dare christen even with a glance, and here this woman comes and has convulsions in it! Go on, run, get her up, tear off the bedclothes!

FÉLIX. But sir . . .

FADINARD. Tell them I've found the article, that I'm on the trail.

FÉLIX. What article?

FADINARD, *pushing him.* Go on, you wretch!

To himself.

No more shilly-shallying. A sick woman at home, a doctor! I've got to have that hat at all costs, if I have to snatch it off the top of a crowned head, or the Obelisk in the Place de la Concorde! Yes, but what shall I do with my wedding? I know! I'll take them inside the column in the Place Vendôme. That's it. I'll say to the guards, "I've reserved the monument for twelve hours! don't let anyone leave!"

To CLARA, *who comes in astonished, left, gazing offstage.*

Bringing her quickly to the footlights.

Clara, quick, where does she live?

CLARA. Who?

FADINARD. Your Baroness.

CLARA. What Baroness?

FADINARD. The hat Baroness, idiot!

CLARA, *recoiling.* Oh, now, look here!

FADINARD. No, sweet angel—— What I mean is: sweet angel! Give me her address.

CLARA. Monsieur Tardiveau will take you; here he is. But you do promise to marry me?

FADINARD. My dear!

SCENE 9

FADINARD, CLARA, TARDIVEAU, *then the whole* WEDDING PARTY.

TARDIVEAU, *entering left and more and more upset.* What do all these people want? Why the devil are they after me? How can I change?

CLARA. Quick, take Monsieur to the Baroness de Champigny.

TARDIVEAU. But madame . . .

FADINARD. Let's get going, it's urgent.

To TARDIVEAU.

I've got eight cabs, take the first one.

He drags him out by the main door. The whole WEDDING
PARTY *pours in on the left and rushes after* TARDIVEAU *and*
FADINARD.

CHORUS.

(Same as before) Since this dignitary, etc.

CLARA, *seeing her ledger being carried off, tries to hold
onto it. The curtain falls.*

ACT THREE

*An elegant parlor. Three doors upstage center opening
onto a dining room. At left, a door leading to the other
room of the apartment. Near the footlights, a settee. At
right, the main entrance; upstage right a closet door. Near
the footlights, flush against the wall, a piano; magnificent
furnishings.*

SCENE 1

The BARONESS DE CHAMPIGNY, ACHILLE DE ROSALBA.

*When the curtain rises, the three upstage doors are open
and a richly spread table is visible.*

ACHILLE, *entering right and looking into the wings.* Charming! Ravishing! It's done in exquisite taste.

Looking off upstage.

What do I see here—a buffet!

BARONESS, *entering left.* Nosey!

ACHILLE. Oh well, my dear cousin, you ask us to a musical afternoon and here I see preparations for supper. What's the meaning of that?

BARONESS. The meaning, my dear Viscount, is that I intend to keep my guests as long as possible. After the concert, we'll dine, and after supper we'll dance. That's my program.

ACHILLE. It suits me perfectly. Will there be many singers?

BARONESS. Yes. Why?

ACHILLE. Just that I should have asked you to save me a little place. I've composed a song.

BARONESS, *aside.* Ugh!

ACHILLE. The title is delicious: "Evening Breeze."

BARONESS. And so original!

ACHILLE. As for the idea, it's very fresh. People are haying. A young shepherd is sitting in a field . . .

BARONESS. Of course, it would be lovely—for a family evening, while we're playing whist. But today, cousin, you must give way to the *artistes.* We have first rate talents, among them the fashionable singer Nisnardi, from Bologna.

ACHILLE. Nisnardi? Who's he?

BARONESS. He's a tenor who has been in Paris eight days; he's all the rage. Everyone's grabbing for him.

ACHILLE. I've never heard of him.

BARONESS. Nor I, but my heart was set on him. I offered him 3000 francs to sing two pieces.

ACHILLE. You can have "Evening Breeze" for nothing.

BARONESS, *smiling.* That's too much. This morning I got a reply from Signor Nisnardi—here it is.

ACHILLE. Oh, his handwriting. Let's see.

BARONESS, *reading.* "Madame, you ask for two pieces; I shall sing three. You offer me 3000 francs; that is not enough.

ACHILLE. Mercy!

BARONESS. "I will only accept a flower from your bouquet."

ACHILLE. Ah, what delicacy, what—— My word, I think I'll
write a song about it!

BARONESS. He's a charming man. Last Thursday he sang at
the Countess of Bray's; she has very pretty feet, you know.

ACHILLE. What about it?

BARONESS. Guess what he asked her for?

ACHILLE. Dear me, I have no idea. A pot of carnations?

BARONESS. No, an evening slipper!

ACHILLE. A slipper! What a curious fellow!

BARONESS. He's very whimsical.

ACHILLE. That's fine, so long as his whims don't go above the
ankle.

BARONESS. Viscount!

ACHILLE. Oh look here, a tenor you know . . .

The noise of several carriages is heard.

BARONESS. Oh, good heavens! Could it be my guests already?
Cousin, be so good as to take my place; I won't be long.
She exits left.

SCENE 2

ACHILLE, *then a* SERVANT.

ACHILLE, *to the* BARONESS, *as she leaves.* Never fear, my
charming cousin; you can count on me.

SERVANT *entering right.* There's a gentleman here who wishes
to speak to the Baroness de Champigny.

ACHILLE. His name?

SERVANT. He doesn't wish to give it. He says that it was he
who had the honor to write to Madame this morning.

ACHILLE, *aside.* Oh, that's it—the singer, the slipper man. I'm
curious to see him. My word, he's punctual. It's obvious

that he's a foreigner. Never mind, a man who has refused
3000 francs deserves the greatest respect.
To the servant.

Show him in.
Aside.

Besides, he's a musician, a colleague.
The servant closes the upstage door, and leaves.

SCENE 3

FADINARD, ACHILLE.

FADINARD, *appearing right, very timid.* Excuse me, sir!
The servant leaves.

ACHILLE. Come right in, dear sir, come in!

FADINARD, *embarrassed and coming forward with frequent
bows.* Thank you so much. I was quite fine in there.
He puts his hat on his head and takes it off quickly.

Ah!
Aside.

I'm all mixed up! Those servants, this fancy parlor,
Pointing right.

these huge family portraits staring at me as if to say, "Have
the goodness to leave, we don't sell hats." It's all put me
in a state.

ACHILLE, *looking at him through a lorgnette.* How Italian he
looks! What an amusing waistcoat!
Laughs, staring at him.

Heh! Heh! Heh!

FADINARD, *making him several bows.* Sir, may I have the
honor—to address you——
Aside.

He's some majordomo!

ACHILLE. Do sit down!

FADINARD. No, thank you. I'm too tired. I mean, I came in a cab.

ACHILLE, *laughing*. In a cab? How charming!

FADINARD. Not so much charming as—rough.

ACHILLE. We were just speaking of you. Such a gallant man! We hear you're fond of little feet!

FADINARD, *astonished*. With truffles?

ACHILLE. Oh, very good! Just the same, that story about the slipper is adorable, adorable!

FADINARD, *aside*. Indeed! What on earth is he getting at?
Aloud.

Excuse me—if I may be so bold, I would like to speak to the Baroness.

ACHILLE. It's fantastic, my dear sir! You haven't the slightest accent.

FADINARD. Oh, you flatter me!

ACHILLE. Word of honor! You could be from the suburbs.

FADINARD, *aside*. Indeed! What on earth is he getting at?
Aloud.

Excuse me, if I may be so bold, I would like to speak to the Baroness.

ACHILLE. To Madame de Champigny? She'll be right down, she's getting dressed. Meanwhile I, her cousin, the Viscount Achille de Rosalba, have been asked to take her place.

FADINARD, *aside*. A viscount!
He makes him several bows, aside.

With these people I'll never have the courage to haggle over a hat!

ACHILLE, *calling him*. Tell me . . .

FADINARD, *going to him*. Sir?

ACHILLE, *leaning on his shoulder*. What would you think of a song entitled "Evening Breeze?"

FADINARD. Me? But—what would you think?

ACHILLE. It's very fresh. People are haying. A young shepherd . . .

FADINARD, *pulling his shoulder out from beneath* ACHILLE'S *arm.* Excuse me—if I may be so bold, I'd like to speak . . .

ACHILLE. Naturally! I'll run and tell her. Delighted, my dear sir, to have met you.

FADINARD. Oh, Sir Viscount, it is I who . . .

ACHILLE. It's just that he hasn't the slightest accent, not the slightest!

Exits left.

SCENE 4

FADINARD *alone.*

FADINARD. Well, at last I'm at the Baroness's. She knows about my visit. After I left Clara's shop, I quickly wrote her a note asking for an interview. I told her everything and ended with a phrase which I find extremely moving: "Madame, two heads are attached to your hat—remember that generosity is a woman's most beautiful coiffure." I think that will make a good impression, and I signed it: "Count Fadinard." That won't look bad either. After all, a Baroness—what the hell, she takes her time getting dressed! And there's my confounded wedding party sitting downstairs. Needless to say, they didn't want to let me go. Ever since this morning, I've been in the position of a man with a string of cabs tied to his—well, not his stomach. It's very inconvenient for going into society, to say nothing of my father-in-law, the porcupine, who keeps sticking his nose into my carriage and yelling, "Are you all right, my son?" "My son, what is that monument?" "My son, where are we going?" Finally, to put an end to it, I answered, "To the *Nursing Calf,*" and they think they're in the courtyard of that establishment, but I ordered the coachmen not to let anyone get out. I don't feel the need to present my family to the Baroness. What the hell, she takes her time getting dressed—if she only knew that I had two demons at home breaking up my furniture, and that by evening I may not even have a chair to offer my wife—to rest her weary head! My own wife! Oh, yes, I left out one detail. I'm married! It's over! What could I do? My father-in-law was fuming, his daughter was crying, and Bobin was kissing me. So I took advantage of a traffic jam to go into the marriage bureau and from there to the church. Poor Hélène, if you could have seen her looking like a little dove——

Changing his tone.

What the hell, she takes her time getting dressed! Oh, here she is!

SCENE 5

FADINARD, *the* BARONESS.

BARONESS, *entering left, in evening dress, and carrying a bouquet.* A thousand pardons, my dear sir, for having kept you waiting.

FADINARD. Madame, it is I who intrude.

In his confusion, he puts his hat back on and takes it off again quickly. Aside.

Fine thing—I'm getting into another state!

BARONESS. I'm so grateful to you for coming early. We'll be able to talk. You aren't too chilly?

FADINARD, *wiping his forehead.* Thank you. I came in a cab.

BARONESS. Alas! There is one thing I cannot give you, and that's the sunny sky of Italy.

FADINARD. Oh, madame, in the first place I wouldn't accept it, I'd be too embarrassed. And in the second, that's not where what I'm looking for is.

BARONESS. I should think not! What a magnificent country, Italy!

FADINARD. Oh, yes!

Aside.

What does she mean, talking about Italy?

BARONESS.

AIR: *La Fée aux Roses.*

> *The memory brings back to my enchanted soul*
> *Its palaces divine, its beaches wide and flat,*

FADINARD, *to remind her of the purpose of his visit.*

> *And its hat!*

BARONESS.

> *Its scented orange groves through which the breezes roll,*
> *Mingling song of bird with trusting lovers' chat,*
> *Its harbors calm, which greet*
> *A peaceful shipping fleet,*
> *Its golden fields of wheat,*

FADINARD, *imitating her.*

> *From which they make hats so sweet,*
> *For horses to eat!*

BARONESS *astonished.* What?

FADINARD, *a bit emotionally.* Madame has doubtless received the note which she had the honor—no, which I gave myself the honor—that is, which I had the honor to write to her.

BARONESS. Of course, and so subtle too!

She sits down on the settee and motions FADINARD *to take a chair.*

FADINARD. You must have thought me very indiscreet.

BARONESS. Not at all!

FADINARD, *seating himself on a chair near the* BARONESS. Perhaps Madame will let me recall to her that generosity is a woman's most beautiful coiffure.

BARONESS, *astonished.* I beg your pardon?

FADINARD. I said: generosity is a woman's most beautiful coiffure.

BARONESS. Of course!

Aside.

What can he mean by that?

FADINARD, *aside*. She understood! She's going to give me the hat!

BARONESS. Don't you agree that music is a wonderful thing?

FADINARD. Sorry?

BARONESS. What a voice! What fire! What passion!

FADINARD, *pretending great ardor*. Oh, don't even talk about it—music! music!! music!!!

Aside.

She's going to give me the hat!

BARONESS. Why don't you have Rossini compose for you?

FADINARD. Me?

Aside.

This woman says the most disconnected things.

Aloud.

I would like Madame to remember that I had the honor to write her a note . . .

BARONESS. A delicious note, which I will keep forever, believe me, forever!

FADINARD, *aside*. Is that all she's going to do?

BARONESS. What do you think of Alboni?

FADINARD. Not much at all—but I would like Madame to recall that in that note—I asked her . . .

BARONESS. Oh, what a fool I am!

Looking at her bouquet.

You can't do without it?

FADINARD, *getting up, forcefully*. Can I do without it? Can the Arabian do without his steed?

BARONESS, *rising*. Oh! Oh! What southern fire!

She goes toward the piano to take a flower from the bouquet.

It would have been cruel to make you wait any longer.

FADINARD, *down by the footlights; aside*. At last, I'm going to get that miserable hat. I'll be able to go home.

Pulling out his purse.

Now it's only a matter of—shall I bargain? No, she's a Baroness, let's not be crass.

BARONESS, *graciously handing him a flower.* Here you are, sir. Cash on the line!

FADINARD, *taking the flower with stupefaction.* What's that? A marigold! What happened? Didn't she get my letter? I shall sue the postman!

SCENE 6

FADINARD, *the* BARONESS, *guests of both sexes. The guests enter right.*

CHORUS.
  AIR: *Nargeot.*

GUESTS.

> *Grateful we*
> *Are to be*
> *Asked to come*
> *To your home,*
> *And to spend*
> *With our friend,*
> *Happy hours without end.*

BARONESS.

> *Grateful she*
> *Is to see*
> *That you've come*
> *To her home,*
> *Here to spend*
> *With your friend*
> *Happy hours without end.*

> *I promised there would be*
> *A great celebrity.*
> *Clap your hands, it's he,*
> *The singer, Nisnardi!*

FADINARD.

> *What the devil, me?*
> *The singer, Nisnardi?*

BARONESS.

> *Great Rubini's rival, he!*

FADINARD.

> *Madame, you have erred!*

BARONESS.

> *Not another word!*
> *From far off Italy, the cheers*
> *Have reached our ears.*

FADINARD.

> *I've got to join this party,*
> *So I'll become Nisnardi*
> *And goodbye Fadinardi.*

Spoken.

I won't deny it, ladies. I am Nisnardi, the great Nisnardi!

Aside.

Otherwise, they'd kick me out.

ALL, *bowing.* Signor!

BARONESS. We shall have to wait until everyone has arrived before we can applaud the nightingale of Bologna, so perhaps you ladies would like to take a stroll in the gardens.

REPRISE:

> *Guests—Grateful we, etc.*
> *Baroness—Grateful she, etc.*
> *Fadinard—Grateful he*
> > *Is to be*
> > *Madly chasing after hats,*
> > *And on this day,*
> > *Going bats,*
> > *When love should sweep his cares away.*

Aside.

As a matter of fact, I may get somewhere.

Going over to the BARONESS, *who is about to exit left with her guests.*

Excuse me, madame, I would like to ask a little favor, but I hardly dare . . .

SCENE 7

FADINARD, *the* BARONESS, *then a* CHAMBERMAID.

BARONESS. Speak! You know there is nothing I can refuse Signor Nisnardi.

FADINARD. It's just that—my request is going to seem very strange, very mad.

BARONESS, *aside.* Oh good Lord, I think he's looking at my shoes!

FADINARD. Confidentially, you know, I'm a pretty queer egg. You understand—artists—a thousand whims run through my head!

BARONESS. How well I know!

FADINARD. That's good—and if I can't satisfy them, it gets me here—in the throat. My voice goes like this.
Pretending to lose his voice.

Singing's out of the question!

BARONESS, *aside.* Oh, good Heavens, my concert!
Aloud.

Speak, sir, tell me what you need, what you must have!

FADINARD. Oh dear, it's very hard to tell you——

BARONESS, *aside.* I'm terrified! He's not looking at my shoes any more.

FADINARD. I'm afraid if you don't give me a little encouragement—it's such an out-of-the-way thing.

BARONESS, *quickly.* My bouquet, perhaps?

FADINARD. No, it's not that. It's a thousand times more unusual.

BARONESS, *aside.* The way he looks at me! I'm almost sorry I announced him to my guests!

FADINARD. Oh God! What beautiful hair you have!

BARONESS, *recoiling suddenly, aside.* My hair! Heaven forbid!

FADINARD. It reminds me of an enchanting hat you were wearing yesterday.

BARONESS. At Chantilly?

FADINARD, *quickly.* Exactly! Oh, the enchanting hat, the ravishing hat!

BARONESS. You mean, sir—is that it?

FADINARD, *with passion.*

AIR: *Quand les oiseaux.*

> *What it was I dared not say,*
> *But you have guessed, I will admit.*
> *Your hat is that for which I pray,*
> *My happiness depends on it.*
> *Underneath your lovely hair*
> *My eyes behold your face divine;*
> *If far away I'm forced to pine,*
> *And if from me a fate unfair*
> *The image of your face must tear,*
> *The frame at least will still be mine.*

Aside.

> *These verses don't exactly shine!*

Aloud.

> *Oh yes, the frame will still be mine.*

BARONESS, *bursting into laughter.* Ha! Ha! Ha!

FADINARD, *laughing also.* Ha! Ha! Ha!

Aside, serious.

I'm going to get it!

BARONESS. I see! It's to match the slipper!

FADINARD. What slipper?

BARONESS, *with bursts of laughter.* Ha! Ha! Ha!

FADINARD, *laughing.* Ha! Ha! Ha!

Aside, serious.

What slipper?

BARONESS, *still laughing.* Don't worry, sir, that hat . . .

FADINARD. Ah!

BARONESS. I'll send it to you tomorrow.

FADINARD. No, right now, right now!

BARONESS. But I'm afraid . . .

FADINARD, *losing his voice again.* Look, you see? My voice—it's slipping! Hoo! hoo!

BARONESS, *wildly ringing a bell.* Oh my Lord! Clothilde! Clothilde!

A chambermaid appears right; the BARONESS *whispers quickly to her; she leaves.*

In five minutes your wish will be granted.

Laughing.

Please forgive me—ha! ha! ha! After all, a hat—it's so original! Ha! ha! ha!

She exits left, laughing.

SCENE 8

FADINARD, *then* NONANCOURT, *then a* SERVANT.

FADINARD, *alone.* In five minutes I'll have absconded with the hat. I'll leave my wallet to pay for it.

Laughing.

Ha! Ha! When I think of old man Nonancourt, how he must be fuming in his cab!

NONANCOURT *appears at the dining-room door; he has a napkin in his buttonhole and ribbons of many colors in the lapel of his coat.* Where the devil is my son-in-law?

FADINARD. My father-in-law!

NONANCOURT, *a bit tipsy.* My son, it's all off!

FADINARD, *turning around.* You again! What are you doing here?

NONANCOURT. We're eating.

FADINARD. Where?

NONANCOURT. In there.

FADINARD, *aside.* Heavens! The Baroness's dinner!

NONANCOURT. Good old *Nursing Calf!* What a swell joint! I'm going to come back here sometime.

FADINARD. Look here . . .

NONANCOURT. Just the same, you've been acting like a good-for-nothing!

FADINARD. Father!

NONANCOURT. Abandoning your wife on your wedding day, letting her dine without you!

FADINARD. What about the others?

NONANCOURT. They're gorging themselves.

FADINARD. What a mess! I'm in a cold sweat.

Seizes the napkin from NONANCOURT *and wipes his forehead with it.*

NONANCOURT. I'm not sure what's the matter with me. I think I'm a bit tipsy.

FADINARD. That's just fine! And the rest of them?

NONANCOURT. Same as me. Bobin fell on his face trying to catch the bride's garter. Did we laugh!

Shaking his foot.

Damn!

FADINARD, *aside, putting the napkin in his pocket.*
Whatever will the Baroness say? And what's keeping that hat? If I only had it, I'd clear out.

Cries from the dining room.

Three cheers for the Bride! Hip hip hooray!

FADINARD, *going upstage.* Will you shut up? Will you shut up?

NONANCOURT, *seated on the settee.* I don't know what I did with my myrtle. Fadinard?

FADINARD, *coming back to* NONANCOURT. You get out of here, quick!

He tries to make him get up.

NONANCOURT, *resisting him.* No! I potted it the day she was born.

FADINARD. You'll find it again. It's in the cab.

A servant, entering right, crosses the set with an unlighted candelabra; he opens the door upstage and utters a cry when he sees the wedding guests at the table.

SERVANT. Oh!

FADINARD. I'm finished!

He lets go of NONANCOURT, *who falls back onto the settee, leaps at the throat of the servant and grabs the candelabra.*

Hush! Not a word!

He pushes him into a closet right and locks him in.

If you move I'll throw you out the window!

The BARONESS *appears left.*

SCENE 9

FADINARD, NONANCOURT, *the* BARONESS.

FADINARD, *holding the candelabra.* The Baroness!

BARONESS, *to* FADINARD. Whatever are you doing with that candelabra?

FADINARD. Me? I'm—looking for my handkerchief, which I've lost.

He turns around as if to search; the napkin is sticking out of his pocket.

BARONESS, *laughing.* But it's in your pocket.

FADINARD. Dear me, you're right—it's in my pocket.

BARONESS. Well, sir, did they bring you what you wanted?

FADINARD, *getting in front of* NONANCOURT *to hide him.* Not yet, madame, not yet, and I'm in a great hurry.

NONANCOURT, *to himself, rising.* I don't know what's the matter with me. I think I'm a bit tipsy.

BARONESS, *pointing to* NONANCOURT. Who is that gentleman?

FADINARD. He's my—this gentleman is accompanying me.

Gives him the candelabra mechanically. NONANCOURT *holds
it in his arm as if it were his myrtle.*

BARONESS, *to* NONANCOURT. Congratulations. To accompany
well is an art!

FADINARD, *aside.* She thinks he's a musician.

NONANCOURT. Madame, I salute you!

Aside.

What a pretty woman.

In a low voice, to FADINARD.

Is she with the wedding party?

FADINARD, *aside.* If he talks, I'm lost. And what's keeping that
hat?

BARONESS, *to* NONANCOURT. Are you Italian, sir?

NONANCOURT. I'm from Charentonneau.

FADINARD. Yes, a little village near Rome.

NONANCOURT. Can you beat it, madame, I've lost my myrtle!

BARONESS. What myrtle?

FADINARD. A song, *"The Myrtle."* It's very charming.

BARONESS, *to* NONANCOURT. Would you like to try the piano,
sir? It's a Pleyel.

NONANCOURT. Come again?

FADINARD. No, it's hopeless!

BARONESS, *seeing the ribbons in* NONANCOURT'S *buttonhole.*
My, what are all those ribbons?

NONANCOURT. The garter.

FADINARD. That's it, the Order of the Garter of—Santo Campo,
Pietro Nero.

Aside.

God, I'm hot.

BARONESS. Oh, how funny. I hope, gentlemen, that you will
do us the honor of dining with us.

NONANCOURT. Maybe tomorrow. I'm full for today.

BARONESS, *laughing.* What a pity!

To FADINARD.

I'm going to get my guests. They can't wait to hear you sing.

FADINARD. They're too kind!

NONANCOURT, *aside.* More guests! What a swell wedding!

BARONESS, *to* NONANCOURT. Your arm, sir?

FADINARD, *aside.* That's done it!

NONANCOURT, *shifting his candelabra to the left hand and offering the right to the* BARONESS, *while leading her out.* Can you beat it, madame? I've lost my myrtle.

SCENE 10

FADINARD, *then a* CHAMBERMAID *with a lady's hat in a scarf, then* BOBIN.

FADINARD, *falling into an armchair.* They're going to throw us kerplunk out the window!

CHAMBERMAID, *entering.* Here's the hat, sir.

FADINARD, *getting up.* The hat! The hat!

Takes the hat and kisses the girl.

Here, that's for you, and my wallet too!

CHAMBERMAID, *aside.* What's the matter with him?

FADINARD, *while opening the scarf.* At last I've got it!

He pulls out a hat.

A black hat—in *crêpe de Chine?*

He tramples on it. Bringing back the CHAMBERMAID, *who is just going out.*

Come back here, you little wretch! The other one! The other one! Answer me!

CHAMBERMAID, *frightened.* Don't hurt me, sir!

FADINARD. Where's the Italian straw hat? I've got to have it!

CHAMBERMAID. Madame gave it as a present to her god-daughter, Madame de Beauperthuis.

FADINARD. Curses! Here we go again! Where does she live?

CHAMBERMAID. 12, rue de Ménars.

FADINARD. All right, get out, you make me sick!

The girl picks up the hat and escapes.

I'd better take off. I'll leave my father-in-law and the wedding party to work things out with the Baroness.

BOBIN, *poking his head through the dining-room door.* Cousin! Cousin!

FADINARD. What?

BOBIN. Aren't we going to dance?

FADINARD. Sure, I'm just about to go out and find some fiddles.

BOBIN *disappears.*

Now, off we go to 12, rue de Ménars.

He exits excitedly.

SCENE 11

The BARONESS, NONANCOURT, GUESTS, *then* FADINARD *and* ACHILLE, *then the* WEDDING PARTY.

NONANCOURT *is still holding the* BARONESS's *arm and also the candelabra; the guests follow them.*

CHORUS.
    AIR: *Valse de Satan*

> What a treat, we're going to hear
> The singer on whom Paris dotes.
> People say both heart and ear
> Are ravished by his tender notes.

BARONESS, *to the* GUESTS. Please sit down, the concert is about to begin.

The GUESTS *seat themselves.*

But where is Monsieur Nisnardi?

NONANCOURT. I don't know.

Yelling.

Monsieur Nisnardi! You're wanted!

ALL. Here he is, here he is!

ACHILLE, *leading back* FADINARD. What's this, signor? You're deserting us?

NONANCOURT, *aside.* Him? Nisnardi?

FADINARD, *to* ACHILLE, *who is leading him in.* I wasn't going anywhere, I assure you!

ALL. Bravo! Bravo!

They applaud him wildly.

FADINARD, *bowing right and left.* Ladies and gentlemen!

Aside.

Nabbed on the very step of the carriage!

BARONESS, *to* NONANCOURT. Sit at the piano.

She seats herself on the settee, next to a lady.

NONANCOURT. You want me to sit at the piano? Sure, I'll sit at the piano.

He puts down the candelabra and sits at the piano. The whole company is seated left, so as not to mask the center door.

BARONESS. Signor Nisnardi, we are ready to applaud you.

FADINARD. Of course, madame—too kind.

A FEW VOICES. Hush, hush.

FADINARD, *near the piano at the far right.* What a mess! I sing like a rusty gate.

Aloud, coughing.

Ahem, ahem!

ALL. Shhhh!

FADINARD, *aside.* What ever am I going to sing to them?

Aloud and coughing.

Ahem, ahem!

NONANCOURT. You want me to play? I'll play.

He bangs the keys very hard without playing any tune.

FADINARD, *singing at the top of his lungs.* Hail, hail, the gang's
all here——

Cries from in back.

Three Cheers for the Bride!

The gathering is astounded. The WEDDING PARTY *is heard
singing a polka. The three doors in back open and the* WED-
DING PARTY *explodes into the room, yelling.*

Take your places for the polka!

NONANCOURT. To the devil with the music! Here's the whole
wedding party.

To FADINARD.

You, go dance with your wife!

FADINARD. Go fly a kite!

Aside.

Every man for himself!

*The wedding guests manage to override the protests of the
society ladies and dance with them. Shouts, confusion. The
curtain falls.*

ACT FOUR

*A bedroom in the house of Beauperthuis. Upstage, a cur-
tained alcove. An open screen down left. An entrance door
at the right of the alcove. Another door left. Side doors. A
table at right against the wall.*

SCENE 1

BEAUPERTHUIS, *alone.*

When the curtain opens, BEAUPERTHUIS *is seated in front
of the screen. He is taking a footbath. A towel covers his*

legs. *His shoes are beside the chair. A lamp is on the table. The alcove curtains are open.*

BEAUPERTHUIS. It's very funny. My wife says to me this morning at seven o'clock, "Beauperthuis, I'm going to buy some suède gloves." And at nine forty-five in the evening, she hasn't come back. No one's going to convince me that it takes twelve hours and fifty-two minutes to buy suède gloves, short of going to the factory to get them. I worked up a splitting headache, just from wondering where my wife was. So I stuck my feet in a tub and sent the maid to all our friends and relatives. No one's seen her. Oh, I forgot to check with my aunt Grosminet. Perhaps Anaïs is there. *He rings and calls.*

Virginie! Virginie!

SCENE 2

BEAUPERTHUIS, VIRGINIE.

VIRGINIE, *carrying a kettle.* Here's your hot water, sir.

BEAUPERTHUIS. Fine! Put it there. Listen . . .

VIRGINIE, *placing the kettle on the floor.* Watch out, sir, it's boiling.

BEAUPERTHUIS. Do you remember how my wife was dressed this morning when she went out?

VIRGINIE. She had on her new dress with ruffles, and her beautiful Italian straw hat.

BEAUPERTHUIS, *to himself.* Yes, a gift from the Baroness, her godmother. A five hundred franc hat, at least—to go buy suède gloves in!

He pours the hot water into the tub.

Very funny.

VIRGINIE. If I may say so, it is rather strange.

BEAUPERTHUIS. It's very clear that my wife has gone visiting somewhere.

VIRGINIE, *aside*. In the Bois de Vincennes.

BEAUPERTHUIS. I want you to go to Madame Grosminet's.

VIRGINIE. At Gros-Caillou?

BEAUPERTHUIS. I'm sure she's there.

VIRGINIE, *forgetting herself*. Oh, sir! I'm sure she's not.

BEAUPERTHUIS. What? How do you know?

VIRGINIE, *quickly*. Oh, I don't at all, sir. I said, "I *think* not."
It's just that you've had me running around for two hours,
sir. I'm absolutely dead. Gros-Caillou isn't just around the
corner, you know.

BEAUPERTHUIS. Well, take a carriage.

Giving her some money.

Here's three francs. Off with you. Run along!

VIRGINIE. Yes, sir.

Aside.

I'll go have a cup of tea with the florist lady on the fifth
floor.

BEAUPERTHUIS, *seeing her still there*. Well?

VIRGINIE. All right, sir, I'm going.

Aside.

Just the same, I'm waiting till I see the straw hat again.
My goodness wouldn't that be funny?
She leaves.

SCENE 3

BEAUPERTHUIS, *then* FADINARD.

BEAUPERTHUIS, *alone*. My head's splitting. I should have put
some mustard in.

With concentrated fury.

Oh, Anaïs! If I really believed—— There's no revenge, no
torture . . .

The bell rings. Radiant.

At last. There she is. Come in.

The bell rings very loudly.

I'm taking a footbath. Just turn the knob. Come in, my dear one.

FADINARD *enters. He is disordered, exhausted, out of breath.*

FADINARD. Monsieur Beauperthuis, if you please.

BEAUPERTHUIS. A stranger! Who is this man? I'm not at home!

FADINARD. Oh, wonderful! It's you.

To himself.

I'm exhausted! They beat us up at the Baroness's. I didn't mind, but Nonancourt is furious. He wants to write to the papers exposing the *Nursing Calf.* What utter madness!

Panting.

Oof!

BEAUPERTHUIS. Get out, sir! Get out!

FADINARD, *taking a chair.* Thank you, sir. You live pretty high up. Your stairs are very steep.

He has seated himself next to BEAUPERTHUIS.

BEAUPERTHUIS, *covering his legs with the towel.* Sir, you don't break into people's houses. I repeat . . .

FADINARD, *lifting the towel a little.* You're taking a footbath? Don't get up. I'll only be a minute.

He lifts the kettle.

BEAUPERTHUIS. But I'm not at home. I'm in no state to listen to you. I've a horrible headache.

FADINARD, *pouring the hot water into the tub.* Let me heat up your water.

BEAUPERTHUIS, *yelling.* Eeeh!

Snatching the kettle from him and putting it on the floor.

Put that down! What do you want, sir? Who are you?

FADINARD. Léonidas Fadinard, twenty-five, landlord, just married. My eight cabs are at your door.

BEAUPERTHUIS. What's that to me, sir? I've never met you!

FADINARD. Same here, and I don't want to meet you, either. I want to see your wife.

BEAUPERTHUIS. My wife! Do you know her?

FADINARD. Oh no, but I know beyond any doubt that she has an article of clothing which I'm in great need of. I've got to have it.

BEAUPERTHUIS. What?

FADINARD, *rising.*

> AIR: *Ces bosquets de lauriers.*

> *I've got to have it, sir, and mark you well*
> *How ruthlessly my purpose I express.*
> *I'll triumph, if I have to go through hell*
> *For this accursed article of dress.*
> *Is it for sale? All right, I'll pay the price.*
> *There is no sum to which I will not climb.*
> *Do you refuse? I'll steal it in a trice!*
> *I care not if the method isn't nice.*
> *I will not even stop at crime,*
> *Not even at the blackest crime!*

BEAUPERTHUIS, *aside.* He's a desperate thief!

> FADINAND *sits down again and pours in more hot water. Yelling.*

> Eeeh! For the last time, sir, will you get out?

FADINARD. Not till I've seen Madame.

BEAUPERTHUIS. She's not in.

FADINARD. At ten o'clock at night? A likely story!

BEAUPERTHUIS. I tell you, she's not in.

FADINARD, *angrily.* Are you telling me that you let your wife run around at all hours of the night? You're not that dumb, sir.

> *He empties in a great deal of boiling water.*

BEAUPERTHUIS. Eeeeh! Christ Almighty! I'm boiled alive!

> *He furiously puts the kettle on the other side.*

FADINARD, *getting up and setting his chair down on the right.*

> I understand! Madame is in bed, but I don't care. My intentions are pure. I'll shut my eyes and we'll settle this business blind.

BEAUPERTHUIS, *standing up in his bath and brandishing the kettle; choking with anger.* Sir!!!

FADINARD. Could you please tell me where her bedroom is?

BEAUPERTHUIS. I'll bash your brains out!

He swings the kettle; FADINARD *wards off the blow by shutting the screen on* BEAUPERTHUIS. BEAUPERTHUIS' *shoes are left outside the screen.*

FADINARD. I told you that I wouldn't stop at crime.

He enters the room off right.

SCENE 4

BEAUPERTHUIS *behind the screen,* NONANCOURT.

BEAUPERTHUIS, *unseen.* Hold on, murderer! Just a minute, thief!

He is heard dressing.

NONANCOURT, *entering with his myrtle and limping.* How did I ever get mixed up with a boor like that? He goes up to his apartment and leaves us standing outside. Well, at last I'm at my son-in-law's. I can change my socks.

BEAUPERTHUIS, *hurrying.* Just wait! Just you wait!

NONANCOURT. Well, well, he's in there, getting undressed.

Seeing the shoes.

Shoes! What a piece of luck!

Takes them and exchanges his own shoes for those of BEAUPERTHUIS. *With relief.*

Ah!

Puts his own shoes where BEAUPERTHUIS' *were.*

That's better. And what about this myrtle I'm beginning to feel sprouting from my arms? I'll go put it in the conjugal bower.

BEAUPERTHUIS, *sticking out his arm and taking the shoes, which* NONANCOURT *has set down.*

My shoes!

NONANCOURT, *knocking on the screen.* Hey, you! Where's your bedroom?

BEAUPERTHUIS. My bedroom? Yes, yes, just a minute! I'm ready.

NONANCOURT. Don't bother. I'll find it myself.

He goes into the room at upstage left of the alcove. At the same time VÉZINET *enters by the main door.*

SCENE 5

BEAUPERTHUIS, VÉZINET.

BEAUPERTHUIS. Damn! My feet have swollen—but never mind.

He comes out from behind the screen limping and jumps on VÉZINET, *whom he at first takes for* FADINARD, *and seizes him by the throat.*

I'll get you, villain!

VÉZINET, *laughing.* Please, please, I've danced plenty! I'm all worn out!

BEAUPERTHUIS, *stupefied.* It's not the same one—it's another! A whole gang! What happened to the first one? You bandit, where's your chief?

VÉZINET, *very amiably.* Thank you—I won't take anything else. I'm terribly sleepy.

Noise of falling furniture in the room where FADINARD *is.*

BEAUPERTHUIS. There he is!

He plunges into the room at right.

SCENE 6

VÉZINET, NONANCOURT, HÉLÈNE, BOBIN, LADIES OF THE
WEDDING PARTY.

VÉZINET. I didn't recognize that guest either. He was wearing
a dressing gown. I guess everyone's going to bed. Well,
I've no objection.

He looks about and peers into the alcove.

NONANCOURT, *coming back. He is carrying his myrtle.* The
nuptial chamber is in there. But I've reconsidered. I've got
to have my myrtle for my ceremonial speech.

He puts it on the table. Speaking to the screen.

Get your clothes on, my son. I'm bringing the bride in.

VÉZINET, *who has been looking under the bed.* No boot jack.

BOBIN, HÉLÈNE, *and the other ladies appear in the main
door.*

BOBIN *and the* LADIES.

CHORUS.

AIR: *Werther*

> *Love is here*
> *To bid you cheer,*
> *So step inside,*
> *Madame the bride.*
> *The fading light*
> *Gives way to night,*
> *Protector of*
> *Your licensed love.*

HÉLÈNE, *hesitating to come in.* No, I don't want to—I don't
dare!

BOBIN. All right, Cousin, let's go out again.

NONANCOURT. Be quiet, Bobin. Your role of best man expires
on this threshold.

BOBIN, *sighing.* Oh!

NONANCOURT. Come in, my daughter! Enter without childish fear the conjugal domicile.

HÉLÈNE, *overcome.* Is my husband—already there?

NONANCOURT. He's behind that screen. He's putting on his night cap.

HÉLÈNE, *frightened.* Oh, I'm going!

BOBIN. Let's go out again, Cousin.

NONANCOURT. Be quiet, Bobin.

HÉLÈNE. Papa, I'm trembling all over.

NONANCOURT. So you should be! Your situation requires it. My children, the time has come, I believe, for me to address you with a few heartfelt words. Come along, my son, put on a dressing gown and place yourself at my right hand.

HÉLÈNE, *quickly.* Oh no, Papa!

NONANCOURT. Very well, stay behind your screen and be so good as to give me your devoted attention. Bobin, my myrtle.

BOBIN, *taking it from the table and giving it to him.* Here.

NONANCOURT, *holding his myrtle, emotionally.* My children!
He hesitates a moment, then blows his nose noisily. Repeating.

My children!

VÉZINET, *to* NONANCOURT, *standing at his right.* Do you know where the boot jack is?

NONANCOURT, *furious.* In the cellar. Go hang yourself!

VÉZINET. Thank you.
He continues his search.

NONANCOURT. Now where was I?

BOBIN, *sobbing.* You were at "In the cellar. Go hang yourself!"

NONANCOURT. Ah yes!
Starting over and putting the myrtle in his other arm.

My children, it is a tender moment for a father, when he

sees depart from him his beloved daughter, the hope of his declining years, the staff of his grey hairs.

Turning toward the screen.

This fragile flower now belongs to you, my son! Love her, cherish her, adore her!

Aside, indignantly.

He doesn't even answer, the brute!

To HÉLÈNE.

Daughter, do you see this shrub? I potted it on the day of your birth. Let it be your emblem!

With mounting emotion.

Let its branches evergreen remind you always that you have a father—a husband—children! Let its branches—evergreen—let its branches—evergreen——

Changing his tone, aside.

Hang it all, I've forgotten the rest!

During this speech, BOBIN *and the* LADIES *have gotten out their handkerchiefs and are sobbing.*

HÉLÈNE, *throwing herself in his arms.* Oh Papa!

BOBIN, *weeping.* What an old silly you are, Uncle!

NONANCOURT, *to* HÉLÈNE, *after blowing his nose.* I felt the need to address you with a few heartfelt words. Now let's go to bed.

HÉLÈNE, *trembling.* Papa, don't leave me!

BOBIN. Don't let's leave her!

NONANCOURT. Don't worry, my angel. I anticipated your reaction. I've arranged for fifteen cots for the grown-ups. The youngsters can sleep in the cabs.

BOBIN. At hourly rates!

VÉZINET, *holding a boot jack; to* NONANCOURT. Look, I've found a boot jack.

NONANCOURT. So what? Go, my daughter.

With a sigh.

Oof!

BOBIN, *sighing.* Oof!

CHORUS.

AIR: *Zampa.*

> The clock at last has rung the mystic hour
> Which holds for you (me) the key to happiness.
> May Hymen keep you (me) safely in his power,
> And spare you (me) from all sorrow and distress.

The LADIES *take the bride into the room upstage left.* BOBIN *tries to rush in too;* NONANCOURT *stops him and makes him go into the room on the right, giving him his myrtle.* VÉZINET *disappears behind the curtains of the alcove in the back, which close upon him.*

SCENE 7

NONANCOURT, *then* FADINARD.

NONANCOURT, *looking at the screen, indignantly.* Well really, now! I can't even hear him moving around. The monster, he was probably sleeping all during my speech.

Opens the screen abruptly.

No one's there!

Seeing FADINARD *come in excitedly by the door upstage left, which was hidden by the screen.*

Ah!

FADINARD *rushes in quickly and searches the room. To himself.* It's not here! I've searched the whole apartment—it's not here!

NONANCOURT. My son, what does this mean?

FADINARD. You again! You're not a father-in-law, you're a piece of sticky glue!

NONANCOURT. At such a solemn time, my son . . .

FADINARD. Let me alone!

NONANCOURT, *following him*. I fear that your unstable temperature is to blame. My son, you've cooled off.

FADINARD, *irritated*. Oh, go to bed!

NONANCOURT. Just as you wish, sir. But tomorrow, after daybreak, we will embark once more upon this subject.

He goes into the room at right where BOBIN *is.*

SCENE 8

FADINARD, BEAUPERTHUIS.

FADINARD, *pacing about, agitated*. It's not here! I've looked everywhere, overturned everything. I dug up a whole collection of hats of every color—blue, yellow, green, grey, the entire rainbow, but not a wisp of straw!

BEAUPERTHUIS, *entering the same door as* FADINARD. There he is! He went right round the apartment. I've got you! *He grabs him by the collar.*

FADINARD. Let me go!

BEAUPERTHUIS, *trying to drag him to the staircase*. You'd better give up. I've a pistol in each pocket.

FADINARD. I don't believe it!

While BEAUPERTHUIS' *two hands are about his neck,* FADINARD *plunges his own into* BEAUPERTHUIS' *pockets, takes the pistols and aims at him.*

BEAUPERTHUIS, *letting go and recoiling in terror*. Help! Thief!

FADINARD, *yelling*. Don't yell—or I'll commit an unfortunate news item.

BEAUPERTHUIS. Give me back my pistols!

FADINARD, *beside himself*. Give me the hat! The hat or your life!

BEAUPERTHUIS, *exhausted and choking*. An experience probably unique in the annals of history! I'm taking a footbath, waiting for my wife, and a man comes in yelling about a hat and threatening me with my own pistols!

FADINARD, *forcefully, dragging him to the middle of the stage.*
It's a tragedy—you don't understand—my horse ate a straw
hat, in the Bois de Vincennes, while its owner was running
around the woods with a soldier!

BEAUPERTHUIS. What of it?

FADINARD. But don't you see, they're dug in at my apartment,
on an indefinite lease!

BEAUPERTHUIS. Can't you make the young widow go home?

FADINARD. Young widow! If only she were! But there's a husband.

BEAUPERTHUIS, *laughing.* Oh, so! Ha! ha! ha!

FADINARD. A cad! a brute! a fool! who would trample her un-
derfoot like a frail grain of pepper!

BEAUPERTHUIS. I can understand that.

FADINARD. Yes, but we'll fix his hash, that old husband—
thanks to you, you naughty old scamp, you old joker—now
won't we fix his hash?

BEAUPERTHUIS. Sir, I don't see how I can lend myself . . .

FADINARD. Let's hurry! Here's the sample.

He shows it to him.

BEAUPERTHUIS, *aside, looking at the sample.* Good God!

FADINARD. Italian straw—poppies.

BEAUPERTHUIS, *aside.* It certainly is! It's hers! And she's at his
house! The suède gloves were just a trick!

FADINARD. See here, how much do you want?

BEAUPERTHUIS, *aside.* There are going to be some atrocities!
Aloud.

Let's go, sir.

FADINARD. Where to?

BEAUPERTHUIS. To your house.

FADINARD. Without the hat?

BEAUPERTHUIS. Hush!

Cocks his ear toward the room where HÉLÈNE *is.*

VIRGINIE, *coming in by the main door.* Sir, I've just been to
Gros-Caillou. No one's there.

BEAUPERTHUIS, *listening.* Hush!

FADINARD, *aside.* Good Lord! The lady's maid!

VIRGINIE, *aside.* Mercy, Félix's employer!

BEAUPERTHUIS, *to himself.* I hear voices in my wife's room.
     She's come back! We'll get to the bottom of this, by God!
     He goes excitedly into the room where HÉLÈNE *is.*

SCENE 9

FADINARD, VIRGINIE.

FADINARD. What are you doing here, you little wretch?

VIRGINIE. What am I doing? Just coming back where I work!

FADINARD. Where you work? You mean—Beauperthuis? Your
     employer?

VIRGINIE. What's wrong with that?

FADINARD, *aside, beside himself.* Oh my Lord! He's the hus-
     band—and I told him everything!

VIRGINIE. What about Madame?

FADINARD. Get out of here, you silly fool! Get out, or I'll chop
     you into little bits!
     Pushes her out.

And the hat I've been chasing all day with my wedding
on my tail, my nose on the scent like a bloodhound—I get
here, I track it down—it's the one that got chewed up!

SCENE 10

FADINARD, BEAUPERTHUIS, HÉLÈNE, NONANCOURT, BOBIN,
VÉZINET, LADIES OF THE WEDDING.

Cries from HÉLÈNE'S *room.*

FADINARD. He's going to massacre her! To the rescue!
     He is about to rush in when the door opens. HÉLÈNE, *in*

her nightclothes, enters weeping, followed by the LADIES
and the stupefied BEAUPERTHUIS.

LADIES, *offstage.* Help! Help!

FADINARD, *petrified.* Hélène?

HÉLÈNE. Papa! Papa!

BEAUPERTHUIS. What's everybody doing in my wife's bedroom?

NONANCOURT *comes out of the room right, in a cotton
nightcap, shirt sleeves, his coat on his arm, carrying his
myrtle.* BOBIN *follows in similar costume.*

NONANCOURT *and* BOBIN. What's the matter? What is it?

BEAUPERTHUIS, *stupefied.* More of them!

FADINARD. The whole wedding! That's the limit!

CHORUS.

AIR: *Neveu du Mercier*

BEAUPERTHUIS.

> I am all at sea!
> Tell me why is everyone
> Breaking in on me?
> It simply isn't done!

NONANCOURT.

> I am all at sea!
> Why these screams from everyone?
> My boy, don't count on me.
> It's all off, my son.

FADINARD.

> I am all at sea!
> Why in hell is everyone
> Upstairs here with me?
> I guess I'd better run.

BOBIN.

> I am all at sea!
> Cousin, say, what have they done?
> You can lean on me,
> I'll save you, dearest one!

HÉLÈNE.

> I am all at sea!
> What a strange idea of fun!
> Breaking in on me,
> My nerves are all undone!

LADIES.

> *We are all at sea!*
> *Who is that ungodly one,*
> *Who so brutally*
> *Broke in on everyone?*

BEAUPERTHUIS. What are you doing in my house?

NONANCOURT *and* BOBIN, *with a cry of astonishment.* Your house?

HÉLÈNE *and the* LADIES, *at the same time.* Good Heavens!

NONANCOURT, *shocked, giving* FADINARD *a push.* His house? Not your house? His house?

FADINARD, *yelling.* Father! You make me tired!

NONANCOURT, *shocked.* What? You shameless and immoral creature! You took us to stay at a stranger's house? And you don't even object to your young bride—at a stranger's? My son, it's all off!

FADINARD. You make me sick!

> *To* BEAUPERTHUIS.

Sir, you must forgive this little mistake.

NONANCOURT. Let's get our clothes on, Bobin.

BOBIN. Yes, Uncle.

FADINARD. That's right, and we'll go home. I'll go ahead with my wife.

Goes toward her. BEAUPERTHUIS *restrains him.*

BEAUPERTHUIS, *in a low voice.* Sir, my wife has not returned.

FADINARD. She probably missed the bus.

BEAUPERTHUIS, *who takes off his dressing gown and puts on his coat.* She's at your house.

FADINARD. I doubt it. The lady who is staying at my house is a Negress. Is your wife a Negress?

BEAUPERTHUIS. What sort of crazy loon do you think I am?

FADINARD. I never heard of that bird.

NONANCOURT. Bobin, my sleeve.

BOBIN. Here, Uncle.

BEAUPERTHUIS. Where are you staying, sir?

FADINARD. I'm not staying!

NONANCOURT. At . . .

FADINARD, *quickly.* Don't tell him!

NONANCOURT, *yelling.* Eight, Place Baudoyer—you tramp!

FADINARD. That's done it!

BEAUPERTHUIS. Excellent!

NONANCOURT. Come along, my daughter!

BOBIN. Come along, everyone!

BEAUPERTHUIS *to* FADINARD, *taking his arm.* Come along, sir!

FADINARD. She's a Negress!

CHORUS—ALL.

> AIR: *Final song from* PLASTRON
>
>> *Upon your wedding night,*
>> *To be in a stranger's place,*
>> *What an ignoble plight,*
>> *What an absurd disgrace!*
>
> BEAUPERTHUIS.
>> *Revenge I'll have tonight,*
>> *For acts so low and base!*
>> *I go with bloody spite*
>> *To blot out my disgrace!*
>
> FADINARD.
>> *Oh what a ghastly sight,*
>> *His grim, determined face!*
>> *With blood and thunder quite*
>> *He'll inundate my place!*

SCENE 11

VIRGINIE, VÉZINET.

VIRGINIE, *entering by the door upstage right. She is carrying a cup and saucer; opening the curtains of the alcove.* Sir, here's your tea.

VÉZINET, *sitting upright.* Thank you, I won't take anything else.

VIRGINIE, *uttering a piercing cry and letting the cup drop.* Oh!

VÉZINET. Same to you!

He lies down again.

ACT FIVE

A square. Streets right and left. Upstage right, FADINARD'S *house; another house downstage right. Downstage left, a post of the National Guard with a sentry box. It is night. The scene is lighted by a street lamp hanging on a wire which crosses from downstage left to upstage right.*

SCENE 1

TARDIVEAU, *in uniform of the National Guard; a* CORPORAL, SOLDIERS OF THE GUARD.

A soldier is on sentry duty. Eleven o'clock strikes. Several soldiers come out of the post.

CORPORAL. Eleven o'clock! Who's next on guard?

SOLDIERS. Tardiveau! Tardiveau!

TARDIVEAU. But Trouillebert, I stood guard three times today so I wouldn't have to tonight. The evening dew gives me a cold.

CORPORAL. Shut up, you old hypocrite! The dew never hurt a do-nothing.

All laugh.

Come along, men. Shoulder arms! Fall into line!

CHORUS.

AIR: *J'aime l'uniforme.*

> *The sleeping city*
> *Is in our care.*
> *We know no pity,*
> *So thieves beware!*

The patrol goes out right.

SCENE 2

TARDIVEAU, *then* NONANCOURT, HÉLÈNE, VÉZINET, BOBIN, *the* WEDDING PARTY.

TARDIVEAU, *alone, placing his rifle and shako in the sentry box, and putting on a black silk cap and a scarf.* Lord, I'm hot! That's just how you catch those bad colds. They've got a roaring fire inside. I kept saying to Trouillebert, "Trouillebert, you're putting too much wood on." A lot of good it did! And now I'm all sweaty. I almost feel like changing to a flannel undershirt.

He undoes three of his jacket buttons and stops.

No, some ladies might come by.

Extending his hand.

Oh, fine, that's just fine, it's raining again!

He puts on the army overcoat.

Wonderful! Wonderful! All we needed was some more rain.

He takes shelter in the sentry box. The whole WEDDING PARTY *enters left, with umbrellas.* NONANCOURT *carries his myrtle.* BOBIN *is holding* HÉLÈNE'S *arm.* VÉZINET *has no umbrella and shelters himself first under one, then another, but their owners keep moving so as to uncover him.*

NONANCOURT, *coming in first with his myrtle.* This way, my children, this way. Jump over the puddle.

He jumps; the rest of the WEDDING PARTY *follow suit.*

CHORUS.
AIR: *"Deux Cornuchet"*

> What a dreadful fate
> To be about so late,
> And have to wander all around
> Instead of sleeping safe and sound!

NONANCOURT. What a wedding! What a wedding!

HÉLÈNE, *looking about her*. Oh, Papa! Where is my husband?

NONANCOURT. What do you know, we've lost him again!

HÉLÈNE. I'm all worn out.

BOBIN. I'm exhausted.

A GENTLEMAN. My feet are dropping off.

NONANCOURT. It's lucky I changed my shoes.

HÉLÈNE. Please, Papa, why did you send the cabs back?

NONANCOURT. What do you mean? Isn't three hundred sixty-five francs enough? I refuse to throw away your dowry on cab fares!

ALL. Of course, but where are we?

NONANCOURT. Damned if I know. I was following Bobin.

BOBIN. You're crazy, Uncle. We were following you.

VÉZINET. Why did we have to get up so early? Are we going to another party?

NONANCOURT. Yes. Tra la la la! Tra la la la!
Furious.

That wretch, Fadinard!

HÉLÈNE. He said to come to his house. Place Baudoyer.

BOBIN. This looks like a square.

NONANCOURT. The point is, is it Place Baudoyer?
To VÉZINET, *who is sheltering under an umbrella.*

Hey, you're from Chaillot, you ought to know.
Yelling.

Is this Place Baudoyer?

VÉZINET. Yes, yes, nice weather for growing peas.

NONANCOURT, *turning away rudely*. Pease porridge hot. Pease porridge cold.
He is near the sentry box.

TARDIVEAU, *sneezing*. Atchoo!

NONANCOURT. God bless you! Oh, it's a sentry. Excuse me, sir, which way to Place Baudoyer?

TARDIVEAU. Keep moving.

NONANCOURT. Thank you!— No one's in sight, not a living soul.

BOBIN. It's 11:45 P.M.

NONANCOURT. Wait a minute, we'll find out.

He knocks at a door, side right.

HÉLÈNE. What are you doing, Papa?

NONANCOURT. We have to ask directions. They say Parisians are always glad to direct strangers.

A GENTLEMAN *in a nightcap and dressing gown appears at the window.* What the hell do you want?

NONANCOURT. Excuse me, sir, can you tell me if this is Place Baudoyer?

GENTLEMAN. Just wait a minute, you good for nothing tramp! *Empties a pot of water from the window and shuts it.*

NONANCOURT *jumps clear;* VÉZINET, *without an umbrella, gets it on the head.*

VÉZINET. Drat it! I was under the drain pipe!

NONANCOURT. What a hothead! He must be from Marseilles.

BOBIN, *who has climbed a signpost to read the name of the square.* It's Baudoyer, Uncle, Place Baudoyer. We're here!

NONANCOURT. What luck! Now let's find Number Eight.

ALL. Here it is! Let's go in, let's go in!

NONANCOURT. Thunderation! No porter, and that rascally son-in-law never gave me the key!

HÉLÈNE. Papa, I'm all worn out. I'm going to sit down.

NONANCOURT, *quickly.* Not on the ground, my child! We're surrounded by asphalt.

BOBIN. There's a light in the house.

NONANCOURT. It's Fadinard's apartment. He must have got here first.

Knocks and calls loudly.

Fadinard! My son-in-law!

All call with him.

Fadinard!

TARDIVEAU, *to* VÉZINET. Not so much noise, sir.

VÉZINET, *graciously.* You're too kind, sir. I'll brush myself off in the house.

NONANCOURT, *yelling.* Fadinard!!!

BOBIN. Your son-in-law doesn't give a damn!

HÉLÈNE. He doesn't want to let us in, Papa.

NONANCOURT. Let's go to the police station.

ALL. Yes, yes, to the police station!

CHORUS.
> *He thinks we're just a joke!*
> *Heavens, what iniquity!*
> *Let us then invoke*
> *The sanctions of authority!*

SCENE 3

The same, FÉLIX.

FÉLIX, *entering by the street at right.* My goodness, what a crowd!

NONANCOURT. His valet! Advance, Mr. Punch!

FÉLIX. What do you know, my master's wedding party! Have you seen my master, sir?

NONANCOURT. Have you seen my monster of a son-in-law?

FÉLIX. I've been chasing after him for two hours.

NONANCOURT. We can get along without him. Open up the door, Pierrot!

FÉLIX. Oh, I can't, sir. I've orders not to. The lady is still up there.

ALL. A lady!

FÉLIX. Yes, sir. The one who's staying there—without a hat, you know—since this morning, with . . .

NONANCOURT, *beside himself.* That's enough!

> *He pushes* FÉLIX *to the right.*

A mistress! On his wedding day!

BOBIN. Without a hat!

NONANCOURT. Warming her feet at the conjugal hearth! And here we are, his wife, his relatives, chasing around for fifteen hours with pots of myrtle!

Giving VÉZINET *the myrtle.*

Infamy! Infamy!

HÉLÈNE. Papa! Papa! I'm going to faint.

NONANCOURT. Not on the ground, my daughter. You'll spoil your fifty-three franc dress.

To everyone.

My children, let us spit upon that shameless creature and go back to Charentonneau.

ALL. Yes! Yes!

HÉLÈNE. But Papa, I don't want to leave my jewelry and my wedding gifts behind.

NONANCOURT. Spoken like a practical woman, my child.

To FÉLIX.

Climb up there, nincompoop, and bring down the wedding presents, jewelry boxes, and all my daughter's stuff.

FÉLIX, *hesitating.* But sir . . .

NONANCOURT. I said climb! Unless you want me to chop off one of your ears!

Pushes him in the house downstage right.

SCENE 4

The same, except for FÉLIX, *then* FADINARD.

HÉLÈNE. Papa, you sacrificed me!

BOBIN. Like Agamemnon and Iffy . . . iffy . . .

NONANCOURT. What could I do? He was a landowner—an attenuating circumstance in any father's eyes. He was a landowner, the cad!

FADINARD, *running in left, terrified, exhausted*. Oh, I've a stitch in my side!

ALL. There he is! There he is!

FADINARD. Dear me, there's my wedding party. Father, may I sit on your lap?

NONANCOURT. We're not interested, sir. It's all off!

FADINARD, *listening*. Shut up!

NONANCOURT, *outraged*. What?

FADINARD. Well shut up, for goodness' sakes!

NONANCOURT. Shut up yourself, you little pipsqueak!

FADINARD, *reassured*. No, I'm wrong. He's lost track of me, and anyway his shoes were hurting him. He was limping like old Vulcan himself. We still have a few minutes in which to avert the frightful massacre.

HÉLÈNE. A massacre?

NONANCOURT. What's this new installment?

FADINARD. The beast has my address. He's on his way, armed to the teeth with daggers and pistols. We've got to help that lady escape.

NONANCOURT, *indignantly*. So you confess it, Sardanapalus!

ALL. He confesses it!

FADINARD, *bewildered*. Pardon?

SCENE 5

The same, FÉLIX, *carrying the wedding presents, packages, a woman's hatbox.*

FÉLIX. Here are the things.
Puts them down.

FADINARD. What's all that?

NONANCOURT. Friends and relatives! Let each of us take a package, and we'll engineer the retreat.

FADINARD. What? My Hélène's trousseau?

NONANCOURT. She isn't yours any longer. I'm taking her back bag and baggage to my nurseries at Charentonneau.

FADINARD. You're abducting my wife, at midnight? I'm opposed to it!

NONANCOURT. I challenge your opposition!

FADINARD, *trying to wrench a hatbox away from* NONANCOURT. Don't you dare touch the trousseau!

NONANCOURT. Will you let go, bigamist!

> *Sits down hard.*

Ah! It's all off, my son!

> *The bottom of the box, containing the hat, is left in his hands and the top in* FADINARD'S.

VÉZINET. See here, be careful. It's an Italian straw hat.

FADINARD, *yelling.* What? Italian?

VÉZINET, *examining it.* My wedding present. I had it sent from Florence—five hundred francs.

FADINARD, *bringing out his sample.* From Florence!

> *Taking the hat from him and comparing it with the sample under the lamp.*

Give it here! I can't believe it! Here I've been chasing around—and all the time——

> *Choking with joy.*

Of course! It's the same! The same! The same! And poppies too!

> *Yelling.*

Hurray for Italy!

> *Puts it back in the box.*

ALL. He's crazy!

FADINARD, *jumping, singing, and embracing everyone.* Hurray for Vézinet! Hurray for Nonancourt! Hurray for my wife! Hurray for Bobin! Hurray for the army!

> *Embraces* TARDIVEAU.

TARDIVEAU, *bewildered.* Keep moving, drat it!

NONANCOURT, *while* FADINARD *madly embraces everybody.*

> A five hundred franc hat! You're not getting it, you scoundrel!
>
> *Takes the hat out of the box and shuts the lid again.*

FADINARD, *who hasn't noticed, taking the box by the string, wildly.* Wait here! I'll stick it on her head and then I'll throw her down the stairs. We're going home! We're going home!
>
> *Exits wildly into the house.*

SCENE 6

The same, except for FADINARD, *the* CORPORAL, SOLDIERS OF THE GUARD.

NONANCOURT. Complete alienation! Marriage null and void! Bravo! Forward march, my friends; let's find our cabs again.

> *They go upstage and encounter the patrol which is just entering.*

CORPORAL. Halt, gentlemen. What are you doing with those packages?

NONANCOURT. We're moving house, Corporal.

CORPORAL. In the middle of the night?

NONANCOURT. If you please, I . . .

CORPORAL. Silence!

> *To* VÉZINET.

> Your papers?

VÉZINET. Yes indeed, sir, five hundred francs, not counting the ribbons!

CORPORAL. Oh, a wise guy!

NONANCOURT. Not at all, sir, the poor old man . . .

CORPORAL. Your papers?

In response to his signal, two guards take NONANCOURT *and* BOBIN *by the collar.*

NONANCOURT. Look here!

HÉLÈNE. Sir, that's Papa!

CORPORAL, *to Hélène.* Your papers?

BOBIN. But don't you see, we don't have any. We just came . . .

CORPORAL. No papers? Come along to the police station. You can do your explaining to the officer.

The patrol prods them toward the station.

NONANCOURT. I protest before the face of Europe!

CHORUS.

> AIR: *C'est assez de débats.* PETIT MOYENS

> PATROL.
>> *Into jail, into jail!*
>> *If you protest you will fail.*
>> *Come and tell your shady tale.*
>> *Into jail, into jail!*

> WEDDING PARTY.
>> *What, you're taking us to jail?*
>> *Such a notion turns us pale!*
>> *If our freedom you curtail,*
>> *Deign at least to hear our tale.*

They are pushed into the guardhouse. NONANCOURT *is still carrying the hat.* FÉLIX, *who struggles, is shoved in with the others. The patrol goes in with them.*

SCENE 7

TARDIVEAU, *then* FADINARD, ANAÏS, ÉMILE.

TARDIVEAU. The patrol is back. I'd sure like to go have my toast and milk.

During what follows, he takes off his grey overcoat, which he hangs on his gun, and puts his shako on the bayonet, so as to make it resemble a sentry at ease.

FADINARD, *leaving the house with the box, followed by* ANAÏS *and* ÉMILE. Come on, madame, come on! I've got the hat—it's going to save your life! Your husband knows everything—he's on my trail—put the hat on and go!

He is carrying the carton. ANAÏS *and* ÉMILE *open it, look inside and cry out loudly.*

ALL THREE. Oh!

ANAÏS. Alas!

ÉMILE, *looking into the box.* It's empty!

FADINARD, *bewildered, holding the box.* It was just there—it was! It's my old shyster of a father-in-law who's spirited it away.

Turning around.

Where is he? Where's my wife? Where's my wedding?

TARDIVEAU, *about to leave.* In the guardhouse, sir. They're all in jail.

Goes out right.

FADINARD. In jail! My wedding—and the hat, too! What's to be done?

ANAÏS, *in despair.* I'm lost!

ÉMILE, *struck with an idea.* Oh, I'll go and explain! I know the officer.

He goes into the guardhouse.

FADINARD, *joyous.* He knows the officer! We'll get it back!

Noise of a carriage off left.

BEAUPERTHUIS, *offstage.* Coachman, let me off here.

ANAÏS. Heavens, my husband!

FADINARD. He took a carriage, the coward.

ANAÏS. I'm going back upstairs!

FADINARD. Stop! He's going to search my apartment!

ANAÏS, *terrified.* Here he is!

FADINARD, *pushing her into the sentry box.* Get in there!

To himself.

And this is what they call a wedding day!

SCENE 8

ANAÏS (*hidden*), FADINARD, BEAUPERTHUIS.

BEAUPERTHUIS *enters, limping a bit.* So there you are, sir!
You got away from me.
Shakes his fist.

FADINARD. Just to buy a cigar. I'm looking for a match. Do
you have a match?

BEAUPERTHUIS. Sir, I command you to open that door—and if
I find her! I'm well armed, sir!

FADINARD. First floor, lefthand door, turn the knob, please.

BEAUPERTHUIS, *to himself.* Ow! Funny, my feet are still swollen.
Enters.

FADINARD, *following him with his eyes a moment.* There's a
deer's-foot door knocker.

SCENE 9

FADINARD, ANAÏS, *then* ÉMILE *at the guardhouse window.*

ANAÏS, *coming out of the sentry box.* I'm dying of fright!
Where shall I hide, where shall I go?

FADINARD, *losing his head.* Don't worry, madame! I only hope
he doesn't find you up there.
A second-floor window in the guardhouse opens.

ÉMILE, *at the window.* Quick! Quick! Here's the hat!

FADINARD. We're saved! The husband is upstairs. Throw it
down!
*ÉMILE throws the hat, which gets caught on the hanging
street light.*

ANAÏS, *uttering a cry.* Oh!

FADINARD. Hell!

Jumps with his umbrella to try and dislodge it but can't reach it. The sound of a fall is heard from the staircase of FADINARD'S *house and* BEAUPERTHUIS *cries out.*

BEAUPERTHUIS, *from the staircase.* Christ Almighty!

ANAÏS, *terrified.* It's he!

FADINARD, *excitedly.* Oh Lord!

Throws the grey National Guard overcoat over ANAÏS' *shoulders, pulls the hood over her head and puts the gun in her hands.*

If he comes close, stick to your guns! Ten-shun! Keep moving!

ANAÏS. But the hat! He's bound to see it!

SCENE 10

ANAÏS *on guard duty,* FADINARD, BEAUPERTHUIS, *then* ÉMILE, *then* TARDIVEAU.

FADINARD, *running to head off* BEAUPERTHUIS *and covering him with his umbrella so that he won't see the straw hat, which is balancing above his head.* Watch out! You'll get wet!

BEAUPERTHUIS, *limping more noticeably.* To the Devil with your unlighted staircase!

FADINARD. The lights are put out at eleven.

ÉMILE, *coming out of the guardhouse, in a low voice.* Keep the husband busy!

He goes downstage right, climbs on the lamppost and begins to cut the wire with his sword.

BEAUPERTHUIS. Let me alone! It's not raining any more. The stars are out.

He tries to look up.

FADINARD. I don't care, you'll get wet.

BEAUPERTHUIS. Damn it, sir! What an utter fool I am!

FADINARD. Yes, sir!

He holds the umbrella very high and jumps to dislodge the hat; as he is holding BEAUPERTHUIS' *arm, the movement makes* BEAUPERTHUIS *jump involuntarily.*

BEAUPERTHUIS. You helped her to escape.

FADINARD. What do you think I am?

He jumps again.

BEAUPERTHUIS. What are you jumping for, sir?

FADINARD. I've cramps in my stomach.

BEAUPERTHUIS. Damn it! I'm going to ask that sentry.

ANAÏS, *aside.* Oh God!

FADINARD, *holding him back roughly.* It won't do any good, sir.

Aside, watching ÉMILE.

Hurray, he's cutting the wire.
Aloud.

He won't answer you. They're forbidden to talk on duty.

BEAUPERTHUIS, *trying to get away.* Let me go!

FADINARD. No, you'll get wet!

He covers him more than ever and jumps.

TARDIVEAU, *coming back in right, and stupefied at seeing a sentry.*

Someone's taken my place!

ANAÏS. Keep moving!

BEAUPERTHUIS. Hum—that voice!

FADINARD, *sticking the umbrella between him and* ANAÏS. A recruit.

TARDIVEAU, *noticing the hat.* Why, what's that?

BEAUPERTHUIS. What?

He pushes the umbrella away and lifts his head.

FADINARD. Nothing.

Shoves his hat over his eyes. At the same time the cord is cut and the light falls.

BEAUPERTHUIS. Hey!

TARDIVEAU, *crying out*. To arms! To arms!

FADINARD, *to* BEAUPERTHUIS. Don't pay any attention to him, the street light fell down.

Here the soldiers of the National Guard come out of the station. People with lanterns appear at the windows. During the song, FADINARD *untangles the hat from the light and gives it to* ANAÏS, *who puts it on her head.*

CHORUS.
   AIR: *Vivent les hussards de Berchini.* TENTATIONS D'ANTOI-
   NETTE, *Act II.*

   > What is this infernal din?
   > This revel Bacchanalian?
   > It's illegal, it's a sin!
   > We'll call a lawyer in!

By the end of the chorus, BEAUPERTHUIS *has finally managed to get his hat off from over his eyes.*

BEAUPERTHUIS. May I say once more, gentlemen . . .

ANAÏS *approaches, the hat on her head, her arms crossed, with dignity.* So! At last I've found you, sir!

BEAUPERTHUIS, *petrified.* My wife!

ANAÏS. What a way to behave!

BEAUPERTHIUS, *aside.* She's got the hat!

ANAÏS. Brawling about in the streets at such an hour!

BEAUPERTHUIS. Italian straw!

FADINARD. And poppies!

ANAÏS. And letting me come home alone, at midnight, when I've been waiting for you since this morning at Cousin Eloa's.

BEAUPERTHUIS. If you don't mind, madame, your cousin Eloa . . .

FADINARD. She's got the hat!

BEAUPERTHUIS. You went to buy suède gloves. It doesn't take fourteen hours to buy suède gloves.

FADINARD. She's got the hat!

ANAÏS, *to* FADINARD. Sir, I don't think I've had the honor . . .

FADINARD. Nor I, madame, but you've got the hat!

Turning to the SOLDIERS.

Has Madame got the hat?

SOLDIERS *and People at the Windows.* She's got the hat! She's got the hat!

BEAUPERTHUIS, *to* FADINARD. But sir, what about that horse in the Bois de Vincennes?

FADINARD. He's got the hat!

NONANCOURT, *appearing at the station window.* It's all right, my boy. We're friends again.

FADINARD, *to* BEAUPERTHUIS. Sir, may I present my father-in-law?

NONANCOURT, *at the window.* Your valet told us the whole story. So beautiful! So chivalrous! So French! Take back my daughter, take back the wedding presents, take back the myrtle! Get us out of these dungeons.

FADINARD, *addressing the* CORPORAL. Sir, may I be so bold as to ask you to give me back my wedding party?

CORPORAL. With pleasure, sir!

Yelling.

Let the wedding party go!

The whole WEDDING PARTY *pours out of the guardhouse.*

CHORUS.

AIR: *C'est l'amour, Act IV.*

> *Fadinard has set us free!*
> *Brave is he,*
> *And great of soul!*
> *Let the whole*
> *Wedding praise*
> *This Amadis of modern days!*

During the chorus, the members of the WEDDING PARTY *surround and embrace* FADINARD.

VÉZINET, *recognizing the hat on* ANAÏS' *head.* Mercy me! That lady . . .

FADINARD, *quickly.* Get that deaf old man out of here!

BEAUPERTHUIS, *to* VÉZINET. What did you say, sir?

VÉZINET. She's got the hat!

BEAUPERTHUIS. All right, all right, I admit I'm in the wrong. She's got the hat!

Kisses his wife's hand.

CHORUS.

AIR: *Final song from* TOUR D'UGOLIN.

> Oh happy day,
> Oh wedding so gay,
> Our cares fly away,
> And love reigns instead!
> { Our young couple can now
> { I'm glad I can now
> Take a last bow.
> { They're impatient, we know,
> { I'm impatient I vow
> { To get them to bed.
> { To get me to bed.

VÉZINET.

> New air by Hervé.
>
> This wedding was lovely!

FADINARD.

> Oh, certainly, quite,
> But a time and a place for every delight.
> Let's all go to bed.

NONANCOURT, *holding his myrtle.*

> Now that's talking sense.

FADINARD, *taking his wife's arm.*

> Come to my bower, my sweet.
> But please take a lesson from all these events,
> My husbandly head you never must greet
> With a hat which a horse couldn't possibly eat!

ALL.

> His husbandly head you never must greet
> With a hat which a horse couldn't possibly eat!

(Curtain)

ONE DAY MORE

A Play in One Act
by

JOSEPH CONRAD

Characters

CAPTAIN HAGBERD, *a retired coasting skipper*
JOSIAH CARVIL, *formerly a shipbuilder—a widower—blind*
HARRY HAGBERD, *son of* CAPTAIN HAGBERD, *who as a boy, ran away from home*
A LAMPLIGHTER
BESSIE CARVIL, *daughter of Josiah Carvil*

PLACE: *A small sea-port.*

TIME: *The present—early autumn, towards dusk.*

STAGE REPRESENTS: *To right—two yellow brick cottages belonging to* CAPTAIN HAGBERD, *one is inhabited by himself, the other by the* CARVILS. *A lamp-post in front. The red roofs of the town in the background. A sea-wall to left.*

NOTE. The division into scenes is made in a purely dramatic sense. It has nothing to do with the scenery. It relates only to the varied grouping of the characters with the consequent changes into the mental and emotional atmosphere of the situation.

Curtain rises disclosing CARVIL *and* BESSIE *moving away from sea-wall.* BESSIE *about twenty-five. Black dress, black straw hat. A lot of mahogany-coloured hair loosely done up. Pale face. Full figure. Very quiet.* CARVIL, *blind, unwieldy. Reddish whiskers; slow, deep voice produced without effort. Immovable, big face.*

CARVIL, *hanging heavily on* BESSIE'S *arm.*

Careful! Go slow!

Stops; BESSIE *waits patiently.*

Want your poor blind father to break his neck?

Shuffles on.

In a hurry to get home and start that everlasting yarn with your chum the lunatic?

BESSIE. I am not in a hurry to get home, Father.

CARVIL. Well, then, go steady with a poor blind man. Blind! Helpless!

Strikes the ground with his stick.

Never mind! I've had time to make enough money to have ham and eggs for breakfast every morning—thank God! And thank God, too, for it, girl. You haven't known a single hardship in all the days of your idle life. Unless you think that a blind, helpless father—

BESSIE. What is there for me to be in a hurry for?

CARVIL. What did you say?

BESSIE. I said was nothing for me to hurry home for.

CARVIL. There is, tho'. To yarn with a lunatic. Anything to get away from your duty.

BESSIE. Captain Hagberd's talk never hurt you or anybody else.

CARVIL. Go on. Stick up for your only friend.

BESSIE. Is it my fault that I haven't another soul to speak to?

CARVIL *snarls*. It's mine, perhaps. Can I help being blind? You fret because you want to be gadding about—with a helpless man left all alone at home. Your own father, too.

BESSIE. I haven't been away from you half a day since Mother died.

CARVIL, *viciously*. He's a lunatic, our landlord is. That's what he is. Has been for years—long before those damned doctors destroyed my sight for me.

Growls angrily, then sighs.

BESSIE. Perhaps Captain Hagberd is not so mad as the town takes him for.

CARVIL, *grimly*. Don't everybody know how he came here from the North to wait till his missing son turns up—here—of all places in the world. His boy that ran away to sea sixteen years ago and never did give a sign of life since! Don't I remember seeing people dodge round corners out of his way when he came along High Street. Seeing him, I tell you.

Groan.

He bothered everybody so with his silly talk of his son being sure to come back home—next year—next spring—next month—— What is it by this time, hey?

BESSIE. Why talk about it? He bothers no one now.

CARVIL. No. They've grown too fly. You've got only to pass a remark on his sail-cloth coat to make him shut up. All the town knows it. But he's got you to listen to his crazy talk whenever he chooses. Don't I hear you two at it, jabber, jabber, mumble, mumble——

BESSIE. What is there so mad in keeping up hope?

CARVIL, *scathing scorn*. Not mad! Starving himself to lay money by—for that son. Filling his house with furniture he won't let any one see—for that son. Advertising in the papers every week, these sixteen years—for that son. Not mad! "Boy," he calls him, "Boy Harry." His boy Harry. His lost boy Harry. Yah! Let him lose his sight to know what real trouble means. And the boy—the man, I should say—must've been put away safe in Davy Jones's locker for many a year—drowned—food for fishes—dead. . . . Stands to reason, or he would have been here before, smelling around the old fool's money.

Shakes BESSIE's *arm slightly.*

Hey?

BESSIE. I don't know. Maybe.

CARVIL, *bursting out.* Damme if I don't think he ever had a son.

BESSIE. Poor man. Perhaps he never had.

CARVIL. Ain't that mad enough for you? But I suppose you think it sensible.

BESSIE. What does it matter? His talk keeps him up.

CARVIL. Aye! And it pleases you. Anything to get away from your poor blind father . . . Jabber, jabber—mumble, mumble—till I begin to think you must be as crazy as he is. What do you find to talk about, you two? What's your game?

During the scene CARVIL *and* BESSIE *have crossed stage from L. to R. slowly with stoppages.*

BESSIE. It's warm. Will you sit out for a while?

CARVIL, *viciously.* Yes, I will sit out.

Insistent.

But what can be your game? What are you up to?

They pass through garden gate.

Because if it's his money you are after——

BESSIE. Father! How can you!

CARVIL, *disregarding her.* To make you independent of your poor blind father, then you are a fool.

Drops heavily on seat.

He's too much of a miser to ever make a will—even if he weren't mad.

BESSIE. Oh! It never entered my head. I swear it never did.

CARVIL. Never did. Hey! Then you are a still bigger fool. . . .
I want to go to sleep!

*Takes off his hat, drops it on ground, and leans his head
back against the wall.*

BESSIE. And I have been a good daughter to you. Won't you
say that for me?

CARVIL, *very distinctly.* I want—to—go—to—sleep. I'm tired.

Closes his eyes.

During the scene CAPTAIN HAGBERD *has been seen hesitating at the back of stage, then running quickly to the door
of his cottage. He puts inside a tin kettle—from under his
coat—and comes down to the railing between the two
gardens, stealthily.*

SCENE 2

CARVIL *seated.* BESSIE. CAPTAIN HAGBERD *white beard, sail-
cloth jacket.*

BESSIE, *knitting.* You've been out this afternoon for quite a
long time, haven't you?

CAPTAIN HAGBERD, *eager.* Yes, my dear.

Slyly.

Of course you saw me come back.

BESSIE. Oh, yes. I did see you. You had something under your
coat.

CAPTAIN HAGBERD, *anxiously.* It was only a kettle, my dear. A
tin water-kettle. I am glad I thought of it just in time.

Winks, nods.

When a husband gets back from his work he needs a lot of
water for a wash. See?

Dignified.

Not that Harry'll ever need to do a hand's turn after he
comes home . . .

Falters—casts stealthy glances on all sides.

. . . to-morrow.

BESSIE *looks up, grave.* Captain Hagberd, have you ever thought that perhaps your son will not . . .

CAPTAIN HAGBERD, *paternally.* I've thought of everything, my dear—of everything a reasonable young couple may need for housekeeping. Why, I can hardly turn about in my room up there, the house is that full.

Rubs his hands with satisfaction.

For my son Harry—when he comes home. One day more.

BESSIE, *flattering.* Oh, you are a great one for bargains.

CAPTAIN HAGBERD, *delighted.*

But Captain Hagberd—if—if—you don't know what may happen—if all that home you've got together were to be wasted—for nothing—after all.

Aside.

Oh, I can't bring it out.

CAPTAIN HAGBERD, *agitated; flings arms up, stamps feet; stuttering.* What? What d'ye mean? What's going to happen to the things?

BESSIE, *soothing.* Nothing! Nothing! Dust—or moth—you know. Damp, perhaps. You never let any one into the house . . .

CAPTAIN HAGBERD. Dust! Damp!

Has a throaty, gurgling laugh.

I light the fires and dust the things myself.

Indignant.

Let any one into the house, indeed! What would Harry say!

Walks up and down his garden hastily with tosses, flings, and jerks of his whole body.

BESSIE, *with authority.* Now, then, Captain Hagberd! You know I won't put up with your tantrums.

Shakes finger at him.

CAPTAIN HAGBERD, *subdued, but still sulky, with his back to her.* You want to see the things. That's what you're after.

Well, no, not even you. Not till Harry has had his first look.

BESSIE. Oh, no! I don't.

Relenting.

Not till you're willing.

Smiles at CAPTAIN HAGBERD, *who has turned half round already.*

You mustn't excite yourself.

Knits.

CAPTAIN HAGBERD, *condescending.* And you the only sensible girl for miles and miles around. Can't you trust me? I am a domestic man. Always was, my dear. I hated the sea. People don't know what they let their boys into when they send them to sea. As soon make convicts of them at once. What sort of life is it? Most of your time you don't know what's going on at home.

Insinuating.

There's nothing anywhere on earth as good as a home, my dear.

Pause.

With a good husband . . .

CARVIL, *heard from his seat, fragmentarily.* There they go . . . jabber, jabber . . . mumble, mumble.

With a groaning effort.

Helpless!

BESSIE *has glanced round at him.*

CAPTAIN HAGBERD *mutters.* Extravagant ham-and-eggs fellow.

Louder.

Of course it isn't as if he had a son to make a home ready for. Girls are different, my dear. They don't run away, my dear, my dear.

Agitated.

BESSIE *drops her arms, wearily.* No, Captain Hagberd—they don't.

CAPTAIN HAGBERD, *slowly.* I wouldn't let my own flesh and blood go to sea. Not I.

BESSIE. And the boy ran away.

CAPTAIN HAGBERD, *a little vacantly.* Yes, my only son Harry.
Rouses himself.

Coming home to-morrow.

BESSIE *looks at him pityingly; speaks softly.* Sometimes, Captain Hagberd, a hope turns out false.

CAPTAIN HAGBERD, *uneasy.* What's that got to do with Harry's coming back?

BESSIE. It's good to hope for something. But suppose now——
Feeling her way.

Yours is not the only lost son that's never . . .

CAPTAIN HAGBERD. Never what? You don't believe he's drowned?

Crouches, glaring and grasping the rails.

BESSIE, *frightened, drops knitting.* Captain Hagberd—don't.
Catches hold of his shoulders over the railings.

Don't—my God! he's going out of his mind!
Cries.

I didn't mean it! I don't know.

CAPTAIN HAGBERD *has backed away. An affected burst of laughter.* What nonsense! None of us Hagberds belonged to the sea. All farmers for hundreds of years.
Paternal and cunning.

Don't alarm yourself, my dear. The sea can't get us. Look at me! I didn't get drowned. Moreover, Harry ain't a sailor at all. And if he isn't a sailor, he's bound to come back—to-morrow.

BESSIE *has been facing him; murmurs.* No. I give it up. He scares me.

Aloud, sharply.

Then I would give up that advertising in the papers.

CAPTAIN HAGBERD, *surprised and puzzled.* Why, my dear? Everybody does it. His poor mother and I have been advertising for years and years. But she was an impatient woman. She died.

BESSIE. If your son's coming, as—as you say—what's the good of that expense? You had better spend that half-crown on yourself. I believe you don't eat enough.

CAPTAIN HAGBERD, *confused*. But it's the right thing to do. Look at the Sunday papers. Missing relatives on top page —all proper.

Looks unhappy.

BESSIE, *tartly*. Ah, well! I declare I don't know what you live on.

CAPTAIN HAGBERD. Are you getting impatient, my dear? Don't get impatient—like my poor wife. If she'd only been patient she'd be here. Waiting—only one day more.

Pleadingly.

Don't be impatient, my dear.

BESSIE. I've no patience with you sometimes.

CAPTAIN HAGBERD, *flash of lucidity*. Why? What's the matter?

Sympathetic.

You're tired out, my dear, that's what it is.

BESSIE. Yes, I am. Day after day.

Stands listless, arms hanging down.

CAPTAIN HAGBERD, *timidly*. House dull?

BESSIE, *apathetic*. Yes.

CAPTAIN HAGBERD, *as before*. H'm. Wash, cook, scrub. Hey?

BESSIE, *as before*. Yes.

CAPTAIN HAGBERD, *pointing stealthily at the sleeping* CARVIL. Heavy?

BESSIE, *in a dead voice*. Like a millstone.

A silence.

CAPTAIN HAGBERD, *burst of indignation*. Why don't that extravagant fellow get you a servant?

BESSIE. I don't know.

CAPTAIN HAGBERD, *cheerily*. Wait till Harry comes home. He'll get you one.

BESSIE, *almost hysterical: laughs.* Why, Captain Hagberd, perhaps your son won't even want to look at me—when he comes home.

CAPTAIN HAGBERD, *in a great voice.* What!

Quite low.

The boy wouldn't dare.

Rising choler.

Wouldn't dare to refuse the only sensible girl for miles around. That stubborn jackanapes refuse to marry a girl like you!

Walks about in a fury.

You trust me, my dear, my dear, my dear. I'll make him. I'll—I'll——

Splutters.

Cut him off with a shilling.

BESSIE. Hush!

Severe.

You mustn't talk like that. What's this? More of your tantrums?

CAPTAIN HAGBERD, *quite humble.* No, no—this isn't my tantrums—when I don't feel quite well in my head. Only I can't stand this. . . . I've grown as fond of you as if you'd been the wife of my Harry already. And to be told——

Can't restrain himself, shouts.

Jackanapes!

BESSIE. Sh——! Don't you worry!

Wearily.

I must give that up, too, I suppose.

Aloud.

I didn't mean it, Captain Hagberd.

CAPTAIN HAGBERD. It's as if I were to have two children tomorrow. My son Harry—and the only sensible girl—— Why, my dear, I couldn't get on without you. We two are reasonble together. The rest of the people in the town are crazy.

The way they stare at you. And the grins—they're all on the grin. It makes me dislike to go out.

Bewildered.

It seems as if there was something wrong about—somewhere. My dear, is there anything wrong—you who are sensible . . .

BESSIE, *soothingly tender.* No, no, Captain Hagberd. There is nothing wrong about you anywhere.

CARVIL, *lying back.* Bessie!

Sits up.

Get my hat, Bessie. . . . Bessie, my hat. . . . Bessie . . . Bessie . . .

At the first sound BESSIE *picks up and puts away her knitting. She walks towards him, picks up hat, puts it on his head.*

Bessie my . . .

Hat on head: shouting stops.

BESSIE, *quietly.* Will you go in, now?

CARVIL. Help me up. Steady. I'm dizzy. It's the thundery weather. An autumn thunderstorm means a bad gale. Very fierce—and sudden. There will be shipwrecks to-night on our coast.

Exit BESSIE *and* CARVIL *through door of their cottage. It has fallen dusk.*

CAPTAIN HAGBERD *picks up spade.* Extravagant fellow! And all this town is mad—perfectly mad. I found them out years ago. Thank God they don't come this way staring and grinning. I can't bear them. I'll never go again into that High Street.

Agitated.

Never, never, never. Won't need to, after to-morrow. Never!

Flings down spade in a passion.

While CAPTAIN HAGBERD *speaks, the bow window of the* CARVILS' *is lit up, and* BESSIE *is seen settling her father in a*

big armchair. Pulls down blind. Enter LAMPLIGHTER. CAP-
TAIN HAGBERD *picks up the spade and leans forward on it
with both hands; very still, watching him light the lamp.*

LAMPLIGHTER, *jocular.* There! You will be able to dig by
lamplight if the fancy takes you.

Exit LAMPLIGHTER *to back.*

CAPTAIN HAGBERD, *disgusted.* Ough! The people here . . .
Shudders.

LAMPLIGHTER'S VOICE, *heard loudly beyond the cottages.* Yes,
that's the way.

Enter HARRY *from back.*

SCENE 3

CAPTAIN HAGBERD. HARRY. *Later,* BESSIE.

HARRY HAGBERD, *thirty-one, tall, broad shoulders, shaven
face, small moustache. Blue serge suit. Coat open. Grey
flannel shirt without collar and tie. No waistcoat. Belt with
buckle. Black, soft felt hat, wide-brimmed, worn crushed
in the crown and a little on one side. Good nature, reckless-
ness, some swagger in the bearing. Assured, deliberate
walk with a heavy tread. Slight roll in the gait. Walks
down. Stops, hands in pockets. Looks about. Speaks.* This
must be it. Can't see anything beyond. There's somebody.
Walks up to CAPTAIN HAGBERD'S *gate.*

Can you tell me . . .
Manner changes. Leans elbow on gate.

Why, you must be Captain Hagberd himself.

CAPTAIN HAGBERD, *in garden, both hands on spade, peering,
startled.* Yes, I am.

HARRY, *slowly.* You've been advertising in the papers for your
son, I believe.

CAPTAIN HAGBERD, *off his guard, nervous*. Yes. My only boy
    Harry. He's coming home to-morrow.

Mumbles.

For a permanent stay.

HARRY, *surprised*. The devil he is!

Change of tone.

My word! You've grown a beard like Father Christmas
    himself.

CAPTAIN HAGBERD, *impressively*. Go your way.

Waves one hand loftily.

What's that to you? Go your way.

Agitated.

Go your way.

HARRY. There, there. I am not trespassing in the street—where
    I stand—am I? Tell you what, I fancy there's something
    wrong about your nerves. Suppose you let me come in—for
    a quiet chat, you know.

CAPTAIN HAGBERD, *horrified*. Let you—*you* come in!

HARRY, *persuasive*. Because I could give you some real infor-
    mation about your son. The—very—latest—tip. If you care
    to hear.

CAPTAIN HAGBERD *explodes*. No! I don't care to hear.

*Begins to pace to and fro, spade on shoulder. Gesticulating
    with his other arm.*

Here's a fellow—a grinning town fellow, who says there's
    something wrong.

Fiercely.

I have got more information than you're aware of. I have
    all the information I want. I have had it for years—for
    years—for years—enough to last me till to-morrow! Let you
    come in, indeed! What would Harry say?

BESSIE CARVIL *enters at cottage door with a white wrap on
    her head and stands in her garden trying to see.*

BESSIE. What's the matter?

CAPTAIN HAGBERD, *beside himself.* An information fellow.
Stumbles.

HARRY, *putting out arm to steady him, gravely.* Here! Steady
a bit! Seems to me somebody's been trying to get at you.
Change of tone.

Hullo! What's this rig you've got on? . . . Storm canvas
coat, by George!
He gives a big, throaty laugh.

Well! You *are* a character!

CAPTAIN HAGBERD, *daunted by the allusion, looks at coat.* I—I
wear it for—for the time being. Till—till—to-morrow.
Shrinks away, spade in hand, to door of his cottage.

BESSIE, *advancing.* And what may you want, sir?

HARRY *turns to* BESSIE *at once; easy manner.* I'd like to know
about this swindle that's going to be sprung on him. I
didn't mean to startle the old man. You see, on my way
here I dropped into a barber's to get a twopenny shave,
and they told me there that he was something of a character. He has been a character all his life.

BESSIE, *very low, wondering.* What swindle?

CAPTAIN HAGBERD. A grinning fellow!
*Makes sudden dash indoors with the spade. Door slams.
Lock clicks. Affected gurgling laugh within.*

SCENE 4

BESSIE *and* HARRY. *Later,* CAPTAIN HAGBERD *from window.*

HARRY, *after a short silence.* What on earth's upset him so?
What's the meaning of all this fuss? He isn't always like
that, is he?

BESSIE. I don't know who you are; but I may tell you that his
mind has been troubled for years about an only son who
ran away from home—a long time ago. Everybody knows
that here.

HARRY, *thoughtful*. Troubled—for years!

Suddenly.

Well, I am the son.

BESSIE *steps back*. You! . . . Harry!

HARRY, *amused, dry tone*. Got hold of my name, eh? Been making friends with the old man?

BESSIE, *distressed*. Yes . . . I . . . sometimes . . .

Rapidly.

He's our landlord.

HARRY, *scornfully*. Owns both them rabbit hutches, does he? Just a thing he'd be proud of. . . .

Earnest.

And now you had better tell me all about that chap who's coming to-morrow. Know anything of him? I reckon there's more than one in that little game. Come! Out with it!

Chaffing.

I don't take no . . . from women.

BESSIE, *bewildered*. Oh! It's so difficult . . . What had I better do?

HARRY, *good humoured*. Make a clean breast of it.

BESSIE, *wildly, to herself*. Impossible!

Starts.

You don't understand. I must think—see—try to—I, I must have time. Plenty of time.

HARRY. What for? Come. Two words. And don't be afraid for yourself. I ain't going to make it a police job. But it's the other fellow that'll get upset when he least expects it. There'll be some fun when he shows his mug here to-morrow.

Snaps fingers.

I don't care that for the old man's dollars, but right is right. You shall see me put a head on that coon, whoever he is.

BESSIE *wrings hands slightly*. What had I better do?

Suddenly to HARRY.

It's you—you yourself that we—that he's waiting for. It's *you* who are to come to-morrow.

HARRY, *slowly*. Oh! it's me!

Perplexed.

There's something there I can't understand. I haven't written ahead or anything. It was my chum who showed me the advertisement with the old boy's address, this very morning—in London.

BESSIE, *anxious*. How can I make it plain to you without . . .

Bites her lip, embarrassed.

Sometimes he talks so strangely.

HARRY, *expectant*. Does he? What about?

BESSIE. Only you. And he will stand no contradicting.

HARRY, *stubborn*. Eh? The old man hasn't changed much from what I can remember.

They stand looking at each other helplessly.

BESSIE. He's made up his mind you would come back . . . to-morrow.

HARRY. I can't hang about here till morning. Got no money to get a bed. Not a cent. But why won't to-day do?

BESSIE. Because you've been too long away.

HARRY, *with force*. Look here, they fairly drove me out. Poor Mother nagged at me for being idle, and the old man said he would cut my soul out of my body rather than let me go to sea.

BESSIE *murmurs*. He can bear no contradicting.

HARRY, *continuing*. Well, it looked as tho' he would do it, too. So I went.

Moody.

It seems to me sometimes I was born to them by a mistake . . . in that other rabbit hutch of a house.

BESSIE, *a little mocking*. And where do you think you ought to have been born by rights?

HARRY. In the open—upon a beach—on a windy night.

BESSIE, *faintly*. Ah!

HARRY. They were characters, both of them, by George! Shall I try the door?

BESSIE. Wait. I must explain to you why it is to-morrow.

HARRY. Aye. That you must, or . . .

Window in CAPTAIN HAGBERD'S *cottage runs up.*

CAPTAIN HAGBERD'S VOICE, *above.* A—grinning—information—fellow coming to worry me in my own garden! What next?

Window rumbles down.

BESSIE. Yes. I must.

Lays hand on HARRY'S *sleeve.*

Let's get further off. Nobody ever comes this way after dark.

HARRY, *careless laugh.* Aye. A good road for a walk with a girl.

They turn their backs on audience and move up the stage, slowly. Close together. HARRY *bends his head over* BESSIE.

BESSIE'S VOICE, *beginning eagerly.* People here somehow did not take kindly to him.

HARRY'S VOICE. Aye. Aye. I understand that.

They walk slowly back towards the front.

BESSIE. He was almost ready to starve himself for your sake.

HARRY. And I had to starve more than once for his whim.

BESSIE. I'm afraid you've a hard heart.

Remains thoughtful.

HARRY. What for? For running away?

Indignant.

Why, he wanted to make a blamed lawyer's clerk of me.

From here this scene goes on mainly near and about the street lamp.

BESSIE, *rousing herself.* What are you? A sailor?

HARRY. Anything you like.

Proudly.

Sailor enough to be worth my salt on board any craft that swims the seas.

BESSIE. He will never, never believe it. He mustn't be contradicted.

HARRY. Always liked to have his own way. And you've been encouraging him.

BESSIE, *earnestly.* No!—not in everything—not really!

HARRY, *vexed laugh.* What about that pretty to-morrow notion? I've a hungry chum in London—waiting for me.

BESSIE, *defending herself.* Why should I make the poor old friendless man miserable? I thought you were far away. I thought you were dead. I didn't know but you had never been born. I . . . I . . .

HARRY *turns to her. She desperately.*

It was easier to believe it myself.

Carried away.

And after all it's true. It's come to pass. This is the to-morrow we've been waiting for.

HARRY, *half perfunctorily.* Aye. Anybody can see that your heart is as soft as your voice.

BESSIE, *as if unable to keep back the words.* I didn't think you would have noticed my voice.

HARRY, *already inattentive.* H'm. Dashed scrape. This is a queer to-morrow, without any sort of to-day, as far as I can see.

Resolutely.

I must try the door.

BESSIE. Well—try, then.

HARRY, *from gate looking over shoulder at* BESSIE. He ain't likely to fly out at me, is he? I would be afraid of laying my hands on him. The chaps are always telling me I don't know my own strength.

BESSIE, *in front.* He's the most harmless creature that ever . . .

HARRY. You wouldn't say so if you had seen him walloping me with a hard leather strap.

Walking up garden.

I haven't forgotten it in sixteen long years.

Rat-tat-tat, twice.

Hullo, Dad.

BESSIE *intensely expectant. Rat-tat-tat.*

Hullo, Dad, let me in. I am your own Harry. Straight. Your son Harry come back home—a day too soon.

Window above rumbles up.

CAPTAIN HAGBERD, *seen leaning out, aiming with spade.* Aha!

BESSIE, *warningly.* Look out, Harry!

Spade falls.

Are you hurt?

Window rumbles down.

HARRY, *in the distance.* Only grazed my hat.

BESSIE. Thank God!

Intensely.

What'll he do now?

HARRY *comes forward, slamming gate behind him.* Just like old times. Nearly licked the life out of me for wanting to go away, and now I come back he shies a confounded old shovel at my head.

Fumes. Laughs a little.

I wouldn't care, only poor little Ginger—Ginger's my chum up in London—he will starve while I walk back all the way from here.

Faces BESSIE blankly.

I spent my last two-pence on a shave . . . Out of respect for the old man.

BESSIE. I think, if you let me, I could manage to talk him round in a week, maybe.

A muffled periodical bellowing has been heard faintly for some time.

HARRY, *on the alert.* What's this? Who's making this row? Hark! Bessie, Bessie. It's in your house, I believe.

BESSIE, *without stirring, drearily.* It's for me.

HARRY, *discreetly, whispering.* Good voice for a ship's deck in a squall. Your husband?

Steps out of lamplight.

BESSIE. No. My father. He's blind.

Pause.

I'm not married.

Bellowings grow louder.

HARRY. Oh, I say. What's up? Who's murdering him?

BESSIE, *calmly.* I expect he's finished his tea.

Bellowing continues regularly.

HARRY. Hadn't you better see to it? You'll have the whole town coming out here presently.

BESSIE *moves off.*

I say!

BESSIE *stops.*

Couldn't you scare up some bread and butter for me from that tea? I'm hungry. Had no breakfast.

BESSIE *starts off at the word "hungry," dropping to the ground the white woollen shawl.* I won't be a minute. Don't go away.

HARRY, *alone; picks up shawl absently, and, looking at it spread out in his hands, pronounces slowly.* A—dam'—silly—scrape.

Pause. Throws shawl on arm. Strolls up and down. Mutters.

No money to get back.

Louder.

Silly little Ginger'll think I've got hold of the pieces and given an old shipmate the go by. One good shove—

Makes motion of bursting in door with his shoulders.

would burst that door in—I bet.

Looks about.

I wonder where the nearest bobby is? No. They would want to bundle me neck and crop into chokey.

Shudders.

Perhaps. It makes me dog sick to think of being locked up. Haven't got the nerve. Not for prison.

Leans against lamp-post.

And not a cent for my fare. I wonder if that girl now . . .

BESSIE, *coming hastily forward, plate with bread and meat in hand.* I didn't take time to get anything else.

HARRY *begins to eat.* You're not standing treat to a beggar. My dad is a rich man—you know.

BESSIE, *plate in hand.* You resemble your father.

HARRY. I was the very image of him in face from a boy—

Eats.

—and that's about as far as it goes. He was always one of your domestic characters. He looked sick when he had to go to sea for a fortnight's trip.

Laughs.

He was all for house and home.

BESSIE. And you? Have you never wished for a home?

Goes off with empty plate and puts it down hastily on CARVIL'S *bench—out of sight.*

HARRY, *left in front.* Home! If I found myself shut up in what the old man calls a home, I would kick it down about my ears on the third day—or else go to bed and die before the week was out. Die in a house—ough!

BESSIE, *returning; stops and speaks from garden railing.* And where is it that you would wish to die?

HARRY. In the bush, in the sea, on some blamed mountain-top for choice. No such luck, tho', I suppose.

BESSIE, *from distance.* Would that be luck?

HARRY. Yes! For them that make the whole world their home.

BESSIE *comes forward shyly.* The world's a cold home—they say.

HARRY, *a little gloomy.* So it is. When a man's done for.

BESSIE. You see!

Taunting.

And a ship's not so very big after all.

HARRY. No. But the sea is great. And then what of the ship! You love her and leave her, Miss—Bessie's your name—isn't it? . . . I like that name.

BESSIE. You like my name! I wonder you remembered it. . . .
That's why, I suppose.

HARRY, *slight swagger in voice.* What's the odds! As long as a
fellow has lived. And a voyage isn't a marriage—as we
sailors say.

BESSIE. So you're not married—

Movement of HARRY.

—to any ship.

HARRY, *soft laugh.* Ship! I've loved and left more of them than
I can remember. I've been nearly everything you can think
of but a tinker or a soldier; I've been a boundary rider; I've
sheared sheep and humped my swag and harpooned a
whale; I've rigged ships and skinned dead bullocks and
prospected for gold—and turned my back on more money
than the old man would have scraped together in his whole
life.

BESSIE, *thoughtfully.* I could talk him over in a week. . . .

HARRY, *negligently.* I dare say you could.
Joking.

I don't know but what I could make shift to wait if you
only promise to talk to me now and then. I've grown quite
fond of your voice. I like a right woman's voice.

BESSIE, *averted head.* Quite fond!
Sharply.

Talk! Nonsense! Much you'd care.
Business-like.

Of course I would have to, sometimes. . . .
Thoughtful again.

Yes. In a week—if—if only I knew you would try to get on
with him afterwards.

HARRY, *leaning against lamp-post; growls through his teeth.*

More humouring. Ah! well, no!
Hums significantly.

Oh, oh, oh, Rio, . . .
And fare thee well
My bonnie young girl,
    We're bound for Rio Grande.

BESSIE, *shivering*. What's this?

HARRY. Why! The chorus of an up-anchor tune. Kiss and go.
A deep-water ship's good-bye. . . . You are cold. Here's
that thing of yours I've picked up and forgot there on my
arm. Turn round a bit. So.

Wraps her up—commanding.

Hold the ends together in front.

BESSIE, *softly*. A week is not so very long.

HARRY *begins violently*. You think that I——

Stops with sidelong look at her.

I can't dodge about in ditches and live on air and water.
Can I? I haven't any money—you know.

BESSIE. He's been scraping and saving up for years. All he has
is for you, and perhaps . . .

HARRY *interrupts*. Yes. If I come to sit on it like a blamed toad
in a hole. Thank you.

BESSIE, *angrily*. What did you come for, then?

HARRY, *promptly*. For five quid—

Pause.

—after a jolly good spree.

BESSIE, *scathingly*. You and that—that chum of yours have
been drinking.

HARRY *laughs*. Don't fly out, Miss Bessie—dear. Ginger's not
a bad little chap. Can't take care of himself, tho'. Blind
three days.

Serious.

Don't think I am given that way. Nothing and nobody
can get over me unless I like. I can be as steady as a rock.

BESSIE, *murmurs*. Oh! I don't think you are bad.

HARRY, *approvingly*. You're right there.

Impulsive.

Ask the girls all over——

Checks himself.

Ginger, he's long-headed too, in his way—mind you. He sees the paper this morning, and says he to me, "Hallo! Look at that, Harry—loving parent—that's five quid, sure." So we scraped all our pockets for the fare. . . .

BESSIE, *unbelieving.* You came here for that?

HARRY, *surprised.* What else would I want here? Five quid isn't much to ask for—once in sixteen years.

Through his teeth with a sidelong look at BESSIE.

And now I am ready to go—for my fare.

BESSIE, *clasping her hands.* Whoever heard a man talk like this before! I can't believe you mean it.

HARRY. What? That I would go? You just try and see.

BESSIE, *disregarding him.* Don't you care for any one? Didn't you ever want any one in the world to care for you?

HARRY. In the world!

Boastful.

There's hardly a place you can go in the world where you wouldn't find somebody that did care for Harry Hagberd.

Pause.

I'm not of the sort that go about skulking under false names.

BESSIE. Somebody—that means a woman.

HARRY. Well! And if it did?

BESSIE, *unsteadily.* Oh, I see how it is. You get round them with your soft speeches, your promises, and then . . .

HARRY, *violently.* Never!

BESSIE, *startled, steps back.* Ah—you never . . .

HARRY, *calm.* Never yet told a lie to a woman.

BESSIE. What lie?

HARRY. Why, the lie that comes glib to a man's tongue. None of that for me. I leave the sneaking off to them soft-spoken chaps you're thinking of. No! If you love me you take me.

And if you take me—why, then, the capstan-song of deep-water ships is sure to settle it all some fine day.

BESSIE, *after a short pause, with effort.* It's like your ships, then.

HARRY, *amused.* Exactly, up to now. Or else I wouldn't be here in a silly fix.

BESSIE, *assumed indifference.* Perhaps it's because you've never yet met—
Voice fails.

HARRY, *negligently.* Maybe. And perhaps never shall. . . . What's the odds? It's the looking for a thing. . . . No matter. I love them all—ships and women. The scrapes they got me into, and the scrapes they got me out of—my word! I say, Miss Bessie, what are you thinking of?

BESSIE *lifts her head.* That you are supposed never to tell a lie.

HARRY. Never, eh? You wouldn't be that hard on a chap.

BESSIE, *recklessly.* Never to a woman, I mean.

HARRY. Well, no.
Serious.
Never anything that matters.
Aside.
I don't seem to get any nearer to my railway fare.
Leans wearily against the lamp-post with a far-off look.
BESSIE *looks at him.*

BESSIE. Now what are *you* thinking of?

HARRY *turns his head; stares at* BESSIE. Well, I was thinking what a fine figure of a girl you are.

BESSIE *looks away a moment.* Is that true, or is it only one of them that don't matter?

HARRY, *laughing a little.* No! No! That's true. Haven't you ever been told that before? The men . . .

BESSIE. I hardly speak to a soul from year's end to year's end. Father's blind. He don't like strangers, and he can't bear to think of me out of his call. Nobody comes near us much.

HARRY, *absent-minded.* Blind—ah! of course.

BESSIE. For years and years . . .

HARRY, *commiserating.* For years and years. In one of them hutches. You are a good daughter.

Brightening up.

A fine girl altogether. You seem the sort that makes a good chum to a man in a fix. And there's not a man in this whole town who found you out? I can hardly credit it, Miss Bessie.

BESSIE *shakes her head.*

Man, I said!

Contemptuous.

A lot of tame rabbits in hutches I call them. . . .

Breaks off.

I say, when's the last train up to London? Can you tell me?

BESSIE *gazes at him steadily.* What for? You've no money.

HARRY. That's just it.

Leans back against post again.

Hard luck.

Insinuating.

But there was never a time in all my travels that a woman of the right sort did not turn up to help me out of a fix. I don't know why. It's perhaps because they know without telling that I love them all.

Playful.

I've almost fallen in love with you, Miss Bessie.

BESSIE, *unsteady laugh.* Why! How you talk! You haven't even seen my face properly.

One step towards HARRY, *as if compelled.*

HARRY, *bending forward gallantly.* A little pale. It suits some.

Puts out his hand, catches hold of BESSIE's *arm. Draws her to him.*

Let's see. . . . Yes, it suits you.

It's a moment before BESSIE *puts up her hands, palms out, and turns away her head.*

BESSIE, *whispering.* Don't.

> *Struggles a little. Released, stands averted.*

HARRY. No offence.

> *Stands, back to audience, looking at* CAPTAIN HAGBERD'S *cottage.*

BESSIE, *alone in front; faces audience; whispers.*

> My voice—my figure—my heart—my face. . . .
> *A silence.* BESSIE's *face gradually lights up. Directly* HARRY *speaks, expression of hopeful attention.*

HARRY, *from railings.* The old man seems to have gone to sleep waiting for that to-morrow of his.

BESSIE. Come away. He sleeps very little.

HARRY *strolls down.* He has taken an everlasting jamming hitch round the whole business.

> *Vexed.*

> Cast it loose who may.

> *Contemptuous exclamation.*

> To-morrow. Pooh! It'll be just another mad to-day.

BESSIE. It's the brooding over his hope that's done it. People teased him so. It's his fondness for you that's troubled his mind.

HARRY. Aye. A confounded shovel on the head. The old man had always a queer way of showing his fondness for me.

BESSIE. A hopeful, troubled, expecting old man—left alone—all alone.

HARRY, *lower tone.* Did he ever tell you what Mother died of?

BESSIE. Yes.

> *A little bitter.*

> From impatience.

HARRY *makes a gesture with his arm; speaks vaguely but with feeling.* I believe you have been very good to my old man. . . .

BESSIE, *tentative.* Wouldn't you try to be a son to him?

HARRY, *angrily*. No contradicting; is that it? You seem to know my dad pretty well. And so do I. He's dead nuts on having his own way—and I've been used to have my own too long. It's the deuce of a fix.

BESSIE. How could it hurt you not to contradict him for a while—and perhaps in time you would get used . . .

HARRY *interrupts sulkily*. I ain't accustomed to knuckle under. There's a pair of us. Hagberds both. I ought to be thinking of my train.

BESSIE, *earnestly*. Why? There's no need. Let us get away up the road a little.

HARRY, *through his teeth*. And no money for the fare.
Looks up.

Sky's come overcast. Black, too. It'll be a wild, windy night . . . to walk the highroad on. But I and wild nights are old friends wherever the free wind blows.

BESSIE, *entreating*. No need. No need.
Looks apprehensively at CAPTAIN HAGBERD's *cottage. Takes a couple of steps up as if to draw* HARRY *further off.* HARRY *follows. Both stop.*

HARRY, *after waiting*. What about this to-morrow whim?

BESSIE. Leave that to me. Of course all his fancies are not mad. They aren't.
Pause.

Most people in this town would think what he had set his mind on quite sensible. If he ever talks to you of it, don't contradict him. It would—it would be dangerous.

HARRY, *surprised*. What would he do?

BESSIE. He would—I don't know—something rash.

HARRY, *startled*. To himself?

BESSIE. No. It'd be against you—I fear.

HARRY, *sullen*. Let him.

BESSIE. Never. Don't quarrel. But perhaps he won't even try to talk to you of it.
Thinking aloud.

Who knows what I can do with him in a week! I can, I can,
I can—I must.

HARRY. Come—what's this sensible notion of his that I mustn't
quarrel about?

BESSIE *turns to* HARRY, *calm, forcible.* If I make him once see
that you've come back, he will be as sane as you or I. All
his mad notions will be gone. But that other is quite sensible. And you mustn't quarrel over it.

Moves up to back of stage. HARRY *follows a little behind,
away from audience.*

HARRY'S VOICE, *calm.* Let's hear what it is.

Voices cease. Action visible as before. HARRY *steps back
and walks hastily down.* BESSIE, *at his elbow, follows with
her hands clasped.*

Loud burst of voice.

HARRY, *raving to and fro.* No! Expects me—a home. Who
wants his home? . . . What I want is hard work, or an all-
fired racket, or more room than there is in the whole of
England. Expects me! A man like me—for his rotten money
—there ain't enough money in the world to turn me into
a blamed tame rabbit in a hutch.

He stops suddenly before BESSIE, *arms crossed on breast.
Violently.*

Don't you see it?

BESSIE, *terrified, stammering faintly.* Yes. Yes. Don't look at
me like this.

Sudden scream.

Don't quarrel with him. He's mad!

HARRY, *headlong utterance.* Mad! Not he. He likes his own
way. Tie me up by the neck here. Here! Ha! Ha! Ha!

Louder.

And the whole world is not a bit too big for me to spread
my elbows in, I can tell you—what's your name—Bessie.

Rising scorn.

Marry! Wants me to marry and settle. . . .
Scathingly.

And as likely as not he has looked out the girl, too—dash
my soul. Talked to you about it—did he? And do you happen to know the Judy—may I ask?
Window in CAPTAIN HAGBERD'S *cottage runs up. They start
and stand still.*

CAPTAIN HAGBERD, *above, begins slowly.* A grinning information fellow from a crazy town.
Voice changes.

Bessie, I see you . . .

BESSIE, *shrilly.* Captain Hagberd! Say nothing. You don't understand. For heaven's sake don't.

CAPTAIN HAGBERD. Send him away this minute, or I will tell
Harry. They know nothing of Harry in this crazy town.
Harry's coming home to-morrow. Do you hear? One day
more!
Silence.

HARRY *mutters.* Well!—he *is* a character.

CAPTAIN HAGBERD *chuckles softly.* Never you fear! The boy
shall marry you.
Sudden anger.

He'll have to. I'll make him. Or, if not—
Furious.

—I'll cut him off with a shilling, and leave everything to
you. Jackanapes! Let him starve!
Window rumbles down.

HARRY, *slowly.* So it's you—the girl. It's you! Now I begin to
see. . . . By heavens, you have a heart as soft as your
woman's voice.

BESSIE, *half averted, face in hands.* You see! Don't come near
me.

HARRY *makes a step towards her.* I must have another look
at your pale face.

BESSIE *turns unexpectedly and pushes him with both hands;* HARRY *staggers back and stands still; fiercely.* Go away.

HARRY, *watching her.* Directly. But women always had to get me out of my scrapes. I am a beggar now, and you must help me out of my scrape.

BESSIE, *who at the word "beggar" had begun fumbling in the pocket of her dress, speaks wildly.* Here it is. Take it. Don't look at me. Don't speak to me!

HARRY *swaggers up under the lamp: looks at coin in his palm.*

Half-a-quid . . . My fare!

BESSIE, *hands clenched.* Why are you still here?

HARRY. Well, you *are* a fine figure of a girl. My word. I've a good mind to stop—for a week.

BESSIE, *pain and shame.* Oh! . . . What are you waiting for? If I had more money I would give it all, all. I would give everything I have to make you go—to make you forget you had ever heard my voice and seen my face.

Covers face with hands.

HARRY, *sombre, watches her.* No fear! I haven't forgotten a single one of you in the world. Some've given me more than money. No matter. You can't buy me in—and you can't buy yourself out . . .

Strides towards her. Seizes her arms. Short struggle. BESSIE *gives way. Hair falls loose.* HARRY *kisses her forehead, cheeks, lips; then releases her.* BESSIE *staggers against railings.*

Exit HARRY; *measured walk without haste.*

SCENE 5

BESSIE. CAPTAIN HAGBERD *at window.*

BESSIE, *staring eyes, hair loose, back against railings; calls out.* Harry!

Gathers up her skirts and runs a little way.

Come back, Harry.

Staggers forward against lamp-post.

Harry!

Much lower.

Harry!

In a whisper.

Take me with you.

Begins to laugh, at first faintly, then louder.

Window rumbles up, and CAPTAIN HAGBERD'S *chuckle mingles with* BESSIE'S *laughter which abruptly stops.*

CAPTAIN HAGBERD *goes on chuckling; speaks cautiously.* Is he gone yet, that information fellow? Do you see him anywhere, my dear?

BESSIE, *low and stammering.* N-no, no!

Totters away from lamp-post.

I don't see him.

CAPTAIN HAGBERD, *anxious.* A grinning vagabond, my dear. Good girl. It's you who drove him away. Good girl.

Stage gradually darkens.

BESSIE. Go in; be quiet! You have done harm enough.

CAPTAIN HAGBERD, *alarmed.* Why? Do you hear him yet, my dear?

BESSIE *sobs, drooping against the railings.* No! No! I don't. I don't hear him any more.

CAPTAIN HAGBERD, *triumphant.* Now we shall be all right, my dear, till our Harry comes home to-morrow.

Affected gurgling laugh.

BESSIE, *distracted.* Be quiet. Shut yourself in. You will make me mad.

Losing control of herself, repeats with rising inflection.

You make me mad.

With despair.

There is no to-morrow!

Sinks to ground near middle railings. Low sobs.

Stage darkens perceptibly.

CAPTAIN HAGBERD, *above, in a voice suddenly dismayed and shrill.* What! What do you say, my dear? No to-morrow? *Broken, very feebly.*

No—to-morrow?

Window runs down.

CARVIL, *heard within, muffled bellowing.* Bessie—Bessie—Bessie—Bessie——

At the first call BESSIE *springs up and begins to stumble blindly towards the door. A faint flash of lightning, followed by a very low rumble of thunder.*

You!—Bessie!

(*Curtain*)

JUDITH

A Tragedy in Three Acts
by

JEAN GIRAUDOUX

English version by
JOHN K. SAVACOOL

Characters

ACT ONE

A room in JUDITH's *house. Two doorways and a window.*

Before the curtain rises, we hear a voice which wails with supplication: "Judith! Judith!" This voice is joined by a chorus which repeats the same musical wail. As the curtain rises, the voice is heard again in solo. We see UNCLE JOSEPH *and several servants running around the room, brandishing swords and clubs.*

JOSEPH. Look downstairs! Look in all the closets! And remember the reward! There's silver for the man who catches him!

SERVANT. We'll never find him.

JOSEPH. He's someplace in this house.

SERVANT. No sir, he is; I mean, yes he isn't!

JOSEPH. What do you mean?

SERVANT. His voice is here, no one denies that. But Master, the voice has no body. No body at all! It's a ghost, that's what it is. It's the voice of the dead crying out for your niece, because she's the only one who can save us! Judith! Judith!

This call sounds so much like the cries we first heard, that the servants tremble with fright. Indeed, the cry is echo'd by the wailing chorus outside.

JOSEPH, *shouting.* Quiet! Now get out! All of you!

The servants leave. JOSEPH *looks around the room suspiciously. He leaves.*

A man's face appears in the window. The man makes a trumpet with his hands and bellows out in the same strident voice: "Judith! Judith! Save us!"

The face disappears. Servants and JOSEPH *enter as before.
They surge into the empty room. Then, finding nothing
there, they stand immobile with awe.*

Enter JOHN, *a young army officer. He drags along with
him the man whose face we saw at the window.*

JOHN, *throwing the man onto the floor at* JOSEPH'S *feet.* I
caught him in full flight. We'll teach these filthy mouths
once and for all that certain names are not to be touched.
Who are you?

JOSEPH. He smells as if he needs a bath. He must be one of
the prophets!

SERVANT. The city is full of them. Dying dogs attract flies.
But when it's a city that's sick and dying, then the scav-
engers are called prophets and the buzzing is called
prophecy.

JOHN. What's your name? Answer me!

THE PROPHET, *raising a hand as if to speak.* Judith! Judith!

JOSEPH. It's an epidemic! All the manure piles of the city
are dreaming about Judith. Put a gag in his mouth!

JOHN. Let him finish first. It might help . . .

THE PROPHET. Fairest of the pure, purest of the fair . . .

JOSEPH. Yes we know. The prophecy! The fairest of our
daughters, the purest flower of Israel must surrender herself to Holofernes.

JOHN. And the fairest, he says, is Judith.

THE PROPHET. Judith! Save us!

JOSEPH. Stuff his mouth with rags and lock him in the cellar!

The servants drag off THE PROPHET, *who is still screaming,*
"Judith, save us!"

*One servant lags behind the others and turns at the door-
way.*

JOSEPH. What's wrong with you?

SERVANT. Good Master, please let Judith save us!

A threatening gesture from JOSEPH *and the servant disappears after the others.*

JOHN. I hope she is not in the house.

JOSEPH. No, she is still at the hospital, tending the wounded.

JOHN. Have you told her?

JOSEPH. What is there to tell? She knows that Israel is dying while outside the city gates our enemy listens for the death rattle.

JOHN. Does she know that they've decided to send her—a sacrifice to Holofernes?

JOSEPH. Who has decided?

JOHN. The rabbis. They had a meeting . . . and the High Priest is on his way here now. He's coming to persuade Judith to . . .

JOSEPH. He'll have to persuade me first.

JOHN. It's too late, Joseph. The whole city is behind him. Have you looked into the streets this afternoon?

JOSEPH. I have.

JOHN. Then you saw it, scribbled on the walls all over the city. Scratched with diamonds on shop windows and smeared with charcoal on the backyard fences. The same stupid words: "Judith the fair, purest of the pure, shall go to bed with Holofernes."

JOSEPH. I saw it.

JOHN. Then you saw them too, huddled in groups at the street corners! The same hysterical old men. The same scab-studded crones that huddle together every time the people smell a miracle in the making.

JOSEPH. Listen to them!

From outside comes the sound of voices wailing, "Judith, save us!"

Other tribes can eat candy or chew gum. But not Israel! The children of Israel eternally need a proper name to suck on. It gives us an excuse for minding someone else's business. If our people are pious, John, it's because piety gives them an excuse for telling God how to run the world.

From outside come more cries of "Judith!"

JOHN. Judith! Judith! Listen to them hammer the name, bark it, unveil its mystery. What chance do you have against a thousand voices led by a Grand Rabbi?

JOSEPH. If Judith wants to, she can make even the Grand Rabbi see reason.

JOHN. In times of death and famine, reason is on the side of the priests—who have their own kind of logic which cries for miracles and, on occasion, invents them.

JOSEPH. Is that what you came here to tell me?

JOHN. I came to tell you that I can save your niece from being thrown to the barbarians and defiled in the hut of their General.

JOSEPH. Save Judith? I thought it was Judith who was to save the city.

JOHN. She must agree to nothing. When the rabbis arrive make the girl promise to decide nothing. I'll be back in an hour . . . and in the meantime her answer is no. No!— even to the Grand Rabbi.

JOHN *opens the door. Abruptly the voices stop.*

Silence?

Voices again. This time the wailing has turned into a chant.

More sinister than silence! They've turned her name into a prayer. Pray, cretins, pray. There are times when prayer is more inhuman than cries for blood!

JOSEPH. Go, John.

JOHN *leaves by side door. The chanting grows louder. Then, through the main door, enters the* GRAND RABBI.

JOACHIM. Where is she?

JOSEPH. What do you want of her?

JOACHIM. As High Priest and Grand Rabbi of Israel, I shall announce what I want only to your niece.

JOSEPH. Joachim, you shall not do this to her.

JOACHIM. Shall not! What shall not the High Priest do to Judith?

JOSEPH. Transform a simple girl into a tribal saint for the crowd to sob over.

JOACHIM. That, Joseph, is for the people of Israel to decide. And today Israel speaks with the voice of the prophets. Indeed, for lack of bread, prophecy is all our people have to live on.

JOSEPH. Joachim, you are a rabbi. I am a banker. Don't talk prophecy to me. Let's call it by its name: mass hysteria.

JOACHIM. Am I to believe that on your shoulders sits the only clear head in the city?

JOSEPH. Yes—unless you are a hypocrite.

JOACHIM. And with those clear-sighted eyes, I suppose I see an end to this siege that has starved our people and ruined commerce? I suppose you see the children of Israel still fat and well-fed on God's bounty? As the sole reasonable man left in the city, you smell springtime in the air, I suppose?

JOSEPH. I smell death and pestilence. The slightest breeze from north, south, east or west reminds me that between us and Holofernes's army there is a ring of Jewish corpses, rotting on the ground. But as yet I do not see our people so anxious to save their skins at any price that they can act like ignorant barbarians.

JOACHIM. And what is it you see standing between your family and the certain massacre that will fall on us to-morrow morning—because you must realize that your niece will be brutalized with the rest? I suppose you see what the bourgeoisie always looks for when courage fails and calamity threatens—a miracle! The dead rising from the battlefield and angels descending from heaven with swords of lightning to rout the enemy!

JOSEPH. If you like. Let's wait for the miracle.

JOACHIM. We need wait no longer! The miracle is at hand. After two months of blind martyrdom, our city has heard the name of your niece. And we blind martyrs now see an end of our ordeal. Is she here?

JOSEPH. No—and you will leave this house before she returns.

JOACHIM. The people have chosen Judith to be their miracle,
and the more I hear her name the more I believe in
Judith. I know your niece. I've watched her grow. She is
lovely and she is aware of her beauty. She is rich and she
has a taste for the fruits of her fortune. All the young men
of the city are her suitors. She holds court over writers
and doctors as well as merchants and entertainers. When
a girl like Judith goes to the theatre she steals the show
from the actors, just as right now at the hospital she is
making men forget they are in the act of dying and that
our city is losing a war. Once I despaired to see how
Judith thrives on this adulation. Today I rejoice. For, it is
thanks to this weakness that our Judith will consent to
give herself to God!

JOSEPH. Now that is between God and Judith.

JOACHIM. And what does Judith say about the choice God
offers?

JOSEPH. We have other things to talk about.

JOACHIM. But she knows, does she not?

JOSEPH. How could she help but know. Your priests have besieged this house more thoroughly than the enemy has
besieged the city.

JOACHIM. And has she changed her way of living? Has she
turned her mirrors to the wall? Removed a single feather
from her bed? You wouldn't know, of course. You are
much too busy denying the grace of God in this place
which the Almighty has already made sacred.

JOSEPH. Sacred! I hope that this house will never be sacred.
Why this is where my father had his first stroke, where
Judith used to play with her dolls, where she lost her first
tooth. In this room my family has eaten, cried and spit.
See, I spit! If this place is holy, that is because man has
lived in it and made it human.

JOACHIM. That is for Judith to decide.

JOSEPH. She can decide tomorrow. Tonight she is busy at
the hospital.

JOACHIM. I have already summoned her. And here she is.

JUDITH *enters, accompanied by* LITTLE JACOB.

JUDITH. Greetings, Joachim. Good evening, Uncle. Is there a crust of bread left in the house for little Jacob? Look at him. I found him on the stairway. He's dying of hunger.

LITTLE JACOB. I don't want any bread.

JUDITH. What do you want, little boy?

LITTLE JACOB. I want Judith to go to our enemy Holofernes.

JUDITH. My, but you learned your lesson well, didn't you! And what does Judith do when she gives herself to Holofernes?

LITTLE JACOB. I don't know.

JUDITH. How sweet! And you are not going to eat any more bread until she does?

LITTLE JACOB. I shall not eat any more bread until she gives herself to Holofernes.

JUDITH. And what about meat? Would you eat a piece of meat?

LITTLE JACOB. Meat?

JUDITH. Uncle Joseph, see if there isn't one more slice of meat left in the kitchen.

JOSEPH. The last we have. Send him to the kitchen. And tell him to leave my house in peace!

LITTLE JACOB *runs off to the kitchen.*

JUDITH. Uncle, you must not be angry with him. Poor little Jacob, he is only repeating what they teach him in school. Here, let me smooth down those ruffled white hairs. There, kiss me. I hope the Grand Rabbi will forgive the vulgarity of this family scene.

She runs her hands around her uncle's collar.

Let me fix your collar. Now, leave us, please.

JOSEPH. Don't trust him, Judith. Don't trust Joachim tonight.

JUDITH. Tonight there is no Joachim. Tonight there is only Judith and God.

JOSEPH. Don't trust God either. Not even God!

JOSEPH *leaves the room.*

JOACHIM. Judith! God is indeed in this room tonight.

JUDITH. Then I am afraid He's got the wrong address. This is not the house He was looking for.

JOACHIM. The prophecy says she shall be the fairest of the fair, purest of the pure. It says nothing about her being modest.

JUDITH. Does your prophecy also say that she shall be the most pleasure-loving girl in the city? Because that's what I am, believe me. If people think I am beautiful, that's because I have expensive clothes and I know how to wear them.

JOACHIM. If you know of any one more worthy to fulfill the law, name her now.

JUDITH. Any woman with the courage to do what you propose would seem both beautiful and pure. That's what the prophecy really means.

JOACHIM. I'm afraid not, Judith. Israel is not Greece, and our God does not speak in Homeric metaphors. If we are bound to the letter of the law, that is because our Jewish God calls each one of His creatures by His own rightful name.

JUDITH. Strange, but I've yet to hear Him pronounce the name of Judith!

JOACHIM. Have you heard Him pronounce the name of Martha, Esther, Ruth or any of your friends?

JUDITH. Joachim, you set your sights too high on the social scale. Just once, can't you forget the rich and mighty? There are still plenty of virgins in the middle class.

JOACHIM. Judith!

JUDITH. And what about the working girls? The church should be more democratic, Joachim. Why don't you give a chance at glory to a name like Cohan or Levy?

JOACHIM. These Cohans and Levys are the very ones who have designated you.

JUDITH. And I have no interest in choices made by people who have not, themselves, been chosen, chosen by God.

JOACHIM. Somehow, I did not expect to find Judith so resistant to the voice of God.

JUDITH. I repeat: to me it is their voice, not Jehovah's, that I hear. And, I've been listening. The tiniest of signs and I would have been convinced.

JOACHIM. What do you want? A burning bush?

JUDITH. A flash of warmth would do. Or a single word. All day I've been listening for it. I even provoked the wounded to make them cry out. But when the words came they were no more than the words of dying men. Two of them died in my arms this afternoon. I held them against me until I held nothing but death.

LITTLE JACOB *appears in the doorway.*

LITTLE JACOB, *putting a slice of meat on the table.* I don't want any meat either.

JUDITH. But you're so hungry, little fellow.

LITTLE JACOB. And I don't want any cheese either. And no cake.

JUDITH. And what about a kiss, if Judith gives it to you?

LITTLE JACOB. Not if that means breaking the fast.

JUDITH. Not if I kiss you on the neck, behind the ear. That's permitted. Now, would you like an apple? There is just one apple left in the house.

LITTLE JACOB. An apple?

JOACHIM. Don't give it to him. They'll only make him give it back.

JUDITH. Off with you then.

LITTLE JACOB. But maybe an apple . . .

JUDITH. Here's your apple. Now go!

LITTLE JACOB *leaves.*

JUDITH. I'm grateful to you, Joachim, for not suggesting that this was God talking to me through the voice of a child.

JOACHIM. If to be worthy of you, a child of Israel has found a way of equating fast with famine, then his voice might well cause you to reflect . . .

JUDITH. Children have no idea of what happens when a giant and a young girl are locked in a room together.

JOACHIM. Do you?

JUDITH. Vaguely. One night in a dream I wrestled for hours with Goliath.

JOACHIM. Who won?

JUDITH. He did, in my dream. But then I woke up.

JOACHIM. Judith, that was no dream for a proper young girl, but it augurs well for us. When a girl is afraid to fight off an attack, she often has a better chance of winning the battle.

The apple comes hurtling through the window and lands at JUDITH's *feet.*

And there is your apple again!

JUDITH. Please, Joachim, find someone else. Down in the courtyard I met a girl who sees visions. There are stigmata on her breasts and on her tongue, and her name is the same as mine. You don't see any divine ink on me, do you?

JOACHIM. I have seen that girl. It's true her name is Judith, but she is blind in one eye and there are open sores on her face.

JUDITH. Then cure her! In time you can turn her imperfections into something appealing.

JOACHIM. Time? How much time do you think we have?

JUDITH. At the hospital they say Holofernes is low on munitions. They say he is melting down jewels to make heads for his arrows.

JOACHIM. Yes, I've heard the story. In fact, I was the one who put it into circulation. The truth is, Judith, we are the ones who have no more weapons.

JUDITH. What about the thirty thousand horsemen that were coming from Syria to help us?

JOACHIM. They arrived this morning. This afternoon they joined forces with the enemy.

JUDITH. All the greater glory for our army when the day of victory comes.

JOACHIM. Judith, our army no longer exists.

JUDITH. What did you say?

JOACHIM. The truth.

JUDITH. A rabbi's truth.

JOACHIM. Would you rather hear it from a soldier? John, for instance?

JUDITH. Why John?

JOACHIM. Because I see him coming across the courtyard.

JUDITH. It's no use. I still won't believe you.

JOACHIM. Would you believe him? You know him well, of course?

JUDITH. Yes, I know him well.

JOACHIM. You are engaged, I suppose?

JUDITH. What if we are?

JOACHIM, *at door.* Send up Lieutenant John. Tell him the Grand Rabbi requests his presence.
To Judith.

If it's because of John that you are hesitating, I know how to convince you.

JUDITH. Convince me of what?

JOACHIM. Of your duty to become a saint.

JUDITH. A saint who is slightly soiled.

JOACHIM. How dare you talk like that to a rabbi!

JUDITH. John will tell you! Although he certainly won't tell you anything about me that you couldn't learn from Paul, James or Peter, or any of the officers who can dance and kiss just as well as he does. But when he's finished, you will know once and for all time that I am not the Judith referred to in the prophecy.

JOACHIM. John? Enter!
Enter JOHN.

Come in, my son.

JOHN. What do you want, Joachim?

JOACHIM. To ask you a few questions.

JOHN. I'm a soldier, not a rabbi. Your knowledge far exceeds
  mine.

JOACHIM. These will be questions that even a lieutenant can
  answer.

JOHN. Yes, Rabbi.

JUDITH. John, answer me. And I want you to tell the truth,
  even if it debases you, even if it debases me.

JOACHIM. Don't you think that my question takes preced-
  ence over yours?

JUDITH. Oh? Then go ahead and ask it.

JOACHIM. John, is it true that this morning what was left of
  our city guard mutinied against its officers and surrendered to the enemy?

JUDITH. That's a lie!

JOACHIM. Is it a lie that at noon our sacred battalion fled in
  panic and left its flag on the ground for all to see—lying
  in the sun outside the city walls?

JUDITH. False! I know it's false!

JOACHIM. Is it false that the only troops left to defend the
  city are two companies of old men recently pressed into
  service? Answer me!

JUDITH. Well, answer him! One word will do it.

JOHN. Don't be cruel.

JUDITH. Cruel! Where were my eyes? I don't need an answer. It is written on your face.

JOHN. Thank God for that.

JUDITH. I suppose you also thank God for defeat?

JOHN. Careful, Judith. Yours is the first mouth in the city to
  pronounce that word.

JUDITH. It's not the word I'm afraid of. It's what it stands
  for.

JOHN. Judith!

JUDITH. So it's defeat, is it! Our glorious army has been defeated! Our captains in their fancy uniforms and our lieutenants with all their ribbons have been defeated.

JOHN. That makes us less attractive, I suppose?

JUDITH. Hideous, that's what it makes you! Hideous!

JOHN. I can still look you in the face, Judith.

JUDITH. But it's not me you see. If you could really see me, you'd lower your eyes. If you could see what I am like from head to foot, now that our country is broken, beaten and trampled on, you wouldn't be able to stand the sight of me. You'd fly from me faster than you flew from the enemy. I saw you, a little while ago, down in the street with the children running after you and the girls clapping their hands. You even kissed one of the children. You had no right to do that. It was the worst kind of lie. You knew in your heart you were defeated and yet you kissed that child!

JOHN. I suppose kisses are only for the man who wins.

JUDITH. For the old and the weak, or even children, defeat can be a kind of consecration. But for a soldier, no. For a soldier defeat is inadmissible.

JOHN. You are young, Judith, very young.

JOACHIM. Enough, my son. Tonight Judith is the first soldier of the city in our first line of battle.

JOHN. Then she should not insult the face of defeat. That is for the non-combatants. If I'm really defeated, that means I'm no longer responsible to you or anyone else.

JOACHIM. We are always responsible to God, my son.

JOHN. God's never been especially fond of lost causes. When we're losing I think He even welcomes our insults. Insults spare him the bother of being implicated in the catastrophe. Besides he still has Judith. Because, if I understand rightly, this is the night when Judith pulls God's chestnuts out of the fire.

JUDITH. Yes, God still has Judith.

JOACHIM. You've said enough, John.

JOHN. Yes, because no matter what I say, her pride will translate it into flattery.

JUDITH. Is it a crime to insist that Israel be the name for a race of conquerors? Is it my fault if you heroes are too weak to defend our honor and pass the sword to a woman?

JOHN. To you, at least, we pass nothing at all. What was the next question?

JUDITH. There are no more questions.

JOHN. Fairest daughter of Israel? Are you really the fairest? So much of you is the reflection of gold and luxury that one never knows what you are really like. Look at her, Joachim! Look at her well, the subtle dilation of the nostrils, the blood beating at her temples. This girl is the threshold of everything that is passionately human and changing. Beauty it is, but human beauty—beauty of the moment!

JUDITH. And this is the moment, the moment I was made for!

JOHN. With me you were more modest, Judith. With me you were not so sure. Maybe you think God is more easily satisfied?

JUDITH. Tonight I shall be the most beautiful of women. That I swear.

JOHN. Judith, you are not the virgin prescribed by the scriptures—and you know it.

JUDITH. No, I do not know it.

JOHN. Ask her, Joachim, ask where she was two weeks ago. This same time of day, just after she left the hospital.

JUDITH. Where was I?

JOHN. In my arms.

JUDITH. In the arms of a soldier who had been defeated by the enemy.

JOHN. In the arms of a man who wrapped himself around you and pressed his lips against yours——

JUDITH. I suppose I surrendered?

JOHN. No, indeed, you did not. You are not simple enough for that. Everytime I approach Judith, she musters a

mass of guilty feelings to fight me off. Who knows, God
may like His virgins already warmed on the fire, palpitat-
ing with unvirginal desires?

JUDITH. It's you who are simple, my friend. And naïve.

JOHN. Yes, because I'm weary with the weight of my love
for you.

JUDITH. Listen to him, Joachim! One kiss and he thinks I'm
promised to him for life.

JOHN. Don't worry. When you marry Holofernes you'll get
no protests from these lips of mine.

JUDITH, *as if by memory*. Holofernes does not exist. Holofernes is only a name for a special way of suffering necessary to redemption. If I leave here tonight it will not be to
join him, but to give myself to those other things. And
I shall not be the only girl in the world who has used her
beauty and her innocence as if they were intended not
for a man, but for a great moment in history!

JOHN. Holofernes is very much a man.

JOACHIM. John, you've said enough.

JOHN. Holofernes is a giant. He has a giant's hands, a giant's
fingers, a giant's bones in his body . . .

JUDITH. Small soul that you are, have you no pity? Can't
you see that my courage will hold just so long as I shut
off my imagination? Answer my question. Is everything
lost?

JOHN. Everything.

JUDITH. Nothing can save us?

JOHN. Nothing. Holofernes attacks at dawn, and there will
be nothing to stop him.

JUDITH. Nothing to stop him at dawn . . .

JOACHIM. And the sun is setting, Judith.

JUDITH. Thank you, John. You decided for me. I leave tonight.

She takes a step toward Joachim.

That is, if Joachim will still accept me.

JOACHIM. I accept you.

JUDITH. I want you to be sure of this. Look me in the eyes. Touch my skin. Pinch my cheeks. God should know by the arch of my nose that I am more a creature of feeling than intelligence.

JOACHIM. You are the beauty of beauties.

JUDITH. No one has ever seen me without my clothes. But before God I guarantee you and the people that my legs are smooth and my feet unscratched.

JOACHIM. Judith, it is absolutely necessary that you remain unexcited.

JUDITH. I never really loved any of those men, not really. They never really touched me. Does this mean that I am chaste and that God has chosen me to fulfill the prophecy?

JOACHIM. You are chaste, and God has chosen you. Are you ready to leave?

JUDITH. I am.

JOACHIM. You know what is expected of you.

JUDITH. Please, Joachim, no sermons. If you know what I should do, keep it to yourself. I see only too clearly what's to be done.

JOACHIM. Then, Judith, this is farewell.

JUDITH. Judith! I'm beginning to see what this girl Judith is like. Ah, but how I'd like to know what she is really thinking about behind this mask of flesh.

JOACHIM. And Holofernes, do you see him clearly too? A brute, shouting drunken insults at the Jews and their God!

JUDITH. I can see him.

JOACHIM. Do you see his women milling around you, despoiling your robes, tearing your hair, mocking your body?

JUDITH. I can see them.

JOACHIM. Do you see the giant, half asleep on his couch, reaching out to grab you, drawing you to him?

JUDITH. I can almost touch him.

JOACHIM. Are you fighting his embrace?

JUDITH. I'm watching the pulse of a blue vein in his neck, it's throbbing like the artery on the neck of a bull. I'm pressing my finger against it. His face is growing purple. Heavens, where am I?

JOACHIM. In the past, Judith. It's time to move into the future.

JUDITH. When? Now?

JOACHIM. Wait until the moon rises. That gives you time for prayers.

JUDITH. Very well. But you must keep my uncle occupied between now and then.

JOACHIM. John, are you coming?

JOHN. No, I'm staying here.

JUDITH. Let him stay. Like a good soldier, he'll stick to his post until he is relieved.

    JOACHIM *leaves.*

JOHN. Then you have made up your mind? To save an insensitive people ruled by a few unscrupulous priests and scorned even by their God, you are leaving. Judith! In this city of ours even the children are ugly!

JUDITH. To save them, people, priests and children, I am leaving.

JOHN. Now?

JUDITH. Now.

JOHN. Then what can I tell you? What do you want to know?

JUDITH. The password, to get through the lines. What is the password tonight?

JOHN. Can't you guess? It's your name. Tonight, Judith, even Jehovah is flattered because His name starts with the same letter as yours.

JUDITH. What gate do I take out of the city?

JOHN. The gate opposite your house. The guards expect you to pass that way.

JUDITH. Where is Holofernes's tent?

JOHN. North, due north of the gate.

JUDITH. I can understand that. He wanted to be where he
could see the sun beating down on the city he is about to
devour. Is there a road or a trail I can follow?

JOHN. No. Outside the gate follow the stream that crosses
the road. But don't drink, because the water has been
poisoned. And wear a heavy cloak. Are you afraid?

JUDITH. Neither solitude nor silence has ever frightened me.

JOHN. Count on neither solitude nor silence. Outside that
gate, every ten paces you'll be stumbling on a sack of
flesh and bones. There will be dogs and at times it will
seem as if the whole battlefield is wailing in its sleep.

JUDITH. A heavy cloak . . . is that all the advice you have
to give me?

JOHN. That is all I have to say.

JUDITH. Are you sure that's all?

JOHN. Do you want me to tell you how a girl can look a giant
in the face? How a virgin can save the letter of her virginity while she is being raped? Is it now, Judith, that
you finally ask me to teach you how a girl makes love?

JUDITH. I wish you would.

JOHN. It's too late for me, Judith. But outside that door is
just the person you need. Susanna, where are you?

JUDITH. Who is that?

JOHN. A woman I brought here with me. She's not of your
class. But it's my dying wish that you receive her and
listen to what she has to say.

JUDITH. Since when is it the survivors who make the dying
wishes?

JOHN. Judith, for once in your life forget your pride and
listen to this woman. I'll be waiting outside. Susanna, you
may come in now.

JOHN *opens the door for* SUSANNA. *She enters a few steps.
Stands looking at* JUDITH. JOHN *then disappears and
closes the door behind him.*

JUDITH. Who are you?

SUSANNA. A friend.

JUDITH. You've come at an awkward time. This isn't exactly a day for friendships.

SUSANNA. . . . a woman who admires you.

JUDITH. Under the circumstances, admiration would seem like an insult in disguise.

SUSANNA. . . . a woman whose life has been the opposite of yours.

JUDITH. What kind of life is that?

SUSANNA. I have lovers and I give myself to them . . . for money. My name is the best known of all the names that girls like you are not supposed to know.

JUDITH. In that case, you have the right to speak to me to-night. What do you want?

SUSANNA. To save you.

JUDITH. Save the girl who is going to save the city? I see there is nothing modest about you.

SUSANNA. Do you think I am beautiful?

JUDITH. For the sake of your profession, I hope so.

SUSANNA. Look at me closely. Look closely, Judith. If I am beautiful, it is because I look something like you. My beauty, I know, covers nothing, nothing at all. It has nothing to hide. But just the same it is something like yours. I've been told so a hundred times. And I'm your height, too—and my voice . . .

JUDITH. That voice?

SUSANNA. Oh, I know it isn't trained to hide my thoughts, like yours. I have no thought to hide. No silences inside me. But it is your voice!

JUDITH. Have you heard that a hundred times too? Who is he? Who is the man?

SUSANNA. The man? Dozens of them. They come to me after you have warmed them up on the terrace. Dozens of them, trying to forget or seeking revenge. And while they cry in my arms or caress me, they call me Judith.

JUDITH. That's their password again tonight.

SUSANNA. For a year now, I've been watching you. I know how you talk and how you walk. And if I've imitated you it's not just to please your boy friends. It's because I love what you are. It's because you are me. You are the way I'd be if I weren't what I am. What's the harm in that?

JUDITH. No harm. It's theft, that's all.

SUSANNA. But I've stolen none of your haughtiness or pride. When I've bumped into you in the street and you've looked down on me with scorn, I've imagined your resignation. When you were cruel I've imagined your meekness. In front of your need for luxury, I've imagined your modesty. I've been happy, Judith, because I've made myself look just like you.

JUDITH. Do you?

SUSANNA. I make people think I do.

JUDITH. No woman patterned after a human being could ever resemble me. Not tonight!

SUSANNA. But you have never been human before. Not before tonight.

JUDITH. Since you must imitate me, speak clearly and come to the point.

SUSANNA. I want to go in your place.

JUDITH. I expected this!

SUSANNA. I don't believe in prophets. Most of them are spies, anyway, working for the enemy. There are some people who think Holofernes has heard so many men boasting about Judith that he has set a trap to catch her for himself.

JUDITH. What if he has? Couldn't God have put this thought in his head, in order to destroy him?

SUSANNA. If so many men of our own army, who know better, could be taken in by this resemblance how can you expect Holofernes to see the difference? Holofernes is a barbarian. He makes no distinction between the beauty I

wear like a mantle and that other beauty like yours, that
one really sees.

JUDITH. And what about God? Will He see any difference
between us?

SUSANNA. God sees fewer differences than we give Him credit
for, Judith.

JUDITH. And just so this exchange of roles will be complete,
I suppose you'd like me to replace you and lie with the
next man who knocks on the door and that he too will
see no difference between us.

SUSANNA. Judith, you don't understand. It's not just to save
your life, it's not because I think you are afraid! It's something else. Let me go in your place tonight. Tomorrow
morning the people will see you in the street. They'll
look at you and think you have returned from the enemy
. . . and the city will be saved.

JUDITH. If it's not my life, then what is it?

SUSANNA. You must stay . . .

JUDITH. Stay pure? You talk like the catechism. I take it, you
refer to my virginity!

SUSANNA. For once my profession will be an honor.

JUDITH. But doesn't Judith have to be a virgin? And isn't that
precisely what you are not? Or has my virginity sent so
many customers knocking at your door that you want to
keep me the way I am?

SUSANNA. Oh, Judith, when a girl becomes a woman she
changes her sex, her race. I want to preserve the miracle
that you are—Judith, the young girl.

JUDITH. So that's what the foolish virgins dream about? My
virginity! I don't know what yours was like, Susanna, but
I'm beginning to understand mine. It's neither ignorant
nor innocent nor pure, but it's mine. It's a promise I bear
inside me, like a child; a promise of a wonderful defeat,
a great shame that will someday fill me to bursting with
pride. Now God has changed this promise of defeat into
one of victory. That's His business. But even if I were in

love with a young man, tonight I'd say to him: "No, you
shall not be the first."

SUSANNA. Judith! You must save yourself!

JUDITH. Who says I won't?

SUSANNA. But you're a girl. You have no weapons, no
strength.

JUDITH. I have the most dangerous weapon of all.

SUSANNA. Poison?

JUDITH. The gift of speech! Words seethe under pressure
inside me. Answers to a question! To a whole series of
questions I've never heard asked? Just what they are
going to prove, I have no idea. But the words are there.
And when the time comes I'll let them prove whatever
there is to be proven. Why, Susanna, you're crying!

SUSANNA. All that sweetness . . . all that violence . . . all
for nothing!

JUDITH. Susanna, you don't understand me any better than
John or the rabbis. If I object to the way they're pushing
me into this adventure, it's only because I've been dreaming, in my bed at night, of doing something like this on
my own. But I waited too long . . . and now it's God
who's going to get all the credit. Maybe I've known all
along it was really His idea. Maybe God thinks I really
thought it up all by myself. Maybe God's jealous because
I thought of it first . . . maybe this is His revenge.

SUSANNA. Judith!

JUDITH. As for my sweetness. Let me kiss you for that. No,
look at me. Now am I really the one you give to those
poor young men I've driven into your arms? Is this the
way you talk to them? Farewell to my soft skin. Farewell
to my lips. How much easier it is to say goodbye to a sister than to your own image in the mirror.

SUSANNA. Judith!

JUDITH. And now I must leave you.

SUSANNA. No, no!

JUDITH. Stupid woman, can't you recognize the voice of God
when it speaks?

*

SUSANNA. You're not going out like that, without a cloak?

JUDITH. I don't want my uncle to know I'm leaving.

SUSANNA. Here, take mine. You will be wading through streams, pushing through the brush.

JUDITH. Is the street still full of people?

SUSANNA. The streets are empty now, but the whole town is watching. They're looking out their windows, waiting for Judith to pass. Even the children have been allowed to stay up late to watch.

JUDITH. It's time the children went to bed. How do I look?

SUSANNA. The way you always look, Judith.

JUDITH. The way I always look! Thank you, Susanna. May Judith look tonight as she has always looked. What a compliment for all the other days of my life. Now, if you will open the door.

JUDITH *leaves.*

SUSANNA. John! John!

JOHN *enters.*

JOHN. Has she gone? You know what to do? Do you remember the shortcut?

SUSANNA. Esther is going with me. She crosses the lines almost every night on business.

JOHN. You have plenty of time. I sent Judith the long way around.

Exit SUSANNA.

THE PROPHET *appears in the window and calls again for* JUDITH *to save the city.* JOHN *runs to window, grabs* THE PROPHET, *drags him into room, throws him on floor, and kills him.*

JOHN. Now, you've been saved! What next!

Wails from outside the house.

CURTAIN

ACT TWO

An anti-chamber in HOLOFERNES'S *tent.* URI *and* OTTA,
two aides de camp, are joking with SARAH *the procuress.*
EGON, *another aide de camp, enters. In the background
are a few guards and a giant negro named* YAMI.

Laughter as EGON, *a painted, manicured and effeminate
officer, enters.*

OTTA. Egon! Come in! Sarah has an idea!

EGON. And it's about time, Sarah. The officers are beginning
to complain. It seems that your merchandise no longer
satisfies them.

SARAH. It's the best I can offer.

EGON. Your best is no longer good enough. Two months ago
you brought us girls who were not only curious to learn
but also plump enough to teach. But, ever since this
beastly famine in the city, we get nothing but their older
sisters.

OTTA. More like their mothers.

URI. No, their grandmothers.

OTTA. And all they want is food. They rush for the kitchen
like a pack of dogs.

EGON. It's your widows who are the worst offenders. Either
they are cold as icicles or else so wanton that a soldier
loses his self-respect by obliging them.

URI. It's obvious you weren't born to your profession.

SARAH. Certainly not! I'm a direct descendant of Jacob.

EGON. Sarah, you amaze me. Ever since we've come to this
country we've had nothing but famous names to serve us,
whether it's to open the secret gates at night or furnish
young boys for our pleasure. If the descendants of Jacob

can't even be satisfactory procurers of women, what good
does it do them to have him as an ancestor?

OTTA. This is the night that Jacob redeems himself.

EGON. Well, Sarah! And what entertainment do you offer
tonight to celebrate the destruction of your city?

SARAH. A comedy.

EGON. But we've seen what you call comedy! Naked women
with national emblems tattoo'd on their navels, dancing
under colored lights. The only person who's not bored to
death with them is the minister of war. I was hoping
you'd have something more substantial.

SARAH. The funniest scene that a Jewess ever played in the
theatre, or ever will play, if you kill them all tomorrow
morning.

EGON. Nonsense, the theatre will never see the last of Jewish
actresses—Sarah! Who is this Jewess? Is she here?

SARAH. She is on her way.

EGON. She looks like you, I suppose?

SARAH. She is twenty years old.

EGON. Another beggar, I suppose?

SARAH. Her father is a millionaire. For three centuries her
forefathers have been lending, renting and stealing to
make a pedestal of gold for this wonder of charity and
generosity to stand on.

EGON. Then why is she coming to see you?

SARAH. She is not coming to see me. She's coming to see
Holofernes.

EGON. If you and this Jewess are plotting trouble . . .

SARAH. I did not arrange this visit. In fact, I had nothing to
do with it. It's the people of Israel who send her. According to their prophets, they can be saved only if the fairest
and purest girl in the city comes to Holofernes, un-
escorted. Everybody thinks that this is the girl the
prophets were talking about. And, since she agrees with
them, she's on her way.

EGON. This is more like it, providing she has some flesh on her!

SARAH. There is scarcely a hint of hair and when Judith cries, even when she perspires, it is like dew at sunrise. And she was born rich.

EGON. Judith? Did you say "Judith?"

SARAH. Why, do you know her?

EGON. That girl who bribed the Arab porters to massacre the officers of the guard last week, what was her name?

SARAH. It's the same girl.

EGON. And she dares come here after butchering our dearest friends? Otta, remember how poor Lamia looked with his head split open and that green slime in his mouth?

SARAH. At last my comedy is beginning to interest you!

EGON. So she's coming here! The girl who made green slime of a hero's blood is coming here! I can hardly wait the pleasure. What refinements of torture have you prepared to welcome our guest?

SARAH. There is only one for a girl like this: humiliation! May I bring her in?

EGON. If you must. The King is resting in the rear of the tent.

SARAH. Then you sit there, on the royal throne. Otta, hand me the cloak.

EGON. Holofernes's cloak? You want her to think that I am Holofernes?

SARAH. Of course. She'll come in trembling with fear. Obsessed with the idea that she is a queen facing a great king. Encourage her, she'll play the Queen of Sheba for you. She'll plead the cause of love and virtue in front of a modern Solomon.

EGON. But why me?

SARAH. Because you can talk. I told you she was a virgin. That means that above everything else she will be very talkative. And remember, all Israel believes in this girl. The people are spending the night on the parapets waiting.

EGON. Waiting?—for what?

SARAH. For morning—when she will walk out of here, followed by a penitent Holofernes.

OTTA. Now Egon, do you understand your part in this comedy?

EGON. I can always understand revenge.

OTTA. You know, in the royal cloak, you look good.

EGON. In a royal cloak anyone looks good! It's the most flattering garment yet invented by man. Otta, remember how poor dear Lamia died? The anguish of that beautiful body torn by two deaths at once? One side of him swollen until he looked more like a giant tumour than a man. The other side, still slim, controlled and dignified, even to the impeccable grace of a smile on his lips. Tonight only the slim beautiful half of Lamia shall stand by my side. No, Lamia, the other side, please! Guard, is the woman ready to present herself?

SARAH. She is coming.

EGON. How do you know?

SARAH. We've had spies on her trail from the moment she left the city.

EGON. And where did she enter the camp?

SARAH. Near the stream where your enemies made their last attack. The water is polluted with blood, but this girl bent down to drink and quenched her thirst.

EGON. Lamia! She drinks blood.

SARAH. She is now approaching the royal tent. Now she accosts the guard and asks for Holofernes.

EGON, *to the guard.* Bring in this creature, this cannibal of pride!

URI. But what about us? What do we do when she comes in?

SARAH. It's very simple. The rest of us will curse and insult the girl. Egon will be fascinated by her words. Bit by bit, he will let her seduce him into sparing the city.

EGON. She can kiss me, but that's all. One kiss.

URI. Egon! How courageous of you!

EGON. That's because of Lamia. Lamia liked women too. But only those who were blond like him. Sarah, I hope this Judith is not a blond. I hope she hasn't put on a lot of paint, just to soften poor Lamia's heart.

Enter the GUARD. *He holds back the flap of the tent.*

SARAH. See for yourself, Great King!

JUDITH *enters.* EGON *and the officers pretend not to notice her entrance. They continue laughing and joking.*

JUDITH. I am here, Holofernes!

URI. Who dares pronounce the name of the King? Who is this creature so ignorant of the law that she knows not it is forbidden to touch the king, even with a word?

JUDITH. She can tell you who I am.

SARAH. Ah? So Judith condescends to recognize Sarah! Sarah has come up in the world since Judith threw her out of the house, hasn't she?

OTTA. What brings her to us? Hysteria? Hunger, thirst? Does she wish a drink?

JUDITH. I quenched my thirst in the stream outside your camp.

EGON. What did she say?

SARAH. I believe she said she just had a drink of water flavored with Jewish blood, so that she may be as courageous as her brothers. It's what they call a noble thought.

EGON. If it is to recite noble thoughts that you've come to us, my dear, you are wasting your time. Noble thoughts never do anyone any good until centuries after they are said. And even then the only people who have any time for them are actors playing in tragedies.

SARAH. She's acting now.

EGON. Please, save it for the theatre! I'm so rarely touched! If you knew how many women have played this scene before my eyes, wives trying to rescue their husbands from my clutches, sisters tendering vials of poison to their beloved brothers after drinking half of it themselves with a sad little smile on their faces. Such noble thoughts! Such superlative gestures! I'm familiar with the whole repertory, but I've never been touched—here! So you drank the water in Esau's stream? You were quite free to do so, you know. Only please don't come boasting about it to me. What is your name?

JUDITH. Judith.

EGON. Sarah, who is Judith?

SARAH. My Lord, she is a virgin. There has never been a virginity that was petted and desired at closer quarters, but it is a virginity just the same. She has a certificate from the Grand Rabbi to prove it. Would you like to see for yourself?

EGON. Touch her, Sarah, and I'll have you whipped! At least she is pleasant to look at, and considerably less emaciated than your usual recruits.

SARAH. I don't know how she does it. The others dry up with hunger. She thrives on it. I think she nourishes herself on the grandeur of the times.

EGON. We have plenty of that to give her. Princess! How dare you show yourself like this? Hum? That perfume around you! Is that the royal scent of Judah?

SARAH. No, my Lord. That's the aroma of the city bank. I told you, she's rich. But there she stands, captive and broken and shattered with fear.

EGON. Oh no, Sarah, you are mistaken. I recognize courage when I see it.

SARAH. She's afraid, I tell you. See how stiff and pale she is. See, she's afraid to open her mouth. It's not always so easy, is it, dearie? Sometimes those great big words seem out of place.

EGON. One more of them out of you, Sarah, and I'll turn you over to Yami. What brings you to our tent, my dear?

JUDITH. I wanted to see a great King, face to face.

EGON. I trust you see him just the way you imagined him to be.

JUDITH. I'm not sure exactly how I imagined him. But I do know that when I left I was despondent, and now I am hopeful.

EGON. Because of something you see in my eyes? The way I curl my beard?

JUDITH. Something in the way you speak.

SARAH. There, you see! Flattery!

EGON. Something that makes it more soft, I suppose? More trusting?

JUDITH. No. But underneath the harsh hypocritical tones of a ruler, I do sense a kind of playfulness. And then there is a curiosity in you which is very encouraging.

EGON. Beware of your intuitions, my child. Holofernes has made a thousand promises during his life. Once he promised the Queen of Aleppo to spare her eldest son if only that great lady would prostitute herself to a donkey. Another time he promised the God of Phoenicia to spare His temple if only He would materialize himself in the form of a man. The Queen obliged the donkey and the God of Phoenicia appeared in person. I killed the Queen's son and I burned the God's temple to the ground.

SARAH. That's because neither the Queen nor the God was like Judith!

JUDITH. Then you couldn't have been the real Holofernes, not the one I want to speak with tonight.

EGON. Speak then! He is listening.

URI. My Lord! It's this girl or us! You'll have to make your choice.

EGON. Silence! I have already chosen.

OTTA. But it's late, my Lord! There is scarcely time to read our reports.

EGON. Speak, girl. In whose name do you come to us?

JUDITH. Just that. Do you know the difference between a girl and a woman?

EGON. A girl is what Sarah was, a long time ago. She is what once all those women were who are the scourge of the earth.

JUDITH. Do you know what it means to be a girl?

EGON. Everybody knows that, except the girls themselves. Once a girl knows it, she is no longer one of them. She's a woman.

JUDITH. Then I am the exception. Because I know what I am, and I'm not a woman.

EGON. Let's say that you are not a woman yet, but that you are well prepared for the grotesque act which will make you one.

JUDITH. To remain a girl, my Lord, is to be driven by a blind force that inures you to pain, unhappiness and suffering. All in the hope that some day you will encounter grandeur in the form of another human being.

EGON. I hope, my dear, that you don't expect to find *that* here. Grandeur belongs to tragedy, and tragedy is for those who have been defeated. Grandeur is the consolation prize the gods offer to the victims, just before they lose their heads on the altar.

JUDITH. Holofernes! Spare the people of Israel, and your name will be praised with theirs for all eternity!

OTTA. Really now! Only a Jewess could take eternity as seriously as all that!

EGON. Goodness me, Judith, don't you think I've already heard all the arguments one could invent for sparing your people? Besides, I do not have much love for women.

SARAH. You'd never guess it tonight. Touch her, my Lord. Touch her with your hands!

EGON. Yami! Take that woman away and whip her!

SARAH. But, my Lord, what have I said? What have I done?

EGON. You have insulted my guest. Yami!

SARAH. Pity, my Lord! I was joking!

OTTA. It's not right to whip her, my Lord, not if she was only joking!

EGON. Let Judith decide. If Judith takes pity on you, you shall be spared.

SARAH. Judith! Pity me!

EGON. One word, one move of her hand and Judith can save you.

JUDITH *remains silent and motionless.*

Very well, that's settled.

OTTA. Take care, my Lord. Embrace that virgin and you'll produce a new race of usurers and prophets.

EGON. It is for you to take care, Otta. Who do you think I am that you can talk to me in this manner? What sort of man are you to forget that today we commemorate the passing of our dear lamented Lamia? Lamia, who owed so much to this Jewess! In his name, Judith, we listen.

JUDITH. Then listen carefully, my Lord, for the love of this man Lamia, just as if he were standing there behind you.

EGON. He is, indeed. At least, half of him. All right, Judith, we are listening. No, come here. Closer. Don't you think we've played this comedy long enough?

JUDITH. Comedy?

EGON. I lied to you, Judith. I knew you were coming. And not from the mouth of that old procuress, but from the mouths of those exquisite young men who screamed your name as we tore them apart, limb by limb. One would think that the whole army of Israel existed only to defend that name. And now here you are, a prisoner in my tent. It wasn't I who invented the story that you would save the Jews by coming here. And yet, my dear, don't you think it possible that the same popular imagination which can so often distill the wisdom of whole volumes of philosophy into a single proverb may have seen through the confusion of history, and simplified the great struggle of nations and armies by identifying the two real adversaries: you and me. Perhaps this war against the Jews cannot end except in a duel which sees the two of us, the real antagonists, face to face. And so here we are. And so the war is ended! Otta, call the general staff. Tomorrow we move north to attack the Phoenicians. And you, Judith, are free to go home.

JUDITH. Go home?

EGON. Hurry home, my child, and tell the Jews how you saved the city. Yami will see you safely through the lines. Yami, do you understand? And tell your people what it is like to treat with a barbarian.

JUDITH. But . . .

EGON. Yes, my dear, you are very attractive, but we have no taste for your charms. And besides, I'm not in the mood.

JUDITH. My Lord.

EGON. Wait! Am I wrong in thinking that you might be able to conquer your aversion, bring your face close to mine, and gently implant a sisterly kiss on my forehead?

JUDITH. I could.

EGON. Well then, do!

Distrustfully, JUDITH *approaches* EGON *and kisses him on the forehead. Suddenly, she grabs him and kisses him passionately on the mouth.*

Cries of mockery from the others. JUDITH *pushes* EGON *away as they surround her. She raises her hand with a dagger.*

EGON. The little bitch! She might have hurt me. Yami, take her away!

SARAH. Imbecile! Where did you think you were? In the court of love? What a fine picture of Jewish intelligence you've given these men, mistaking a pederast with his painted lips and long eyelashes for King Holofernes!

EGON. Yami! Take her away, she's yours. Do what you like with her.

YAMI. No.

EGON. Do you hear. I'm giving her to you.

YAMI. No.

EGON. You dare refuse? You know the penalty?

YAMI. Yes.

URI. All right, men! Kill him!

The guards drag YAMI *off to be killed.*

SARAH. Give the girl to me, Egon. I can use her. Didn't you
notice how nicely she's learned to kiss?

EGON. No. We are going to avenge poor Lamia, and right
here.

SARAH. Why don't you cry for help, Judith? Call for your
soldiers! Call for the prophets! Or better yet, call for God!

JUDITH. Holofernes! Holofernes! Holofernes!

*The curtains part at the rear of the tent, flooding the stage
with light.* HOLOFERNES *appears.*

HOLOFERNES. Take that woman out of my sight and kill her!

SARAH. But, Holofernes, what have I done?

HOLOFERNES. Let's say that you mispronounced my name.
That should suffice.

SARAH. Pity, my Lord! It was Egon's idea!

HOLOFERNES. Then we'll start your little comedy all over
again, only this time in earnest. We'll ask this young girl
if she wants to pity you.

SARAH. Pity, Judith!

HOLOFERNES. One word, one move of her hand, and Judith
can save you.

SARAH. Save me, Judith! Don't let them kill me.

JUDITH *does not move.*

HOLOFERNES. Take her away! Besides she's a Jew. We should
have killed her long ago.

SARAH. You think you'll kill us all, don't you? Israel will live,
despite you, the Messiah will come and He'll rule over us.
And it won't be because of a stupid bourgeois who walks
around boasting she's still a virgin. It will be because of
Sarah, mistress of whores! Take this city, burn it! But
you'll never kill all the Jews, because for weeks and weeks
I've been smuggling the young ones through your lines
to safety in the hills. That's where they've gone, your play-
mates. But they'll come back. They'll come back and build
again and they'll live to spit on your name!

HOLOFERNES. Poor Sarah! Every night you smuggled them
out of the city, and every morning I'd have to send fresh

horsemen to pursue the caravan and exterminate its Jewish cargo.

SARAH. Murderer!

She hurls herself onto HOLOFERNES. *The guards grab her and drag her back.*

HOLOFERNES. Now leave us alone. All of you!

All leave except HOLOFERNES *and* JUDITH. *He contemplates her. Then, after a silence . . .*

HOLOFERNES. It's as if they come through the air on wings . . .

JUDITH. . . . .

HOLOFERNES. . . . . or come burrowing through the ground like moles. Just when a man least expects to see a woman, there she comes. Flying, burrowing, bringing some new note of sweetness or pain he never heard before.

JUDITH. . . . .

HOLOFERNES. And that's about the sum of what I've learned during ten years of military conquest. The really great adventure comes to those who lock themselves in their offices or retire alone to study in the rear of their tents. While the philosopher meditates, or the banker audits his books, or the general pores over his maps, alone at their desks these men weave an invisible web of thought. And, suddenly, in the next room they hear someone struggling. It's a woman, caught in the web. And then all the man has to do is gently untangle her with his two hands. But where on earth did this one come from, the most perfect of all?

JUDITH. From a battlefield, where men are dying.

HOLOFERNES. I can never remember how a woman slips away from me, disappears from my life, but I never forget a single detail of how she first crosses my path. The dress she was wearing, the time of day, the first smile. When she leaves, she's like all the rest, but when she comes to me, she's like no other creature on earth. But how different you are from the others, Judith. More different than I would ever have thought possible. If you'd like to powder your nose, tidy your hair . . .

JUDITH. After what they did to me, I'm ready for anything that comes.

HOLOFERNES. Even for love?

JUDITH, *with horror.* Egon touched me. I'm no longer worthy.

HOLOFERNES. Wipe away that rouge from the corner of your mouth, and Egon will disappear from your face. Would you like it if I also wiped him off the face of the earth?

JUDITH. Oh no, let him live. Let his filthy marks stay to shame me as long as I live.

HOLOFERNES. Nonsense! You know very well he'll disappear the first time you wash your face.

JUDITH. Do you think that, after what God has done to me, I can ever show the world my face again? I've been shamed, Holofernes. Burned with shame! I can still feel them, Egon's lips, like a white brand on my burning face.

HOLOFERNES. It's the brand that burns, the face is white. Here, let me wipe it off.

JUDITH. You'll never wipe off the false kiss God gave me. His is worse than Egon's. And it's all over my face.

HOLOFERNES, *kissing her lightly.* We'll take care of Egon's first. There! The face is clean, washed clean. It looks as if we've washed off the other ones too, the ones your boy friends must have left there. Anger is the best thing in the world to bring back a look of outraged virginity to a woman's face. It takes anger to reveal her secret.

JUDITH. What is my secret?

HOLOFERNES. The secret behind those cold dry eyes . . .

JUDITH. Yes, what is it?

HOLOFERNES. Sweetness.

JUDITH. Sweetness! Didn't you feel the dagger under my cloak?

HOLOFERNES. Like a part of your body. But it's the only part of that body that wishes me harm. The rest is love.

JUDITH. I've abandoned myself to hatred.

HOLOFERNES. Yes, yes, I know there are complications. But there are times, Judith, when the only place in life we can get a foothold is in the glorious void of pleasure. Is that what you seek? Is that what you want from me?

JUDITH. The only way I can get a foothold now is to debase myself. Do you think that all Israel and God Himself have been flattering me, pampering me, for twenty years just to throw me into a trap like this? And even if they have I refuse to accept it. Body and soul, buried in shame!

HOLOFERNES. But we just wiped that off! Or don't you like me the way I am? Do I have to disappear and make way for a third Holofernes? You wanted to see me. Here I am. You wanted to talk to me. I'm listening. Now, what is it?

JUDITH. Nothing. Nothing, anymore.

HOLOFERNES. Aren't you going to tell me about that God of yours?

JUDITH. Let Him talk for Himself. He's big enough.

HOLOFERNES. But if you were to speak for him I might listen more sympathetically. I've always cared most for Gods that are weak, the ones whose divinity depends on the love men give them. And what about your brothers? When you left them a few hours ago, didn't you promise to work for their salvation?

JUDITH. That was a thousand years ago.

HOLOFERNES. But they're still alive, waiting to be saved. They're still out there, crying for you. Listen! You can hear them from here.

JUDITH. I no longer understand their language. And I'm ashamed that I ever spoke it. Yes, they're singing. I know the song by heart. That's me they are singing about, pure as the lamb, brave as the lion. I'm sick of that sanctified tone that injects God into every word! I'm sick of words. I've said the last one I'll ever say!

HOLOFERNES. No, you must talk. There is nothing to fear, so long as we are in the tent.

JUDITH. I don't understand.

HOLOFERNES. You understand only too well. You are beginning to guess where you are.

JUDITH. Where am I?

HOLOFERNES. What does it feel like?

JUDITH. An island. A clearing in the woods.

HOLOFERNES. You see, you knew all the time.

JUDITH. What did I know?

HOLOFERNES. That this is a place where there is no such thing as God.

JUDITH. Where? Here?

HOLOFERNES. These thirty square yards of tent! One of the rare corners of life where we humans are really free! This poor universe of ours is infested with deities, Judith. From Greece to the Indies, from north to south, there isn't a country that doesn't swarm with them, each with his own particular evils, his own particular odors. They are the air you breathe from the first day you enter the world. But there are still some places off limits to them. This is one of those places. Here you are untouched by original sin. Here you have no need for prayers or singing hymns. I see you are beginning to guess who I am.

JUDITH. Who are you?

HOLOFERNES. I am what in this God-infested world only the King of Kings dares to be: a man. The first one if you like. A man of the world, of *this* world, friend of nature and enemy of God. What is a pretty girl like you doing with all those psalm singers, anyway? Think how sweet life could be if you were freed from fears and had no need for prayers. Think what life would be like if man were really innocent.

JUDITH. So it's innocence you offer me!

HOLOFERNES. I offer you, for tonight and for as long as you like, the gift of utter simplicity and the calm that goes with it. I'm offering you the same words you used as a child. Words as simple as "apples" and "oranges." And inside there are no gods to spoil the fruit, like worms eating away at the core. I offer you songs instead of litanies. Listen. Sounds like those come to rest naturally around us instead of being sucked up to the clouds by that vacuum

in the heavens. I offer you pleasure, Judith. And that is a
word that makes the image of God disappear . . .

JUDITH. He has a way of reappearing afterwards awfully fast.
Hadn't we better hurry?

HOLOFERNES. Hurry? Certainly not! Do you think there is any
lovelier sight than a woman stripped naked of godliness!
Still coltish in her new-found freedom! How beautiful you
are, Judith . . . and, suddenly, so unadorned! That's the
truth your whole body is crying out to me. What is it,
Judith? What is it you want?

JUDITH. To lose myself!

HOLOFERNES. Your body says the same thing, but more gently.

JUDITH. Then I shall not listen to my body.

HOLOFERNES. Your body tells me that it is tired, that it's going
to fall to the ground with its own weight unless a man
forces it to lie down. That it's going to suffocate, unless a
man puts his arms around it so tightly it can scarcely
breathe. Your body wants to be God! What do you want?

JUDITH. To be insulted, beaten, reviled, torn to pieces and
desecrated!

HOLOFERNES. Both of you shall be obliged.

JUDITH. No. Not yet!

OTTA *appears in the doorway of the tent.*

OTTA. My Lord, Judith is waiting outside.

HOLOFERNES. What did you say?

OTTA. There is a woman outside who says her name is Judith.
I told her you were resting, but she insists on seeing you
tonight.

HOLOFERNES. Two Holofernes, and now two Judiths! What
shall we do with this new Judith?

JUDITH. I know who she is. Let her come in and you can
choose between us.

A gesture out the door from OTTA. SUSANNA *enters.*

HOLOFERNES. So you are Judith?

SUSANNA. Yes.

JUDITH. Then why don't you say so? We have no other way of knowing it.

SUSANNA. I am Judith.

JUDITH. You are also Esther, Madeleine or Rose. Must we go over all that again? Now that we've seen you, you may go.

SUSANNA. Not without you.

HOLOFERNES. What does she want?

JUDITH. She wants to save me from you.

HOLOFERNES. You want to save Judith? Is she in danger?

SUSANNA. Yes, but not the danger I anticipated.

JUDITH. You thought you'd find me on my knees, screaming for mercy in front of a bearded ogre, didn't you?

SUSANNA. I did not expect to interrupt a love scene.

JUDITH. . . . written a long time ago by God.

SUSANNA. This is not the way they imagine the scene back in the city. They see Judith on her knees, pleading with a monster.

HOLOFERNES. Oh? And what do you think it is that stands before her? Every girl gets the monster she deserves.

SUSANNA. What stands in front of her? That's obvious: the first man who's ever made Judith feel. She was sent here by God. But now, it's a man who keeps her here. Holofernes, you must save it!

HOLOFERNES. What am I supposed to save now?

SUSANNA. The honor of the world.

HOLOFERNES. You mean Judith's virtue?

SUSANNA. Today they are the same thing.

HOLOFERNES. My dear young lady, there will be plenty of girls to take Judith's place. Nothing reproduces itself so quickly as a virgin.

SUSANNA. She is not the real Judith. Why, I'm more Judith than she is—me. And I am only a pale imitation of what she was yesterday. In all the city she is the only one who isn't Judith tonight. And that goes for women, children, old men, as well as the heroes of the army.

JUDITH. Those heroes sent me here.

SUSANNA. But I came to save you.

JUDITH. Now, God's envoy unveils her holy secret. She is jealous of Holofernes!

SUSANNA. Silence her, my Lord, I beg you.

HOLOFERNES. I find this very interesting.

JUDITH. There's your rival, Holofernes. If you want me, you'll have to take me from her.

SUSANNA. Pity her, my Lord. You may not believe in God but you must believe in beauty, human beauty. She's suddenly seen herself naked, stripped of sainthood, and now she wants to destroy herself.

HOLOFERNES. If it's human, beauty has nothing to fear from me, not at a moment like this. On the contrary.

SUSANNA. Judith! Remember Israel!

JUDITH. Israel! As far as Israel is concerned, Judith came to Holofernes. That's the extent of her responsibility to her people, God and their prophets. From this point on, fate works for or against the Jews quite apart from anything Judith may do. Neither Holofernes nor poor miserable Judith can do anything for them.

SUSANNA. That's blasphemy!

JUDITH. God is only interested in the way things look. Appearance, not the details! God asks us to dress up our acts, make them look like sacrifices. But underneath the appearance He leaves us free to satisfy our own desires, the lowest of them. Why, any streetwalker in the city would know the difference between the real Holofernes and his servant. But not Judith-the-saint! God wants to destroy me. Well, I won't let him. I shall destroy myself!

SUSANNA. Do you hear that, Holofernes? Don't think for one moment that you have seduced this girl. If she comes to you, that's because she is disgusted with life.

JUDITH. Not with life. With women like you!

SUSANNA. And what about men like John?

JUDITH. Women like him too! Everything that's ever touched me before tonight seems to have been of my own sex.

SUSANNA. Praise be to Holofernes! The only man in the world!
Choose, Judith—Holofernes or God!

Exit SUSANNA.

HOLOFERNES. Into my arms, Jewess!

JUDITH. I am the Jewess.

HOLOFERNES. That's a word we Assyrians reserve for insults.

JUDITH. King though you may be, that insult makes this Jewess your equal tonight.

HOLOFERNES. You don't know all the unpleasant things it
means to us: greed, poverty, blood that beats stronger
with fear than with appetite.

JUDITH. It is also the word for generosity and courage. Only
a Jewess knows the force of a human embrace.

HOLOFERNES. That's something I'd like to learn.

JUDITH. God inspires only those who believe in Him.

HOLOFERNES. . . . and so puts them under a curse.

JUDITH. God's never found any other way of singling out one
race or one person except to put them under a curse. The
day God learns to smile, my people will not only be chosen,
they will also be blessed.

HOLOFERNES. Bravo, Judith! When you marry, what wonderful
conversation you'll serve your husband for breakfast—if
they let you live that long.

JUDITH. They? Judith!

HOLOFERNES. Now, you're not going to kill yourself! Purity,
my dear, is only a word.

JUDITH. I am not pure.

HOLOFERNES. No?

JUDITH. Do you think that a virgin could have crossed that
battlefield and come here, alone, to face the unknown?

HOLOFERNES. What else is there for virgins to face?

JUDITH. I gave myself to the man I love, just before I left the
city.

HOLOFERNES. You've never loved anyone. Yesterday you were
in love with the world in general. Today you detest it in
detail. Besides, women like you abhor giving themselves

for love, at least when it's the first time. You prefer to be taken by force.

JUDITH. There is no force but the force of God.

HOLOFERNES. But God has a way of delegating His powers. I've already acted as God's agent on several occasions.

JUDITH. This time you are going to be surprised.

HOLOFERNES. I shall not be surprised, I assure you. A woman is a creature who has discovered her own nature. You are still looking for yours. You are a virgin.

JUDITH. It's my nature to explore.

HOLOFERNES. That's not true. You won't know what you are really like until tomorrow morning. Miserly or spendthrift, angel or shrew, you don't yet know. From my couch you will get up with your first born child—yourself. Wouldn't it be wonderful if Judith were to wake up as a woman and discover that she is all sweetness and loving submission?

JUDITH. I wouldn't count on it.

HOLOFERNES. . . . or if all those Jewish wedding chants were suddenly to resolve into a single word: "Holofernes," pronounced with tenderness.

JUDITH. Tenderness has nothing to do with a name like that.

HOLOFERNES. No? Then why did you call me? If you were so afraid of Egon, why didn't you call on God for help?

JUDITH, *wiping her mouth*. Only a man could help me.

HOLOFERNES. Yet I heard something I'd never heard before: my name, pronounced like a beacon in the dark. You called for me the way you'd call for a life guard to jump off his post, dive into the water, and save you from drowning.

JUDITH. And what can you save me from now?

HOLOFERNES. From everything that threatens to rob your life of meaning.

JUDITH. From love, too, I suppose?

HOLOFERNES. You know very well that if a single hair of my head displeased you, you'd find a means of breaking away from me.

JUDITH. And if the shape of my ears or the spacing of my
teeth failed to meet your taste, would you be able to say
that we were destined to meet?

HOLOFERNES. You mean we like each other?

JUDITH. I mean my torment is complete. My duel with Holofernes has turned into a love match between two bodies,
one fair and one bronzed by the sun.

HOLOFERNES. That God of yours never did believe in real
fights between real enemies. To Him a fight is no more
than a scrap between two of His accomplices who've had
a falling out. And you can be sure that He depends more
on our getting along together than on our mutual hatred.
Come now. And silence!

JUDITH. Silence? How can I hate you in silence?

HOLOFERNES. Like this.

He kisses her.

Have you often dreamed of this moment, Judith?

JUDITH. Yes.

HOLOFERNES. Did you often imagine what it would be like?

JUDITH. I've spent my whole life thinking about it.

HOLOFERNES. And you don't want to wait any longer?

JUDITH. No longer.

HOLOFERNES. Because this is the high mark of your life?

JUDITH. This is as low as I'll ever sink. God has forsaken me.
I don't know why, but God has forsaken me. He wants a
girl to sacrifice herself. He pushes her towards it. But when
the moment comes, God can't stand the details and He
turns His head. I've been too proud of my virtue, Holofernes. Now God wants me to throw it away, for nothing
at all.

HOLOFERNES. For joy!

JUDITH. For nothing at all.

HOLOFERNES. Don't feel sorry for yourself. You are probably
the only girl in the world who has found a way of fulfill-
ing her mission. You'll soon see how it is. God made little
girls to be devoured by monsters, and somehow the little

girls always end up giving themselves to some man. That's where, from God's point of view, they miss their calling.

JUDITH. And that's where I am different!

A silence.

HOLOFERNES *beckons her to rear of tent.* JUDITH *starts to follow.* HOLOFERNES, *amused, turns.* Yes, Judith?

JUDITH. Is there a woman here?

HOLOFERNES. At this time of night there is only Daria. Poor old Daria. But I am afraid she won't be much company to talk to. Daria is deaf and dumb.

JUDITH. If she were deaf, dumb and blind, just so she is a woman.

HOLOFERNES. As you like, I'll send her to you.

He claps his hands.

Judith—
Pause.

It is you who come to me.

Exit HOLOFERNES *to rear of the tent.*
DARIA *enters.*

JUDITH. You are Daria, aren't you? Yes, I know you can't hear me and you have no tongue to talk with. What do I want? Nothing, Daria. Just to spend one last minute with a woman before I become one myself. Maybe it is just as well you cannot answer.

Are you a virgin, Daria? You shake your head "no" as if I were asking if you could hear or speak. Poor Daria! You are not very attractive. Your eyes don't even have any real kindness in them. But tonight you'll have to be mother, sister, and myself to me. He took you by force, I suppose, brutally? What if I were to fight him off? No! He can't soil me now. Since the day God singled me out just because I was pure, I've been soiled as much as I can ever be. Soiled by God Himself! This may sound conceited, but I can say it to you because you can't hear me. It's *me* God is angry with. It's not Holofernes and it's not the Jews in the city. All history is like that. Just God's way of hiding

the fact that He is tracking down one poor lone creature
to destroy her. And now He has me cornered, Daria. He
wins. In a few minutes He'll have written the end of
Judith's story. Or rather, I'll be writing it off for Him.
If only He were a monster, maybe I'd have the strength to
resist.

Ah? Do you think so? It won't be unpleasant? Something
half way between crucifixion and laughter? No, don't open
the curtains yet. One minute more. All right, now! How
silent it is! A great king waiting for a wife . . . a girl
waiting to be reviled . . . a people waiting to die . . . an
army facing defeat . . . such things produce a silence like
this. One would almost believe that God is also deaf and
dumb!

May Jehovah pardon me, Daria. I know that what I've
been saying is blasphemy. But the day will come when
you'll find your tongue and that's the day when the vengeance of heaven and the angels will fall on those like me
who have gone joyfully to their shame.

JUDITH *exits to rear of the tent.*

DARIA, *laughing.* And so amen!

                                                    CURTAIN

ACT THREE

Same as Act Two. SUSANNA *is seated. Over her knees is the
dress* JUDITH *was wearing. One of* HOLOFERNES'S *guards
is stretched out on the bench, dead drunk.*

JOHN *enters, stealthily. As he comes through the doorway
we see the pale light of early morning behind him.*

SUSANNA. John!

JOHN. And did you think it was an archangel? The angels will
never be interested in Judith again, Susanna. After last
night, a man is the best she can expect. Where are they?

SUSANNA. How did you get here?

JOHN. Sarah escaped. She's told them everything. All Israel is up in arms against Judith for betraying their trust. It wasn't hard to get in once Sarah put the guards to sleep. They're drunk, all of them. Like this one.

JOHN kicks the GUARD *asleep on the bench.*

GUARD. Dead drunk!

SUSANNA. What are you going to do?

JOHN. Where the Jewess has failed only the Jew may succeed. I suppose they are still asleep.

SUSANNA. Yes.

JOHN. Get Judith away from him, but quietly.

SUSANNA. But she's still asleep.

JOHN. Asleep! You say it so calmly! Judith is the only child of Israel who slept a wink last night.

SUSANNA. Don't shout!

JOHN. Susanna, if we came here this morning, it was not to whisper like mourners around her marriage bed. Ah! If it were weeping and wailing they wanted, I could tell them tales of sorrow about this wedding night!

SUSANNA. Not so loud, they'll hear you.

JOHN. All night I've seen it in my head, heard it buzzing in my ears.

He is talking in whispers now.

Not a detail in all its horror was spared my imagination, because I know Judith and I know what she is like. Oh, Susanna, I'm so miserable!

SUSANNA. No more miserable than I am.

JOHN. We didn't deserve this. We loved her. What's that?

SUSANNA. Her dress.

JOHN. Then she'll come in here . . .

SUSANNA. But how do we know Holofernes won't come with her?

JOHN. Because I know Judith. She'll squeeze every extra dividend out of this crime. And that means waking up next

to him in the morning, pitilessly examining his face while
he is still asleep. No, there is only one sure way of getting
someone out of the next room, whether she's still asleep
or not, and that is to call her name.

Shouting.

Judith! Judith!

JUDITH *enters, wearing* HOLOFERNES'S *cape.* JOHN *turns
away.*

SUSANNA. Is that you, Judith?

JUDITH. It's me, or almost me. What time is it?

SUSANNA *walks to doorway and pulls back the flap.*

SUSANNA. Look!

JUDITH. Yes, there's no doubt about that. A pincushion of
blood on the horizon. A cold wind blowing through the
hair of a poor soldier lying dead on the battlefield. A sky
all gangrene and gold, and a soldier with a sword full of
rusty menace . . . and Judith full of shame and happiness.
As they say, it's the dawn.

She comes back into the room. JOHN *turns, as if to sneak
out.* JUDITH *stops him.*

John!

JOHN. "John!" Did you enjoy yourself last night?

SUSANNA. John, don't!

JOHN. You're not as curious as I am, Susanna. Judith, did you
have a good night's sleep?

JUDITH. It was brief.

JOHN. And you are no longer . . .

JUDITH. No longer.

JOHN. All Israel knows you have betrayed us.

JUDITH. I'm glad you know. I was trying to think of a way to
tell you.

JOHN. They have stoned your servants, burned your house.
Your uncle is wounded. The people curse your name.

JUDITH. I no longer belong to them.

JOHN. To whom do you belong? To Holofernes?

JUDITH. To death.

JOHN. Death is not far away. It's on its way here now.

JUDITH. And it's welcome! Draw your sword, if you like. I'm ready for it.

JOHN. My sword has a cleaner mission to perform. But unless you want to die, leave this place. The rabbis are going to make one last effort to appease Holofernes. The prophets have formed a procession. They are on their way here now.

JUDITH. What's that to me?

JOHN. Even if Holofernes massacres them, here in this tent, before they die they will find some way of punishing you first, Judith. You have been unfaithful to God.

JUDITH. Who has been unfaithful, God or Judith? That's something we don't yet know.

JOHN. Ah—the panther has sharpened her claws!

JUDITH. Then for once in your life have the courage to be a hunter instead of a mere soldier taking orders. You have a sword. Use it!

JOHN. He's in there, I suppose. Asleep!

JUDITH. Like a piece of marble. Silent and asleep.

JOHN. Then God has not failed me!

JOHN *draws his sword. He disappears into* HOLOFERNES's *chamber at rear of the tent.*

JUDITH. Poor John! He couldn't possibly understand what has happened. But you do, Susanna. You've already guessed.

JOHN *returns. Stands stunned in the doorway.*

JUDITH. . . . .

JOHN *makes an attempt to move, but is transfixed.*

JUDITH. Put away your sword now.

JOHN *runs to* JUDITH. *Kneels.*

JOHN. Judith, can you ever forgive us? Susanna, put your lips to the cloak that covered her as she crossed the battlefield. Blessed be every hair on her head! Blessed be the hatred

in Judith's heart! I'll make myself worthy of you, Judith.
You'll see.

He runs to HOLOFERNES's *chamber.* SUSANNA *kneels in front
of* JUDITH.

JUDITH. You'll spoil your dress . . .

SUSANNA. Judith, you are a saint.

JUDITH. Get off your knees.

SUSANNA. You killed him.

JUDITH. Kill? Assassins kill.

SUSANNA. Even God knows no other word for what you've
done.

JUDITH. Then God has a very limited vocabulary. I hope you
understand *why* I killed him.

SUSANNA. You did it because God transformed you into hatred
itself!

JUDITH. Hatred? Do I look like hatred?

SUSANNA. A kind of hatred we've never seen before.

JUDITH. Do you really believe I could have killed him out of
hatred, at dawn, a few hours after he made me his wife?

SUSANNA. I believe that Judith has been true to her mission.

JUDITH. Far from it! The moment Judith struck that blow
was the moment she forgot who she was, where she came
from, and what she was supposed to do.

SUSANNA. But you are alive and he is . . .

JUDITH. If I am alive it is because I knew that sooner or later
the guards would kill me anyway . . . Now that I have
lived to tell my story, I want you to be my witness before
the judges when they arrive. I want you to tell them that
Judith's story did not end in hatred. The truth is that what
died in that chamber was a man and woman in love.

SUSANNA. But you killed him!

JUDITH. I'd been sleeping, Susanna. No more than a few
winks, but it was all the night to me. And then I awoke,
and for the first time in my life I saw myself at dawn next
to another human being. Everything had already happened! Now all I could look forward to was losing him . . .

Even if it were possible to make him mine, really mine in
face of the Jews and the Assyrians. Even then every morning there would be this awful moment when he'd rise,
face this light, leave me and go back to the world of living
and fighting. So you see, there was no other way to keep
it perfect, the way it was last night. . . . Hasn't the sight
of a sleeping body next to yours ever made you think that
perhaps murder is the tenderest and most enduring embrace of all?

SUSANNA. That's what murderers call it. But for centuries to
come, Judith will be known to history as the one chosen
by God to kill a man she hated because he was the enemy
of her people.

JUDITH. Never! I'll tell them everything, Susanna. Listen!
Those voices . . . They're coming to punish me. You'll
tell them how it was, won't you? Please! If I give you a
kiss? You won't recognize the kiss I gave you last evening.
That was nothing at all.

SUSANNA. I refuse to listen.

JUDITH. All right, stop up your ears. I don't need them. Stupid
that I am, there is a man in the room. Guard, wake up!

SUSANNA. He's drunk.

JUDITH. Drunk or not, he has ears to hear with. And in each
ear there's a little hammer to beat on a little anvil and
make sound on a little drum. That's all I need to transmit
my story down through the ages. Guard!

GUARD. I'm asleep.

JUDITH. Asleep! Listen to me.

GUARD, *half awake*. Who says I'm asleep? Not on duty!

JUDITH. Wake up and I'll make it worth your while.

GUARD. Oh, a woman! Hurrah for women!

JUDITH. Do you know what this woman has done?

GUARD. What has she done?

JUDITH. She has killed your King. She has killed Holofernes.

GUARD. What did she do?

JUDITH. Killed.

GUARD. Killed him? Oh, that's bad!

JUDITH. Do you know why? Because she loved him!

GUARD. Because what?

JUDITH. Because she loved him.

GUARD. Loved him? Oh, that's good!

JUDITH. You see, Susanna!

GUARD, *going back to sleep.* You see, Susanna!

JUDITH. I've hammered the truth into the head of a sleeping man. Some day it will come out again. Maybe it will take centuries, but it will come out again to plague the generals and the rabbis. They're coming here for me, aren't they? Can you see them yet?

SUSANNA *goes to the entrance and looks out of the tent.*

GUARD, *in his sleep.* Because she loved him, she killed Holofernes. But what was her name?

JUDITH, *leaning over the guard.* Judith!

GUARD. But why didn't Holofernes kill Judith?

JUDITH. Don't worry, Judith will be killed.

GUARD. That's good.

SUSANNA. It's the Jews! Joachim and the prophets are leading the procession.

JUDITH. Let them come. Let them tie my hands, spit on me, beat me, insult me with each lash of the whip! That's what I want from them. And with each lash of the whip I'll lash back with my tongue. Blow for blow, I'll make them listen to each joy I've known until I am whipped unconscious.

The Jews burst into the tent. JOACHIM, THE PROPHET *of Act One (anyone knows all prophets look alike), and a group of cantors. They speak in the rounded liturgical tones of men who live in a world of scriptures.*

CANTORS. Praise be to Judith! Glory to her name!

FIRST CANTOR. Pray for me, Judith.

JUDITH. I don't understand.

JOACHIM. Hatred ruled the heart of Judith and vanquished

the enemy of Israel. Israel shall be saved and we prostrate ourselves at the feet of Judith.

SUSANNA, *to Judith.* Don't say a word. Joachim, keep an eye on her.

FIRST CANTOR. Holofernes is already deserted by his allies. Even now Lieutenant John runs in their camps, showing the severed head of the mighty King that Judith killed.

SECOND CANTOR. We have captured whole caravans of food and great casks of wine, and when Judith gives the word all Israel shall drink.

SECOND CANTOR. Judith is the bread we eat.

THIRD CANTOR. Judith is the water we drink.

JUDITH. Jews!

JOACHIM, *intervening.* What are you going to tell them?

JUDITH. The truth!

JOACHIM. They already know the truth. God's truth! Judith's truth does not interest them now. Listen to the cantors. Listen to what they know is true.

The two CANTORS *step forward.*

FIRST CANTOR. And for two days Judith did carry a sword under her mantle. It did cut into her flesh with each step she took, striking her knees like the pendant of a temple bell.

SECOND CANTOR. And Judith did cross the field of battle before the moon did rise. And the better to find her way she did follow the blood red stream of Esau like an angry beast of prey. For hers was the righteous wrath of the Lord our God.

JUDITH. But God was no longer in her heart.

JOACHIM. Silence, girl!

CANTORS IN UNISON. What does Judith say?

FIRST CANTOR. And Holofernes in his tent did have a dream, and he turned from the whore who shared his couch.

SECOND CANTOR. And Holofernes did turn away from the Queen in Damascus crowned, who was painted and rouged down to her heart.

FIRST CANTOR. He did turn from Pharaoh's daughter.

SECOND CANTOR. From the hundred naked Muscovites dancing lewd dances around his couch.

THIRD CANTOR. From the great tiger of Bengal, all garlanded with wreaths of arms and legs and human breasts.

TWO CANTORS IN UNISON. And it was then that Holofernes saw Judith, fairest of the fair.

JUDITH. Lies! Myths! Legends for children! Holofernes was alone, all alone like a priest at the altar.

JOACHIM. Silence, girl.

Chanting like the CANTORS.

"Judith alone, only Judith," the great king cried. "Judith alone is sweetness and light."

TWO CANTORS IN UNISON. Judith alone is balm. Only the touch of Judith's hand, only the velvet touch of Judith's hand caressing lightly from the knee . . .

FIRST CANTOR. And yet she was poison.

SECOND CANTOR. Hardened steel.

THIRD CANTOR. A trap with teeth of iron.

FIRST CANTOR. Vitriol.

SECOND CANTOR. With fangs of a serpent.

SUSANNA. To sting with hatred when the moment came.

JUDITH. Susanna, that's a lie and you know it. Jews! Listen to me!

JOACHIM, *to* CANTORS. Finish the psalm!

FIRST CANTOR. He did lay her naked on the couch.

SUSANNA. But God did cover her nakedness.

SECOND CANTOR. God did clothe her with air and with light. Of transparence God made for Judith a veil.

JUDITH. That's not true!

JOACHIM *to the* CANTORS. Finish the psalm! Finish the psalm!

FIRST CANTOR. Naked he saw her on the couch and looked into her face.

JOACHIM. Face to face, that's true, isn't it, Judith?

JUDITH. Is it true? Yes, it's true.

JOACHIM. Did you hear that? She says it's true!

CANTORS IN UNISON. Glory be to Truth, purest of the pure, fairest of the fair!

SUSANNA, *in the manner of the* CANTORS. But suddenly God did make the monster weak, weak in all his limbs. And Holofernes no longer had the strength to possess our Judith.

CANTORS IN UNISON. He did not possess her! He did not possess her!

JUDITH, *stepping forward.* He did possess her! And she was so full of love for him that there was no room for anyone else, even for God!

ALL THE CANTORS. What did she say?

JOACHIM. Silence! Leave us. Judith wants to talk to me alone.

JUDITH. No, rabbis, don't go. It's *you* I want to talk to. If you'd stop singing your tribal lies, I could tell you the truth. This Jewess lay willingly with Holofernes on his couch and pleasured herself.

ALL THE CANTORS. Don't say it, Judith! It's blasphemy!

JOACHIM. Judith, you are destroying us.

JUDITH. And it wasn't a couch like the one in your psalms. It was a real bed with real pillows and real sheets, and down feathers that blew through the air, mixing memories of home and childhood with every excess of passion.

THE PROPHET, *raising his sword.* Vengeance!

JUDITH. She sought pleasure on that bed and pleasure she got. And in the first chill of the morning she awakened and piously pulled the covers over Holofernes in the manner prescribed for the dutiful wife.

ALL THE CANTORS, *wailing in unison.* Lost, lost, all is lost. The girl has destroyed us!

SUSANNA. It's true, rabbis, it's true! But it was I, Susanna, who did these things. Not her! He never touched her!

JUDITH *strikes* SUSANNA. SUSANNA *falls to the ground.*

JOACHIM. Outside! All of you!

He draws JUDITH *away from the* CANTORS.

THE PROPHET. Why?

JOACHIM. I must explain to Judith how she is to act when we enter the city.

THE PROPHET. Then hurry, rabbi, Israel waits.

SECOND CANTOR. Israel waits.

THIRD CANTOR. Israel waits on the day of the prophets.

All leave except JOACHIM, *the* FIRST CANTOR, JUDITH *and the* GUARD. *As* SUSANNA'S *body is carried past the drunken* GUARD, *he rolls over and mutters in his sleep.*

GUARD. There goes Susanna.

Silence while the group disappears out the doorway.

JOACHIM. What are your conditions?

JUDITH. On what conditions will I tell a lie?

JOACHIM. On what conditions will you live and hold your tongue!

JUDITH. Do I look like someone anxious to live and hold her tongue?

JOACHIM. The slightest slip of that tongue and you deprive the people of their miracle.

JUDITH. And the people must not be deprived of their miracle!

JOACHIM. We quite understand that after what has happened you may want to live apart in solitary contemplation. You know the municipal palace in the gardens by the lake? It's yours. We'll see to it that no one comes to bother you, that no one ruffles your desire to retire from the world. But you must come with us this morning and walk at the head of the procession.

JUDITH. Do you really think that I could be satisfied with a cottage in the park, magnolia trees and a private beach? That is the sort of thing a man gives his mistress when she's outlived her usefulness. Rabbi, I am twenty years old.

FIRST CANTOR. How proud she is this morning!

JUDITH. And I suppose He's not proud!

JOACHIM. Who's that?

JUDITH. God! I've killed a man in the name of someone else,

and now God writhes with jealousy. That divine hypocrite, I can feel Him all around me, grasping, trying to take all the credit for Himself. If I were willing, He'd even accept me as His emissary to the Jews, let me live in a palace by the lake, and give me a halo to wear as long as I live. But I know God! He'd only take it away from me later.

GUARD, *in his sleep.* She killed him because she loved him.

JUDITH. Did you hear that?

JOACHIM. What?

JUDITH. The guard.

JOACHIM. You're hearing things. He didn't say a word.

JUDITH. Oh, yes he did. He told you why I killed Holofernes.

JOACHIM. Why you *think* you killed him. But what you think doesn't matter now. My dear girl, the point is that the deed is done . . . and done just the way the church predicted it.

JUDITH. Did you also predict the joy it would bring me?

FIRST CANTOR. Please! Spare us the details.

JUDITH. Did Joachim spare me any details yesterday when he was describing Holofernes the monster? That's what is missing to drown your triumph, isn't it? You want me to swear under oath that Holofernes was bestial and deformed. Well, he wasn't. His eyes were clear, his body was smooth and strong. There is only one human word to . . .

FIRST CANTOR. My dear girl, you forget we've seen his head on the end of a stick.

JUDITH. I'll get even with John for that!

JOACHIM. If it's revenge you want, Judith, you must live.

JUDITH, *suddenly turning to the* GUARD. What's that the guard is saying?

JOACHIM. Nothing, I assure you. He's asleep.

JUDITH. Then why is he sitting up? Why does he stare at me like that?

FIRST CANTOR. You're imagining things. He's sound asleep, as Joachim says.

JOACHIM. Judith, your very hesitation is a crime against God, since you hesitate between Him and His most hated enemy.

JUDITH. I choose my own kind of hatred.

FIRST CANTOR. Girl, girl! There is a limit to our patience.

JUDITH. Then lose your patience. God won't mind. Not once since last night have I felt His presence in this tent. I waited for Him to turn me into an archangel. He didn't. But you got your miracle just the same. Why is that man sitting up again? What does he want?

FIRST CANTOR. Who?

JUDITH. The guard.

FIRST CANTOR. The man is sound asleep on the bench.

JUDITH. Do you think it's a reflection I see?

FIRST CANTOR. Reflection of what?

JOACHIM. Stick to the subject, Judith. Hasn't God given us exactly what we prayed for? Us and you!

JUDITH. How do you know what I prayed for?

JOACHIM. Can you deny that a miracle has taken place, and by your hands?

JUDITH. Your miracle is a fraud. God gave it to you cheap with a minimum of innocence, and all because I'm rich and spoiled and my name is great enough to conceal the deception.

FIRST CANTOR. You want God to stay a virgin too? Do you think that just because a Jewess desired to . . .

JOACHIM, *simultaneously with* CANTOR. Judith, beware! You are breaking the bond that binds you to God. Never again can you . . .

A chord of music! Angelic thunder! An unearthly light floods the scene.

The two churchmen freeze in preposterous positions, breaking their speeches in mid-sentence. Only JUDITH *is left alive on the strangely lighted stage. Slowly, she turns to the bench where the drunken* GUARD *is sleeping.*

The GUARD *sits up. Grins at* JUDITH.

GUARD. Excuse me, Judith. I don't want to butt in, but . . .

JUDITH. Child of light, who are you?

GUARD. That's no way to talk to a guard.

JUDITH. But there's such a brightness and warmth about you!

GUARD. Brightness? That's because we've reached the moment when sour smells sweet, black is white, when you say clear as mud and mean transparent.

JUDITH. No, I see you as you really are, draped in purples and gold . . .

GUARD. Oh, you're more perceiving than I thought. Very well, Judith, it's just *us* now. A fight to the finish.

JUDITH. But why just us?

GUARD. Because it's time for some body blows. You are God's enemy, Judith, and I know exactly what holds to use on women like you.

JUDITH. I don't understand.

GUARD. Tell me, Judith, since you left home last night, has that lovely body of yours wanted for anything—food, drink or anything else?

JUDITH. . . .

GUARD. No, I think not. Did the bloody water of Esau's stream leave a stain on your dress? Did the mud on the battle-field soil your sandals? Did the thistles in the fields scratch your legs? Look at your hands. Is there a trace of murder left on them? Yes, rub them. See if you can make a spot of blood appear. Rub away, my dear. As long as you live, Judith, your hands will remain white and pure. Not a mark to mar the perfection of your body.

JUDITH. And what about *the* mark, the mark made by Holofernes?

GUARD. Even that can be disputed. You might as well face it, Judith. You are still a virgin.

JUDITH. What right have you to talk to me like this?

GUARD. Obstinate girl! Ever since you left the city the heavenly hosts have been beating their wings around you, guiding you, pitying you, building a sacred cathedral in

the air over you. And, one after another, you have forced
them to turn away their faces. And of all these hosts of
heaven only I remain and I am reduced to making myself
visible—vulgarly visible, in the heavy, sweaty vestments
of a drunken guardsman.

JUDITH. Who are you? If you are God talking to me at last,
it is too late.

GUARD. Do you really think that God is ever going to talk to
you? Do you think that God is ever going to talk to any
man? No, Judith, it is not in words that God is articulate.
Those chosen by Him are anointed with thistle oil, their
ears ring with the silence of the night, they stumble across
the battlefields and where they pass even the dying cease
to cry. In the streams the cold water and hard pebbles flow
silently around their legs, and watchdogs turn the other
way without a single bark. Can you truthfully say you felt
none of this presence along your path last night?

Music.

JUDITH. Don't stop. Tell me more.

GUARD. That's our message to Judith, fairest of Israel's daughters, chosen by God.

JUDITH. Forgive me.

GUARD. Oh, so you can hear me now!

JUDITH. Forgive me.

GUARD. Tell Israel the truth and God will forgive you.

JUDITH. But what truth?

GUARD. That you killed the enemy of God just as God or-
dained, because you hated him.

JUDITH. But you know yourself that is not so!

GUARD. Not so?

JUDITH. Weren't you there? Didn't you see what happened?

GUARD. Think back over your night, from the beginning.
When you entered the alcove, what did you see?

JUDITH. I saw a couch, that's all.

GUARD. Even God hesitates to ask a woman to stay on her
feet when she fights.

JUDITH. I went to him.

GUARD. And we rejoiced because we saw only your sharp nails, your teeth, and every angle of your body.

JUDITH. And then I reached out to touch him and he was real. It was a revelation to me!

GUARD. God does not object if the divine voice occasionally emanates from vulgar bodies or coarse skins. But such things are only filters. God had long before decided that Holofernes would never truly touch you and He draped you in a transparent cloak. The angel Michael was on your lips. Ephraim was the flower in your hair. I was your right hand thrown around his neck. And all night long heaven was a mold enveloping you and your delirium. And in the morning God gave you the idea of killing . . .

JUDITH. Killing myself!

GUARD. If you like. But then you lost sight of everything except a little white circle on the sleeper's chest. As if a tiny mirror, like the one you played with as a child, were concentrating light from above onto that spot in the center of the man you thought you loved. And that spot of light, you struck at it . . . it was a target for you. Isn't that true, Judith?

JUDITH. Maybe.

GUARD. Isn't that true?

JUDITH, *low.* Yes, it is true.

GUARD. And tears of joy flowed in heaven to see hatred on your body. And we forged rivets which would prevent you from withdrawing the dagger once you had plunged it to its mark.

JUDITH. I only wanted to scratch him, prick the skin.

GUARD. And when you raised the dagger in your hand, that circle of light filled your thoughts, multiplied them by ten hundred. Didn't you feel the presence then, Judith?

JUDITH. Oh, was that you?

GUARD. Me and an avalanche of other spirits. And after the deed was done and you were awaiting death, like a bee who dies after stinging its enemy, we returned you to the world of nature. And you heard the spider spinning its web and the mole burrowing his tunnel in the ground under the bed. Then you heard a human voice. That was Susanna. And this, ungrateful child, is what God has done for you. Now open the flaps and go back to your people. Israel is waiting.

JUDITH. No, no! They'll make me into a martyr.

GUARD. Who said you were a martyr?

JUDITH. Since the day I was born everyone knows God intended me for love.

GUARD. Don't be stubborn, Judith. There is love in your story, but that chapter belongs to Susanna.

JUDITH. Do you think I'd suffer like this if I weren't made of tenderness? And why must this miracle be an afterthought? Why must you take a night of blasphemy and make it look as if it were something holy?

GUARD. That is for God to worry about. From where He sits, a thousand years away, God reserves the right to project saintliness on sacrilege and purity on self-indulgence. It's all a question of knowing how to light the stage.

JUDITH. Those lights are so bright they're scorching me.

GUARD. And this is only the beginning. Wait until the sun rises. There it comes now. Rise, sun! And you, Judith, to the city!

JUDITH. The city! In one night I've lost everything I ever lived for. No friends, no . . .

GUARD. You can live without your friends.

JUDITH. And my memories?

GUARD. What memories?

JUDITH. If I am to grow old, what is my desiccated old body to do with the memories of the happy, warm, breathing thing it once was? What will I keep of Holofernes? Shall I have a son? You could at least tell me that?

GUARD. I've said all I can say to Judith before taking up my own life of disgrace. For in order to convince you, I've betrayed God's most hidden secret, and in doing so I've lost my place in heaven.

JUDITH. You, too! You too betrayed God. But what made you do it?

GUARD, *with an angelic smile.* Love?

JUDITH. Love for me?

GUARD. Love for love. I don't see why Judith shouldn't tell her people that somewhere outside the gates of heaven there is a fallen angel who still believes that Judith is a name for tenderness. But you must do as I say, immediately, or else I shall have to seize you and press your throat until I've squeezed out the truth.

JUDITH. The truth?

GUARD. The truth, Judith, is God's lie to the world! And you must shout it, for all to hear!

With one gesture, he bends JUDITH's *shoulders to the ground. Then he flops back onto the bench and sinks back into a drunken sleep.*

The scene between the CANTOR *and the* HIGH PRIEST *continues where it left off, as if nothing has happened.*

FIRST CANTOR. . . . that just because she wants to hear His voice God will send a special messenger to her?

JOACHIM. . . . that just because you want to see what He looks like God will appear in the flesh?

JUDITH, *blinded.* Is that you, Joachim?

Enter JOHN. *A flash of light as he opens the tent flap attracts* JUDITH's *attention. She turns.*

JUDITH. Oh, it's you—John!

She walks to him, as if trying to imagine that he is someone else. JOHN *recoils. Pulls his cape over an object cradled in one arm.*

Did you . . . ? Is that . . . ?

JUDITH *makes a gesture of appeal to* JOHN. *After protecting the object in his arms with the cape, he draws his sword to prevent her approach.*

The rest of the scene is a pantomime played in counterpoint against the dialogue of the churchmen.

When JUDITH *replies to* JOACHIM's *questions she does so in a tired, faraway voice—as if she were replying to* JOHN.

JOACHIM. If anybody ever finds God's hiding place in the universe, my girl, it won't be you!

JUDITH, *looking at* JOHN. Don't worry, I'm going with you.

JOACHIM. To the city?

FIRST CANTOR. Where you can stir up this scandal all over again? Oh no, we don't leave this tent until everything is settled between us. What are your conditions?

JUDITH, *still staring at* JOHN. I told you, I'm coming with you. With no conditions at all.

JOACHIM. But we have conditions. We have to protect ourselves against a relapse.

JUDITH, *still to* JOHN. Whatever they are, I agree to them in advance.

JOACHIM. You will live in the synagogue. You will see neither friends nor family.

JUDITH, *still to* JOHN. That won't be difficult. God has already crowded them out of my life.

JOACHIM. If any last words of love or pleasure remain in your mouth, say them now. Spit them out here before entering an everlasting silence. Come on, child, spit!

JUDITH, *backing away from* JOHN. My mouth is dry.

JOACHIM. If you wish we can call a servant who will bathe you before we go.

JUDITH, *turning away from* JOHN. My body is dry, too.

JOACHIM. Starting tomorrow morning Judith shall sit in judgment over disorderly families, immoral professors, and prostitutes. She will prescribe their punisments.

JOHN. She will know how to punish them.

JOACHIM. And you will select those who are to fast and pray and wear the sackcloth in her company.

JOHN. She accepts.

JUDITH. I accept.

FIRST CANTOR. Then glory be to Judith, Israel is saved! Wait,

Joachim. Put this cloak over her shoulders. That is more seeming for the bride of God.

GUARD, *drunk.* She told me she was a widow. Holofernes's widow!

JUDITH. What did he say?

FIRST CANTOR. Nothing. Just a hiccup.

GUARD. She loved him. She killed him because she loved him.

JOACHIM. Well, Judith, what are you waiting for?

JUDITH *approaches the* GUARD *on the bench. She looks down at him with a mixture of tenderness and repugnance.*

JUDITH. John, someone should cut out this man's tongue.

GUARD. Her name was Judith. She had a body made for love. All night long, without a break . . .

JUDITH *covers the* GUARD's *mouth with her hand. Turns to* JOHN.

JUDITH. And when the soldiers cut out his tongue, make sure that someone puts wax in their ears.

The GUARD *rises again from the bench.*

JUDITH. What's he doing now?

FIRST CANTOR. Oh, I think he's trying to tell us something— Yes. It's a kiss. But what does it mean?

GUARD. What does it mean? It means that I am Judith, the whore!

JUDITH. John, you had better have him killed.

JOACHIM. He shall be killed.

JUDITH, *after a last look at the guard.* Then let the world make way for Judith-the-Saint!

Chorus of CANTORS *from outside. Exit* JUDITH *and* JOACHIM. JOHN *kneels as the curtain falls.*

THIEVES' CARNIVAL

A Play in Four Acts
by

JEAN ANOUILH

English version by
LUCIENNE HILL

Characters

Thieves

PETERBONO
HECTOR
GUSTAVE

LORD EDGARD
LADY HURF

Her nieces

EVA
JULIETTE

DUPONT-DUFORT SENIOR
DUPONT-DUFORT JUNIOR
TOWN CRIER
POLICEMEN
NURSEMAID
A CHILD
MUSICIAN

ACT ONE

The public gardens of a watering-place which saw its heyday in the 1880's. In the middle, a bandstand. The orchestra is represented by a single musician, who at the rise of the curtain is executing a solo of superlative virtuosity on the clarinet. A woman deckchair attendant goes to and fro. The summer visitors stroll up and down to the rhythm of the music. In the foreground EVA *and* HECTOR *are locked in a dramatic screen embrace. The music stops. So does the kiss, from which* HECTOR *emerges, reeling a little. Applause for the musician.*

HECTOR, *covered in confusion.* I say, steady. They're applauding us!

EVA *bursts out laughing.* Of course not, it's the orchestra. I must say you appeal to me enormously.

HECTOR, *instinctively fingering his hair and moustache.* What do you like about me, specially?

EVA. Everything.

She blows him a kiss.

We mustn't stay here, it's too risky. I'll see you tonight at eight in the Phoenix bar. And if you should meet me with my aunt, whatever you do, pretend you don't know me.

HECTOR, *yearningly.* Your little hand, once more.

EVA. Careful. My aunt's old friend Lord Edgard is over there by the bandstand reading his paper. He'll see us.

She holds out her hand, but turns away to watch LORD EDGARD.

HECTOR, *passionately.* I want to inhale the perfume of your hand!

He bends over her hand, and surreptitiously draws a jeweller's eyeglass from his pocket to take a closer look at EVA'S *rings.* EVA *withdraws her hand, unaware of the manœuvre.*

EVA. Till tonight.

She goes.

HECTOR, *weak at the knees.* My beloved . . .

> *He follows her out of sight, then comes downstage again, putting away his eyeglass, and mutters with icy self-possession.*

A good two hundred thousand. And not a flaw in the lot.

> *At this point the* TOWN CRIER *enters with his drum and the crowd gather round to listen.*

TOWN CRIER. Townsmen of Vichy! The Municipality, anxious to preserve the well-being and security of the invalids and bathers, issues a warning for their information and protection! Numerous complaints from visitors have been lodged at the Town Hall and at the main police station, Market Street. A dangerous pack of picklepockets——

> *He has a little trouble with this word, at which the clarinet plays a little accompaniment. The* TOWN CRIER *swings round on him, furious.*

—a dangerous pack of pockpickets——

> *Again the clarinet renders the word in music.*

—is at this very hour within our gates. The local police is on the watch. Members of the Force, in plain clothes and in uniform, are ready to protect our visitors . . .

> *Indeed, even as he speaks policemen are threading their several ways gracefully through the crowd.*

Visitors are nevertheless requested to exercise the greatest possible caution, particularly on the public highway, in public parks and in all other places of public resort. A reward in kind is offered by the Tourist Association to anyone supplying information leading to the apprehension of the felons! Tell your friends!

> *A roll of drums. During the proclamation* HECTOR *has relieved the* TOWN CRIER *of his enormous copper watch and bulging purse. The crowd scatters, and the drum and the harangue are heard again further off.* HECTOR *takes a seat, and the chair attendant approaches.*

CHAIR ATTENDANT. Will you take a ticket, sir, please?

HECTOR, *largely.* Since it's customary . . .

CHAIR ATTENDANT. That'll be five francs, please.

While HECTOR *feels for the money, the attendant steals his wallet, then the huge watch and the purse he has just taken from the* TOWN CRIER.

HECTOR, *seizing the hand on its next trip into his pocket.* Hey! What do you think you're up to?

The attendant struggles to free herself, and loses her wig.

Have you gone crazy?

He lifts his own wig and moustache a trifle.

It's me!

The chair attendant readjusts her wig. It is PETERBONO.

PETERBONO. Sorry, old chap. It's me too. Had a good day?

HECTOR. The purse and a watch, and a cigarette lighter.

PETERBONO.

Examining them.

I know that watch. It's the Town Crier's and it's made of copper. I put it back into his pocket, the poor devil, that and the purse, which you'll find if you check up contains just fifteen cents and the receipt for a registered parcel. As for the lighter, we've already got nine hundred and three, out of which only a couple work. I've known you do better, my lad!

HECTOR. I've a date tonight with a girl who'll be mine before you can say mischief, and who wears over two hundred thousand francs' worth of diamonds on her middle finger.

PETERBONO. We'll look into it. Have you noticed that little thing over there? The necklace?

HECTOR, *examining the girl through the fieldglasses he wears round his neck.* Phew! The stones are enormous!

PETERBONO. No wishful thinking. They're smaller to the naked eye. Still, off we go. Small change manœuvre. I get offensive and you interfere.

They cross to the girl with a terrible affectation of indifference.

Ticket? Ticket?

The girl gives him a coin; PETERBONO *begins to yell.*

I've got no change! I tell you I've got no change! No change, do you hear? No change at all, I keep on telling you!

HECTOR. What's this? No change, eh? Excuse me, mademoiselle, allow me to put this insolent baggage in her place!

There follows a tussle under cover of which HECTOR *investigates the clasp of the girl's necklace.*

THE GIRL, *violently freeing herself.* No, you don't!

HECTOR, *taken aback.* What do you mean, no you don't!

PETERBONO. No you don't what?

THE GIRL, *lifting her wig. It is* GUSTAVE. It's me.

HECTOR, *falling into a chair.* Charming!

PETERBONO, *exploding.* That's what comes of not working to plan! I can't rely on anybody! Running errands, that's all you're fit for! Errand boys! If it weren't for your poor old mother who put you in my charge to learn the business, you'd be out on your ear, the pair of you. Do you hear me? Out on your ear! And without your week's pay in lieu of notice, make no mistake! And complain to the union if you dare! I'll tell them a thing or two, the dance you've led me, both of you!

To GUSTAVE.

You! You haven't done a stroke today, naturally!

GUSTAVE. Yes I have. I've done two. First, there's this magnificent wallet.

PETERBONO. Let's have a look.

He examines it, then searches himself anxiously.

Where did you get this? Who from?

GUSTAVE. I got it in the Boulevard Ravachol off an old gentleman with a long white beard . . .

PETERBONO, *terrible in his anger.* —check trousers, olive-green jacket and deer-stalker cap, am I right, pigeon-brain?

GUSTAVE, *quaking.* Yes, sir. Did you see me?

PETERBONO *sinks into a chair, flattened by this latest blow.*
That was me, idiot, that was me! At this rate we'll be lucky
if we cover our expenses!

GUSTAVE. But I've got something else, Mr. Peterbono, sir.

PETERBONO, *profoundly discouraged.* If it's something else
you stole from me you can imagine my curiosity.

GUSTAVE. It isn't a thing, it's a girl. And she looks rich.

HECTOR, *jumping up.* Good God! Don't say it's the same girl.
A redhead? About twenty-five? Name of Eva?

GUSTAVE. No. Dark hair, about twenty. Name of Juliette.

HECTOR. Oh, that's all right.

PETERBONO. What did you get?

GUSTAVE. Nothing yet. But I helped her fish a kid out of the
Thermes Fountain. We sat in the sun to dry and we got
talking. She told me she liked me.

PETERBONO. Any jewels?

GUSTAVE. One very fine pearl.

PETERBONO. Good. We must look into that. Hector, can you
spare a moment this afternoon, other engagements permit-
ting?

GUSTAVE. No! I'd like to handle this myself.

PETERBONO. What's this? What's this? Handle it yourself,
would you? Well, whatever next?

GUSTAVE. It was me she took a fancy to.

PETERBONO. All the more reason. Hector will swallow her in
one.

GUSTAVE. No, I tell you! Not this one!

PETERBONO, *severely.* Gustave, listen to me. Your mother put
you in my care, and I took you into the firm as assistant
decoy. You're young and you're ambitious. That's fine. I
was ambitious myself when I was your age. But just a minute! In our profession, as in all professions, you have to
work your way up from the bottom. Hector here is the
finest professional seducer I know this side of Monte Carlo.
There's a chap who hits the bull's eye three times out of
four, and take it from me, that's a pretty handsome aver-

age. You don't mean to tell me that you, a mere apprentice, expect to turn out better work than that?

GUSTAVE. To hell with it! I'll get her for myself.

PETERBONO, *tight-lipped.* If you wish to do a job on the side in your spare time there's nothing to stop you. You'll owe me just the sixty-five per cent on what you make, that's all.

HECTOR, *who has been watching a nursemaid during this altercation.* Peter?

PETERBONO. Hector?

HECTOR. That nursemaid over there. See the gold chain?

PETERBONO, *contemptuously.* Pooh! It's probably gilded fuse wire.

HECTOR. Listen, it's ten to seven. We've ten minutes in hand before supper.

PETERBONO. Very well, if you're set on it. We'll give her the "Three Musketeers" Manœuvre.

HECTOR. Three Musketeers Manœuvre?

PETERBONO. It's the classic routine for nursemaids. Number one gets off with her, number two plays ten little pigs with the baby, and number three starts whistling bugle-calls without a break to make her senses reel.

They go. Enter LADY HURF *and* JULIETTE.

JULIETTE. The little boy was barely five years old. He was only in up to his waist, but he was frightened and he kept falling over. He would have drowned, I'm sure.

LADY HURF. How dreadful! Have you noticed all these little chimney-pot hats everywhere? How absurd they look!

JULIETTE. Fortunately this young man came to the rescue. He was wonderful, and very sweet.

LADY HURF. All children are sweet at five. But at twelve they begin to get silly. That's why I never wanted any.

JULIETTE. I was talking about the young man, Aunt.

LADY HURF. Oh yes, of course. There's another of those grotesque little hats. The young man was very sweet—yes, go on.

JULIETTE. That's all.

LADY HURF. We must invite him to dinner.

JULIETTE. He's gone. I'd never seen him before.

LADY HURF. Good. One always knows far too many people. Besides, I can't stand stories about drowning. Your poor uncle swam like a lump of lead. He drowned himself seven times, I could have hit him. Ah, there's Edgard. Edgard, have you seen Eva?

LORD EDGARD, *appearing from behind his paper*. How are you, my dear?

LADY HURF. I asked if you'd seen Eva.

LORD EDGARD. Eva? No, I haven't. That's very odd. Now what can I have done with her? Perhaps she's at the Baths.

LADY HURF. At seven o'clock at night? Don't be silly.

JULIETTE. Shall we try the Phoenix bar? She often goes there.

LADY HURF. Edgard, don't stir from this spot for any reason whatsoever.

LORD EDGARD. Very good, my dear.

LADY HURF, *going*. But of course if you see her, run after her.

LORD EDGARD. Very good, my dear.

LADY HURF. Or better still, don't; you'd only lose her—just come and tell us which way she went.

LORD EDGARD. Very good, my dear.

LADY HURF. On second thoughts, no. You'd never manage to find us. Send one attendant after her, another attendant to let us know, and put a third in your place to tell us where you've gone so we can pick you up on the way home if we should happen to be passing.

LORD EDGARD. Very good, my dear.

He retires stunned behind his paper. Exit LADY HURF *with* JULIETTE. *Enter the* DUPONT-DUFORTS, *father and son, accompanied by the little jig on the clarinet, which is their signature tune.*

DUPONT-DUFORT SENIOR. Let's follow. We'll meet them casually on the promenade, and try to tempt them to a cocktail. Didier, I don't know what's come over you. You, a hardworking, conscientious lad, brimful of initiative, and look at you. You're not paying an atom of attention to young Juliette.

DUPONT-DUFORT JUNIOR. She snubs me.

DUPONT-DUFORT SENIOR. What does that matter? To begin with, you aren't just anybody. You are Dupont-Dufort junior. Her aunt thinks a great deal of you. She's prepared to make any investment on your recommendation.

DUPONT-DUFORT JUNIOR. That ought to be enough for us.

DUPONT-DUFORT SENIOR. Son, in matters of money there's no such thing as enough. I'd far and away prefer you to pull off this marriage. Nothing short of that will put our bank fairly and squarely on its feet again. So let me see a bit of charm, a little fascination.

DUPONT-DUFORT JUNIOR. Yes, Dad.

DUPONT-DUFORT SENIOR. We couldn't wish for more propitious circumstances. They're bored to tears, and there's nobody here in the least presentable. So let's make ourselves agreeable, superlatively agreeable.

DUPONT-DUFORT JUNIOR. Yes, Dad.

Exeunt the DUPONT-DUFORTS. LORD EDGARD, *who has heard every word, looks over his* Times *to watch them go.* PETER-BONO, HECTOR *and* GUSTAVE *come in dressed as soldiers as the* MUSICIAN *begins his second number. The* POLICEMEN *enter at the same time from the other side. They all perform a flirtatious little ballet round the* NURSEMAID, *the manœuvres of the* POLICEMEN *seriously impeding those of the three thieves. The* NURSEMAID *finally goes; the* POLICEMEN, *twirling their white batons behind their backs, make gallant attempts to hinder her departure. During the ballet* LADY HURF *returns alone and goes to sit beside* LORD EDGARD. *The music stops at the exit of the* POLICE-MEN *and the* NURSEMAID.

PETERBONO, *thwarted.* Lads, that's the first time I've ever known the Three Musketeers Manœuvre to miscarry.

LADY HURF, *to* LORD EDGARD. Well, Edgard my dear, and what have you done with yourself today?

LORD EDGARD, *surprised and embarrassed as always at* LADY HURF's *customary abruptness*. I—er—I read *The Times*.

LADY HURF, *sternly*. The same as yesterday?

LORD EDGARD, *ingenuously*. Not the same copy as yesterday.

HECTOR, *who has been watching the scene, gives a whistle of admiration*. See those pearls?

PETERBONO. Four millions!

HECTOR. How about it? What's it to be? Russian princes?

PETERBONO. No. She knows her onions by the look of her. Ruined Spanish noblemen.

GUSTAVE. That's bright of you. Whenever you masquerade as Spaniards you're rigged out like a couple of rats.

PETERBONO. Quiet, shaver! You're speaking of a trade you know nothing about.

GUSTAVE. Well, anyway, if you think I'm dressing up as your ecclesiastical secretary like the last time, it's no go. I'm not wearing a cassock in this heat.

PETERBONO. Gustave, you're trying my patience! Come along, home! Hector and I will be Spanish Grandees, and you'll put on that cassock, heat or no heat.

The unwilling GUSTAVE *is borne away, to the accompaniment of a little jig on the clarinet*.

LADY HURF, *who has been deep in thought*. Edgard, the situation is grave . . .

LORD EDGARD. I know. According to *The Times*, the Empire . . .

LADY HURF. No, no, here.

LORD EDGARD, *looking round him anxiously*. Here?

LADY HURF. Listen to me. We have two tender creatures in our care. Intrigues are fermenting—marriages are brewing. Personally I can't keep track of them—it gives me the vertigo. Who is to uncover them, Edgard, who is to supervise them?

LORD EDGARD. Who?

LADY HURF. Juliette is a scatterbrain. Eva is a scatterbrain. As for me, I haven't a notion what's going on and the mere idea of it bores me to extinction. Besides, I've no more commonsense than those two senseless girls. That leaves you in the midst of these three scatterbrains.

LORD EDGARD. That leaves me.

LADY HURF. Which is another way of saying nobody. I am perplexed, excessively perplexed. Anything may happen in this watering-place. Intrigues spring up under one's very feet like so much jungle vegetation. Should we do better to leave Vichy, I wonder? Ought we perhaps to bury ourselves in some rustic backwater? Edgard, for heaven's sake say something! You are the guardian of these two young things, aren't you?

LORD EDGARD. We might ask Dupont-Dufort his advice. He seems to be a man of character.

LADY HURF. A deal too much character. What a ninny you are. He's the last man from whom we want advice. The Dupont-Duforts are after our money.

LORD EDGARD. But they're rich.

LADY HURF. Exactly. That's what worries me. They're after a lot of money. An investment or a marriage settlement. Our two little ones with their millions are exceptionally tempting morsels.

LORD EDGARD. Could we not telegraph to England?

LADY HURF. What for?

LORD EDGARD. Scotland Yard might send us a detective.

LADY HURF. That would be a great help, I must say! They're crooked as corkscrews, the lot of them!

LORD EDGARD. The problem, then, is in effect insoluble.

LADY HURF. Edgard, you simply must bestir yourself. Our fate, the girls' and mine, is in your hands.

LORD EDGARD *looks at his hands, very worried*. I don't know that I am very well equipped.

LADY HURF, *sternly*. Edgard, do you call yourself a man? And a gentleman?

LORD EDGARD. Yes.

LADY HURF. Then make a decision!

LORD EDGARD, *firmly*. Very well! I shall nevertheless summon
a detective from Scotland Yard, with a special proviso that
I want him honest.

LADY HURF. Over my dead body! If he's honest, he'll philander
with the kitchen-maids and he won't wash. It will be insufferable. And yet I don't know why I should be telling
you all this. What do I want with absolute security? I'm
as bored as a piece of old carpet!

LORD EDGARD. Oh, my dear . . . !

LADY HURF. That's all I am, a piece of old carpet.

LORD EDGARD. You, who were once so beautiful.

LADY HURF. Yes, in the nineteen-hundreds. Oh, I could scream
with rage! I want to enjoy my last few years—I want to
laugh a little. Sixty years I've spent deluded into thinking
life a serious business. That's sixty years too long. I am in
the mood, Edgard, for a gigantic piece of folly.

LORD EDGARD. Nothing dangerous, I hope?

LADY HURF. I don't know. I'll see what occurs to me.

She leans towards him.

I think I should like to massacre the Dupont-Duforts.

*In they come, accompanied by their particular little tune,
with* EVA *and* JULIETTE.

DUPONT-DUFORT SENIOR. How are you today, milady?

DUPONT-DUFORT JUNIOR. Milady.

DUPONT-DUFORT SENIOR. Ah, dear Lord Edgard.

LORD EDGARD, *drawing him aside*. Take the greatest possible
care.

DUPONT-DUFORT SENIOR. But why, milord?

LORD EDGARD. Hush! I can't tell you. But take care. Leave
Vichy.

DUPONT-DUFORT JUNIOR. We ran into these ladies on the
promenade.

EVA. Vichy's an impossible place. Nothing to do, nowhere to
go, and all the men are hideous.

DUPONT-DUFORT JUNIOR. Oh, how true! Quite, quite hideous,
all of them!

DUPONT-DUFORT SENIOR. All of them!

Aside to his son.

Excellent thing for us.

EVA. I have an engagement tonight, Aunt. I shall be late for dinner—if I'm back at all.

DUPONT-DUFORT SENIOR, *aside to his son.* With you?

DUPONT-DUFORT JUNIOR. No.

JULIETTE. Eva, I haven't told you. I rescued a little boy who fell into the Thermes Fountain, and I met an enchanting young man, who helped me to save him.

LADY HURF. Juliette talks of nothing else.

The DUPONT-DUFORTS *look at each other anxiously.*

DUPONT-DUFORT SENIOR. Wasn't that you?

DUPONT-DUFORT JUNIOR. No.

JULIETTE. We sat in the sun till we were dry, and chatted. You've no idea how pleasant he was! He's slight, with dark hair and—he's not the same as yours by any chance?

EVA. No. Mine's tall, with red hair.

JULIETTE. Thank goodness!

DUPONT-DUFORT SENIOR *whispers.* Sonny, you have absolutely *got* to sparkle.

Raising his voice.

Didier, dear boy, have you been to the swimming-pool with these ladies yet? You must give them a demonstration of your impeccable crawl. You could have rescued the toddler with the greatest of ease.

JULIETTE. Oh, the crawl would have been quite useless. The Thermes Fountain is only eighteen inches deep.

Towards the end of this scene, PETERBONO, *as a very noble —all too noble—old Spanish gentleman,* HECTOR *as a Grandee, an equally spectacular achievement, and* GUS-TAVE, *their ecclesiastical secretary, come in and slowly approach the others.*

PETERBONO. Careful. This is big game. Stay close, and take no risks.

HECTOR. Your monocle.

PETERBONO. The big act, "Noblesse oblige." Wait for the word go. Gustave, two paces behind.

The clarinet strikes up a march, heroic and ultra-Spanish. Suddenly, LADY HURF, *who has been watching this curious trio, runs to them and throws her arms round* PETERBONO's *neck.*

LADY HURF. Why, if it isn't that dear dear Duke of Miraflores!
Music stops.

PETERBONO, *surprised and uneasy.* Uh?

LADY HURF. Don't say you've forgotten! Biarritz 1902. The luncheon parties at Pampeluna! The bull-fights! Lady Hurf.

PETERBONO. Ah . . . ! Lady Hurf. Bull-fights. Lunch. Dear friend.
To the other two.

I must have made up like one of her acquaintances.

LADY HURF. I am so, so happy! I was disintegrating with boredom. But where is the Duchess?

PETERBONO. Dead.
Tremolo from the orchestra.

LADY HURF. Oh, heavens! And your cousin the Count?

PETERBONO. Dead.
Tremolo from the orchestra.

LADY HURF. Oh, heavens! And your friend, the Admiral?

PETERBONO. Also dead.
The orchestra begins a funeral march. PETERBONO *turns to his friends.*

Saved!

LADY HURF. My poor friend. So many funerals.

PETERBONO. Alas! However, may I present my son, Don Hector? And my ecclesiastical secretary, Dom Petrus?

LADY HURF. Lord Edgard, whom you knew years ago. It was he whom you beat each morning at golf, and who was always losing his golf-balls.

PETERBONO. Ha, golf—yes. Dear friend.

LORD EDGARD, *panic-stricken, to* LADY HURF. But, my dear——

LADY HURF, *sternly*. What's the matter? Do you mean to say you don't remember the Duke?

LORD EDGARD. This is insane. Come now, think back——

LADY HURF. Your memory is abominable. Don't say another word or I shall lose my temper. My nieces, Eva and Juliette, who worry me so dreadfully because they're both very marriageable, and their dowries are exceptionally tempting to fortune-hunters.

The DUPONT-DUFORTS *look at each other.*

DUPONT-DUFORT SENIOR. Dignity, lad, dignity.

DUPONT-DUFORT JUNIOR. She can't mean us.

PETERBONO *and* HECTOR *indulge in violent nudging.*

LADY HURF. I am so delighted to have met you again. Vichy is such a dull hole. Tell me, do you remember the Ridottos on the Riviera?

PETERBONO. I should think I do!

DUPONT-DUFORT JUNIOR, *to his father*. We're forgotten.

DUPONT-DUFORT SENIOR. Let's introduce ourselves. Dupont-Dufort, senior.

DUPONT-DUFORT JUNIOR. Junior.

During the introductions, EVA *stares hard at* HECTOR, *who simulates an enormous interest in the conversation.* GUSTAVE *has all but disappeared into his brief-case, and rummages feverishly among his papers to avoid* JULIETTE'S *gaze, which is fixed on him in puzzled interest.*

LADY HURF. You must be as bored as I am. It's an undreamed of stroke of fortune, our meeting, don't you think?

PETERBONO, *nudging* HECTOR. Undreamed of.

HECTOR, *nudging* PETERBONO. Yes. Undreamed of—absolutely undreamed of.

In their glee, they go much too far, but no one seems to notice.

LADY HURF. Your son is most charming. Don't you think so, Eva?

EVA. Yes.

PETERBONO. He was the most dashing officer in the entire Spanish army—before the revolution.

LADY HURF. Alas! You suffered a great deal?

PETERBONO. A great deal.

LADY HURF. Where are you staying? Not at an hotel?

PETERBONO, *vaguely*. Yes.

LADY HURF. It's out of the question, Edgard! The Duke is staying at an hotel!

LORD EDGARD. But, my dearest, I assure you——

LADY HURF. Be quiet! Dear Duke, you cannot, you simply cannot stay at an hotel. Will you do us the honour of accepting our humble hospitality? Our villa is enormous, and we shall put the west wing entirely at your disposal.

PETERBONO. Certainly, certainly, certainly, certainly——

Stupendous nudging between PETERBONO *and* HECTOR. *The* DUPONT-DUFORTS *exchange crestfallen glances.*

LADY HURF. You may, needless to say, bring your entourage.

She looks enquiringly at GUSTAVE.

Is he looking for something?

PETERBONO. A document, yes. Dom Petrus!

GUSTAVE, *emerging from the brief-case*. Your Grace?

He has put on some dark glasses.

LADY HURF. Has he got bad eyes?

PETERBONO. Oh, very bad. His condition requires a certain amount of care. I couldn't burden you with his presence. Dom Petrus, we shall accept Lady Hurf's generous offer of hospitality. Call at the hotel, will you, and have our luggage sent on. And stay there until further notice. You will collect the mail and come to us each morning for instructions.

GUSTAVE, *furious*. But, your Grace . . .

PETERBONO. Enough!

GUSTAVE. Your Grace——

PETERBONO. Off with you!

> HECTOR *gives* GUSTAVE *a push, and he wanders reluctantly away.*

LADY HURF, *moved.* Just as he used to be! That same commanding tone—the vocal magic of the Miraflores! Your cousin had it too.

PETERBONO. Alas!

LADY HURF. How did he die?

PETERBONO. Er, how he died?

LADY HURF. Yes—I was so fond of him.

PETERBONO. You want me to relate the circumstances of his passing?

LADY HURF. Yes.

PETERBONO *turns to* HECTOR *in his panic.* Well, he died . . .

> HECTOR *mimes a motor accident, but this* PETERBONO *cannot grasp.*

PETERBONO. He died insane.

LADY HURF. Ah, poor fellow! He always was eccentric. But your wife, the dear Duchess?

PETERBONO. Dead.

LADY HURF. Yes, I know. But how?

> HECTOR *touches his heart several times.* PETERBONO *is slow to take the suggestion, but as he has no imagination whatever himself, he gives way.*

PETERBONO. Of love.

LADY HURF, *in confusion.* Oh, I beg your pardon! And your friend the Admiral?

PETERBONO. Ah, now the Admiral . . .

> *He looks at* HECTOR, *who indicates that he has run out of ideas. He again misinterprets the pantomime.*

Drowned. But please excuse me, you are re-opening wounds which time has not yet healed.

LADY HURF. Oh, forgive me, dear friend, forgive me!

> *To the others.*

What breeding! What grandeur in adversity! Don't you think so, Edgard?

LORD EDGARD. My dear, I still insist that——

LADY HURF. Do stop insisting. Can't you see the Duke is suffering?

DUPONT-DUFORT SENIOR, *to his son.* Let us join in the conversation.

DUPONT-DUFORT JUNIOR. What an appalling avalanche of misfortunes!

DUPONT-DUFORT SENIOR. Falling on such venerable heads!

No one listens.

LADY HURF, *in a peal of laughter.* How beautiful Biarritz was in those days. Do you remember the balls?

PETERBONO. Ah, the balls . . .

LADY HURF. And Lina Veri?

PETERBONO. Lina Veri. I can't quite recall . . .

LADY HURF. Come, come. Why, you were intimate! *To the others.* He's aged so much.

PETERBONO. Oh, Lina Veri. Of course. The darling of Italian society.

LADY HURF. No, no, no. She was a dancer.

PETERBONO. Oh yes, but her mother was the darling of Italian society.

LADY HURF, *to the others.* He's wandering a little. He's very tired. My dear Duke, I would like to show you your apartments right away. The villa is close by, at the end of the avenue.

PETERBONO. With pleasure.

GUSTAVE comes running in, this time as his own charming self, but magnificently dressed.

GUSTAVE. Good morning, Father!

PETERBONO, *off his balance.* Little basket! Allow me to present my second son, Don Pedro, whom I'd forgotten to mention.

LADY HURF. Gracious, you have another son? By whom?

PETERBONO, *panicking again.* Ah, that's a long story——

He looks at HECTOR, *who signs to him to go carefully.*

But that one also opens wounds as yet unhealed by time.

LADY HURF. Come along, Edgard.

LORD EDGARD. But, my dear——

LADY HURF. And keep quiet!

They go, HECTOR *paying elaborate attentions to* EVA, *who has continued to stare at him.*

JULIETTE, *to* GUSTAVE. Now will you kindly tell me what is going on?

GUSTAVE. Ssh! I'll explain later.

They go too. The DUPONT-DUFORTS *are left alone.*

DUPONT-DUFORT JUNIOR. Father, they've forgotten us——!

DUPONT-DUFORT SENIOR. All the same, we'll follow. And, Didier, twice the affability. Let's hope these young men are already attached or better still that they aren't interested in women!

They go.

ACT TWO

A drawing-room in LADY HURF's *house. It is evening, after dinner, and* JULIETTE *and* GUSTAVE *are sitting side by side; a little romantic air is heard in the distance.*

JULIETTE. It's nice here. No one is disturbing us tonight.

GUSTAVE. Yes, it is nice.

JULIETTE. For three days now you've been sad. Are you home-sick for Spain?

GUSTAVE. Oh no.

JULIETTE. I'm sorry now I wouldn't work at my Spanish at school. We might have spoken it together. It would have been fun.

GUSTAVE. I only speak a few words myself.

JULIETTE. Do you? That's funny.

GUSTAVE. Yes, it is rather.

A silence.

JULIETTE. It must be amusing to be a prince.

GUSTAVE. Oh, one gets used to it, you know.

A silence.

JULIETTE. Don Pedro, what's the matter? We were much friendlier three days ago.

GUSTAVE. Nothing's the matter.

A pause. LORD EDGARD *crosses the room laden with papers.*

LORD EDGARD, *muttering.* Though I should die in the endeavour, I'll set my mind at rest.

He drops his papers. They jump up to help him but he bars their path.

Don't touch them! Don't touch them!

He picks up the papers himself and goes out muttering.

This momentous discovery, if discovery there be, must be surrounded with the greatest possible precautions.

GUSTAVE. What is he looking for? He's done nothing but ferret about among those old papers since we came here.

JULIETTE. I don't know. He's a little mad. Only he's painstaking as well, you see, so sometimes the results are quite prodigious.

A little girl comes in.

Oh, here's my little friend.

CHILD. Mademoiselle Juliette, I've picked some daisies for you.

JULIETTE. Thank you, darling.

CHILD. They haven't very many petals. Daddy says they aren't the ones that lovers use.

JULIETTE. Never mind.

CHILD. Shall I get some others?

JULIETTE. No. Yes. You're very sweet.

She kisses her.

Run away now.

The CHILD *goes.* JULIETTE *turns to* GUSTAVE, *shamefaced.*

JULIETTE. Do you think it's silly of me?

GUSTAVE. No.

JULIETTE. You said you loved me, Don Pedro, yet for three days now you haven't even looked at me.

GUSTAVE. I do love you, Juliette.

JULIETTE. Then why——?

GUSTAVE. I can't tell you.

JULIETTE. My father wasn't titled, I know, but my aunt is a Lady, and my grandfather was an Honourable.

GUSTAVE. How funny you are. It isn't that.

JULIETTE. Do you think the Duke of Miraflores would consent to my marrying you?

GUSTAVE, *smiling.* I'm sure he would.

JULIETTE. Why do you look so sad then, if you love me and everyone approves?

GUSTAVE. I can't tell you.

JULIETTE. But you do feel, don't you, that our lives might meet and join one day?

GUSTAVE. I would be lying if I told you I felt that.

JULIETTE, *turning away.* That's unkind of you.

GUSTAVE. Careful. Here's your cousin.

JULIETTE. Come into the garden. It's getting dark. I want you to tell me everything.

The music fades as they go. EVA *comes in, followed by* HECTOR, *in a totally different make-up from the one he wore in Act One.*

HECTOR. There, you see, they've left us the place to ourselves.

EVA. But I don't in the least need a place to myself—that's the pity of it—I could adapt myself quite easily to a great crowd around us.

HECTOR. How cruel you are!

EVA. I don't like you. I'm cruel to those I dislike. It's in my nature. But on the other hand, when someone appeals to me, there's hardly anything I wouldn't do for him.

HECTOR, *in despair.* Why, why can I not manage to appeal to you a second time?

EVA. You know perfectly well why. You're not the same now.

HECTOR. What abominable absent-mindedness! This disguise, I tell you, is the fancy of an aristocrat wearied to death of his own personality, a pastime which affords him an escape from his oppressive self. And for this accursed fancy, must I lose my love?

EVA. I remember with delight a young man who spoke to me in the park. Find him for me. I might still think him lovable.

HECTOR. This is ridiculous! Won't you even tell me if I'm getting warm? At least tell me, did I have a beard when I first appealed to you?

EVA. But it wouldn't amuse me if I were to tell you.

HECTOR, *who has turned away to change his make-up, turns back again wearing a completely new face.* It wasn't like this, I suppose?

EVA, *in a burst of laughter.* No, oh no!

HECTOR. Yet you remember my voice, my eyes?

EVA. Yes, but it isn't enough.

HECTOR. I'm the same height as I was. I'm tall, well built— I assure you I am, very well built.

EVA. I only judge by faces.

HECTOR. This is horrible! Horrible! I'll never find the face that pleased you, ever! It wasn't as a woman, by any chance?

EVA. What do you take me for?

HECTOR. Or as a Chinaman?

EVA. You're evidently out of your mind. I'll wait till you're in it again.

She goes to sit further off; he starts to follow her and she turns on him.

No, no, no! For heaven's sake will you stop following me about and changing your beard every five minutes! You're making my head spin.

HECTOR, *stricken.* And to think that idiot Peterbono keeps on swearing it was as a test-pilot!

LORD EDGARD *crosses the room laden with papers.*

LORD EDGARD. This is unthinkable! I must find this letter, from which the truth will spring in such a curious fashion.

He sees HECTOR *in his latest make-up, drops his papers and leaps on him.*

At last! The detective from Scotland Yard.

HECTOR. No sir.

He makes to go.

LORD EDGARD. Excellent! The perfect answer. I specially stipulated secrecy. But don't be afraid, I am Lord Edgard in person. You may disclose your identity.

HECTOR. I tell you I'm not the man you're expecting.

He goes.

LORD EDGARD, *following him.* I see! I see! Perfect! You're keeping word for word to my instructions! I stressed the need for caution!

LADY HURF *enters, holding a magazine.*

LADY HURF. My little Eva is bored, isn't she?

EVA *smiles and says nothing. Unseen by* LADY HURF, HECTOR *comes back in another make-up, which he silently shows* EVA. *She shakes her head and he retires, heavy-hearted.* LADY HURF *puts down her magazine with a sigh.*

My little Eva is as bored as she can be.

EVA, *with a smile.* Yes, Aunt.

LADY HURF. So am I, darling, very bored.

EVA. Only I'm twenty-five, so you see, it's rather sad.

LADY HURF. You'll see how much sadder it can be when you are sixty. For you there's always love. As you may guess, it's several years now since I officially renounced it.

EVA. Oh, love!

LADY HURF. *What* a deep sigh! Since you've been a widow, surely you've had lovers?

EVA. I never had a single one who loved me.

LADY HURF. You want the moon. If your lovers bore you, marry one of them. That will give the others an added fascination.

EVA. Marry? Whom?

LADY HURF. Needless to say these Dupont-Duforts exasperate us both. What about the Spaniards?

EVA. Prince Hector chases after me changing his moustache in the hope of rediscovering the one that first appealed to me.

LADY HURF. Truly appealed to you?

EVA, *smiling.* I don't remember.

LADY HURF. They're curious individuals.

EVA. Why?

LADY HURF. Oh, I don't know. I tell you, I'm an old carcass who doesn't know what to do with herself. I've had everything a woman could reasonably, or even unreasonably, wish for. Money, power, lovers. Now that I'm old, I feel as alone inside my skin as I did as a little girl and they made me face the wall when I'd been naughty. And here's the rub; I know that between that little girl and this old woman, there has been, under the charivari and the noise, nothing but an even greater loneliness.

EVA. I've always thought of you as happy.

LADY HURF. You don't see much, do you? I am playing a part. Only, like everything else I do, I play it well, that's all. Yours now, you play badly, little girl.

She strokes her hair.

Child, child, you will always find yourself pursued by desires with changing beards and never have the courage to tell one of them: stay as you are—I love you. Don't think yourself a martyr now. All women are the same. My little Juliette, though, will come through because she is ro-

mantic. Her simplicity will save her. It's a favour only
granted to few.

EVA. There are some who can love.

LADY HURF. Yes. There are some who love a man. Who kill
him with loving, who kill themselves for him, but they
are seldom heiresses to millions.

She strokes her hair again, with a rueful smile.

Ah, you'll finish up like me, an old woman covered in diamonds who plays at intrigues in an effort to forget that
she has never lived. And yet, I'd like to laugh a little.
Here am I, playing with fire, and the fire won't even burn
my fingers.

EVA. What do you mean, Aunt?

LADY HURF. Shush—here come our marionettes.

PETERBONO *and* HECTOR *appear in the doorway, preceded
by the musician, and followed almost at once by the*
DUPONT-DUFORTS. *They all rush towards the ladies, but
it is the thieves who get there first to kiss their hands.*

Jumps to her feet and utters a sudden cry.

Ah! I have an idea!

PETERBONO, *frightened, to* HECTOR. She scares the life out of
me. Every time she screams like that, I think my beard's
loose.

LADY HURF. Where is Juliette?

EVA. In the garden, with Prince Pedro. They're inseparable.

PETERBONO. Ah, the dear children!

LADY HURF, *calling.* Juliette!

JULIETTE, *coming in with* GUSTAVE. Did you want me, Aunt
Emily?

LADY HURF, *drawing her aside.* Your eyes are red, child. Now
mind, you mustn't be unhappy, or I cut the strings and the
puppets will fall down.

JULIETTE. What do you mean, Aunt?

LADY HURF. If I appear to be talking through my hat, it's

precisely so you won't understand me. Come along, both
of you.

*She takes them by the waist and leads them into the
garden.*

I have an idea to brighten up this evening; I want you to
tell me what you think of it.

They go. The DUPONT-DUFORTS *look at each other.*

DUPONT-DUFORT SENIOR. After them, sonny. And a hundred
times more charm. Remember, it's our future that's at stake.

DUPONT-DUFORT JUNIOR. Yes, Pa.

Left alone, the three thieves can unbend.

HECTOR, *offering* PETERBONO *a box of cigars.* Would you care
for a cigar?

PETERBONO, *helping himself.* I'm savouring them. They're re-
markably good.

HECTOR, *pouring out.* A little brandy?

PETERBONO. Thank you.

They drink.

HECTOR. Another cigar, perhaps?

PETERBONO, *grabbing a fistful without more ado.* You're too
kind. No, no really, you embarrass me.

He feels a slight remorse, and takes the box.

But may I in return press you to a cigar?

HECTOR, *pulling them out of his pockets in handfuls.* Thank
you so much. I'm all right just now.

*There is a moment of beatitude and exquisite refinement.
They spread themselves blissfully on the sofa. Suddenly*
HECTOR *indicates* GUSTAVE, *sitting sad and sombre in his
corner.*

PETERBONO *rises and goes to him.* What's wrong, laddie?
Why so sad? Here you are with a wonderful room, lovely
food, and a pretty little thing to flirt with, you're playing
at princes, and for all that you can manage to be gloomy?

GUSTAVE. I don't want to stay here.

The other two give a start.

PETERBONO. Uh? You want to leave?

GUSTAVE. Yes.

PETERBONO. Leave here?

GUSTAVE. Yes—leave here.

PETERBONO. Hector, the boy's lost his reason.

HECTOR. What do you want to leave for?

GUSTAVE. I'm in love with Juliette.

HECTOR. Well then?

GUSTAVE. Really in love.

HECTOR. Well then?

PETERBONO. Why not? You've never been better off. She takes you for a prince, and rich at that. Go in and win, lad, she's as good as yours.

GUSTAVE. I don't want to take her, for a day, and then be forced to leave her.

PETERBONO. You'll have to leave her one day.

GUSTAVE. And—I'm ashamed of this game I have to play with her. I'd rather go away, now, and never see her again.

HECTOR. He's out of his mind.

PETERBONO. Completely.

GUSTAVE. Look, what are we here for?

PETERBONO. What are we here for? We're working, lad. It's the height of our season.

GUSTAVE. We're here to do a job. Let's do it then and go.

PETERBONO. And the preliminaries? Have you spared a single thought for the preliminaries?

GUSTAVE. They've gone on long enough, your damn preliminaries.

PETERBONO. I ask you, Hector, isn't it painful? Having to listen to an apprentice teaching us our trade!

HECTOR. Of course we'll do a job; that's what we came for, but have you even the first idea what that job's going to be?

GUSTAVE. Strip the drawing-room?

PETERBONO. With carpet-bags, eh? Like raggle-taggle gypsies! The lowness, Hector, the abysmal lowness of this youngster's mind! Understand boy, that we haven't yet decided on the job we're going to do. And if our behaviour strikes you, a novice, as peculiar, tell yourself it's because we're in the process of investigating the possibilities of this—establishment.

GUSTAVE. You're lingering on here for the brandy and cigars, and because Hector still hopes he'll get Eva to remember him. But in actual fact you haven't the smallest inkling what you want to do. I may be an apprentice, but I'll tell you something—that's no way to work.

PETERBONO, *running to* HECTOR. Hector, hold me back!

HECTOR, *still blissfully smoking*. Gustave, don't be difficult. Try to understand.

PETERBONO. Hector, hold me back!

HECTOR. You see, we're wavering . . .

PETERBONO. Hold me back, Hector! Hold me back!

HECTOR *takes his arm to please him*. All right, I've got you.

PETERBONO, *deflated*. Just as well.

HECTOR, *to* GUSTAVE. We're wavering between several possible courses of action . . .

GUSTAVE. Which?

HECTOR. Shall we confide in him, Pete? Is it safe to risk the indiscretion of a youth?

PETERBONO *shrugs*. Oh, confide in him, do. Since we're answerable to him now.

HECTOR. Right. Tell him your idea first, Pete.

PETERBONO. After you, Hector, after you.

HECTOR, *embarrassed*. Aaaaaaah . . . well . . .

GUSTAVE. You haven't thought of a thing!

HECTOR, *in righteous rage*. We haven't thought of a thing?!!! We're wavering between the trick of the dud cheque given in exchange for real jewels on a Saturday, which gives the weekend to make our getaway, or the trick of the good cheque received in exchange for dud jewels under the same conditions. We've also considered giving Lady Hurf some orchids sprayed with ether (taking good care not to smell them ourselves) so as to relieve her of the pearls as soon as she nods off.

PETERBONO, *equally incensed.* Or we might provoke the Dupont-Duforts to a duel! We wound them and then in the commotion we make off with the silver!

GUSTAVE. What if you're the ones to get wounded?

PETERBONO. Impossible!

GUSTAVE. Why?

PETERBONO, *yelling.* I don't know. But it's impossible!

HECTOR. Or again we could make out we'd been robbed and demand a colossal sum for hush-money!

PETERBONO. Pretend we found a pearl in the oysters at dinner, for instance, and swap it for a pearl of Lady Hurf's, or something.

GUSTAVE. There's no "r" in the month.

PETERBONO. I said for instance!

GUSTAVE. In other words you just don't know. Well, I'm going to do the job tonight, and then I'm off.

PETERBONO. Tonight? And why not right away?

GUSTAVE. Yes, why not right away? I want to go away. I want to leave here as soon as possible.

PETERBONO. He'll be the ruin of us! Gustave, think of your poor old mother, who put you in my care!

GUSTAVE. No!

PETERBONO. I'll put my curse on you! Naturally you don't care a rap if I put my curse on you?

GUSTAVE. No.

PETERBONO, *bellowing.* Hector! Hold me back!

He seizes GUSTAVE.

Just another fortnight. We'll do the job all right, but it's nice here, and it isn't so often we're in a nice place . . .

GUSTAVE. No. I'm too unhappy.

He goes.

HECTOR *leaps after him.* After him! We've got to stop him before he starts a scandal.

PETERBONO, *calling after him.* I've got an idea! Suppose we pretended not to know him?

HECTOR shrugs his shoulders and goes out, refusing even to consider such a solution.

Enter LORD EDGARD, preceded by the musician playing a succession of tremolos as if he had intimations of a sudden blow of destiny. He is rummaging in his ever-present pile of papers. All of a sudden he utters a loud cry and falls in a dead faint among his scattered letters. The musician runs for help, emitting isolated notes from his instrument.

JULIETTE *comes in.* Uncle, Uncle, what's the matter?

She props him up on a sofa and feels his hands.

Ice-cold! What's this?

She picks up a letter, reads it, and hurriedly thrusts it into her pocket. Running out.

Aunt Emily! Aunt Emily! Come quickly!

The clarinet in great confusion multiplies his tragic tremolos. Everyone comes rushing in shouting at once.

Stroke!
At his age!
No, he's only fainted.
Stand back—give him air.
Get a doctor!
He's coming round.
He's all right now.
A sudden shock.
Perhaps he found what he was looking for.

The music stops. An enormous silence.

PETERBONO *breathes to* HECTOR *in the silence.* The chance of a lifetime.

HECTOR. Yes. But what do we do about it?

PETERBONO. Well, nothing obviously, but it's still the chance of a lifetime.

LORD EDGARD, *sitting up slowly, says in a toneless voice.* My friends, I have a ghastly piece of news for you. The Duke of Miraflores died in Biarritz in 1904.

Everyone looks at PETERBONO, *who is very ill at ease. An impish little jig on the clarinet.*

PETERBONO. Nonsense!

HECTOR, *aside.* Talk about the chance of a lifetime!

PETERBONO. This is a fine time to be funny! Ease over to the window.

LADY HURF. Edgard, are you out of your mind?

LORD EDGARD. No, I tell you. I've found the notification. I knew I'd find it eventually. Ever since the day——
He searches himself.

Where is it? This is too much! Where is it? I had it a moment ago! Oh, my goodness! It's gone again.

DUPONT-DUFORT SENIOR. Everything is coming to light!

DUPONT-DUFORT JUNIOR. We are saved!

To PETERBONO, *who is imperceptibly edging towards the window.*

Aren't you staying to make sure your host is all right?

PETERBONO. Yes, oh yes!

LADY HURF. Edgard, that's a ridiculous joke to play on the dear duke.

LORD EDGARD. But, my dear, I guarantee——

LADY HURF. Come along, dear Duke, and show him you aren't dead.

PETERBONO, *uneasy.* No, no. I'm not dead.

LORD EDGARD. Yet I found the notification . . .

LADY HURF, *pinching him.* Edgard, you're making a mistake, I'm sure. You must apologize.

LORD EDGARD, *rubbing his arm.* Ouch! Why yes, now that you mention it, I think I must have been confusing him with the Duke of Orleans.

LADY HURF. Of course. Shall we call the incident closed?

PETERBONO, *in great relief.* Completely closed.

LADY HURF. Let's go outside, shall we? I've ordered coffee on the terrace. I want to tell you about my idea.

DUPONT-DUFORT SENIOR, *in step with her*. I think it's a wonderful idea.

LADY HURF, *exasperated*. Wait a minute, my dear man, I haven't told you yet. Listen. They're holding a Thieves' Carnival tonight at the Casino. We're all going to dress up as thieves and go to it.

DUPONT-DUFORT SENIOR *and* JUNIOR *immediately burst out laughing*. He! He! He! How terribly, terribly amusing!

DUPONT-DUFORT SENIOR, *to his son as they go out*. Play up to her, son.

Exit.

PETERBONO, *furious, as he goes out with* HECTOR. I call that in very poor taste, don't you?

JULIETTE *is alone. She stands motionless a moment. The music is heard some way away, playing a romantic theme.* JULIETTE *takes out the fatal letter and reads it.*

JULIETTE. "We regret to announce the sad death of His Serene Highness the Duke of Miraflores y Grandes, Marquis of Priola, Count of Zeste and Galba. The funeral will take place . . ."

She stands in thought a moment.

If his father isn't the Duke of Miraflores—then who can he be? Why has he taken the car out of the garage? Why is he hiding from me?

CHILD, *entering*. Mademoiselle Juliette, I found some. Look, daisies with lots of petals.

JULIETTE. Haven't you gone to bed yet?

CHILD. I was picking daisies for you.

JULIETTE. Thank you, you're an angel.

She kisses her.

His father may be an adventurer, but you see, he loves me. He does love me, doesn't he?

CHILD. Yes, of course he does.

JULIETTE. We don't care, do we, if he's an adventurer, or worse? If you were me, you'd love him, wouldn't you, just the same? Only why does that hard look come into his eyes whenever I ask him about himself? If he has designs on me, and he'd be wise to have, because I'm very rich, he should be very pleasant to me all the time—whereas— do you think he prefers Eva? That would be terrible——

CHILD. I don't know.

JULIETTE. No, of course you don't. Come along, I'll take you home. Are you afraid of the dark?

CHILD. No.

JULIETTE. That's a good girl. Nor am I. There's nothing to be afraid of, you know. Thieves won't hurt you.

They go.

ACT THREE

The same set. The room is dark; a figure is seen moving about with a torch. It is GUSTAVE, *dressed in dark clothes and wearing a cap. He is silently examining the objects in the drawing-room. Suddenly he hears a noise and switches off the torch; a low whistle; two dark figures spring up, two torches flash, and focus on* GUSTAVE.

GUSTAVE. Who's that?

FIGURE. Tonight's the night.

GUSTAVE. Peterbono?

FIGURE. No. We're the new ones.

2ND FIGURE. The new bandits.

GUSTAVE. For God's sake, what's going on?

He draws a revolver.

Hands up!

DUPONT-DUFORT SENIOR, *it is no other.* Ha ha ha! That's good! Where did you get the gun? It's magnificent!

GUSTAVE. Stay where you are or I fire!

DUPONT-DUFORT SENIOR. Come quietly! The game's up.

GUSTAVE. Stay where you are, damn you!

He fires.

DUPONT-DUFORT SENIOR, *blissfully unaware of his danger.* Oh, well done! Bravo!

GUSTAVE. What do you mean, Bravo?

He fires again.

DUPONT-DUFORT JUNIOR. It's a wonderful imitation! Where on earth did you buy those caps?

GUSTAVE. For the last time, stay where you are!

He fires again and shatters a vase, which falls with a terrible clatter.

DUPONT-DUFORT SENIOR. Didier, why do you have to be so clumsy!

DUPONT-DUFORT JUNIOR, *protesting in the dark.* But, Dad, I didn't do it!

DUPONT-DUFORT SENIOR. Well, it can't have been I, can it? I'm in the middle of the room.

DUPONT-DUFORT JUNIOR. But, Dad, so am I!

DUPONT-DUFORT SENIOR, *suddenly anxious.* Well, then, who broke the vase?

LORD EDGARD *enters and switches on the light. He is dressed up as a policeman.* Now, now, what is all this noise? How do you like my helmet?

DUPONT-DUFORT SENIOR, *who has got himself up, along with his son, in a terrifying apache disguise.* Superb, my lord, superb!

Exit LORD EDGARD. DUPONT-DUFORT SENIOR *goes to* GUSTAVE.

My word, I don't think much of your costume. It doesn't come off—it's much too simple. It's the little touches that mean so much. For instance, look, this little scar here.

DUPONT-DUFORT JUNIOR. And the black eye patch.

GUSTAVE. What are you doing dressed up like that?

DUPONT-DUFORT SENIOR. We're going to the Casino.

DUPONT-DUFORT JUNIOR. To the Thieves' Carnival. And so are you.

GUSTAVE. Oh? Oh yes, of course. So am I.

DUPONT-DUFORT SENIOR. Only if I were you, I'd touch up your make-up, my boy. It's a shade too simple. You don't look a bit like a thief.

GUSTAVE. You're quite right. I'll see to it at once.

He turns at the door.

Tell me, is everybody going to the Thieves' Carnival?

DUPONT-DUFORT SENIOR. Of course; everybody.

GUSTAVE. That's fine. See you later.

He goes.

DUPONT-DUFORT SENIOR. Not an ounce of imagination in him, that boy.

DUPONT-DUFORT JUNIOR. If the other two have rigged themselves up as absurdly as that, which they probably have, we're well on the way. The girls will have eyes for nobody but us!

DUPONT-DUFORT SENIOR. Have you seen the latest batch of telegrams?

DUPONT-DUFORT JUNIOR. Yes.

DUPONT-DUFORT SENIOR. If we don't leave this house with a fat settlement, it's the colonies for us, I can tell you. Make yourself irresistible, there's a good boy.

DUPONT-DUFORT JUNIOR. I'm doing my best, Dad.

DUPONT-DUFORT SENIOR. I know you are. You're an honest, conscientious lad, but you mustn't slacken for one moment. The success of this evening's entertainment means a great deal to us. What's more, there's something shady about our rivals which is bound to give rise to a scandal one of these days. It was quite obviously Lady Hurf who made the old duffer keep quiet this afternoon, when he insisted the Duke of Miraflores died in 1904. Keep your eyes open, and be ready for any emergency.

DUPONT-DUFORT JUNIOR. We have got to get rid of these galli-
vanters. It's a matter of life and death.

DUPONT-DUFORT SENIOR. We'll let them dig their own graves,
while we'll be more and more agreeable. Ssh! Here comes
Lady Hurf.

Enter LADY HURF *and* EVA, *as thieves in petticoats. The*
DUPONT-DUFORTS *cough desperately to attract attention.*

LADY HURF, *seeing them.* Oh, breathtaking! Aren't they, Eva?
Breathtaking! Who would have thought they had it in
them! What do you think of our guests, Eva?

EVA. What a spectacular effect! How in the world did you
manage it?

DUPONT-DUFORT SENIOR, *simpering.* We're delighted.

DUPONT-DUFORT JUNIOR. That we delight you.

LADY HURF. They always look as though they're waiting for a
tip.

EVA. Which, in a way, they are.

LADY HURF. The Duke and his sons are being very slow.

EVA. I called out to them as I went by. They can't manage to
dress up as thieves, they said.

LADY HURF, *as she goes.* Go up and fetch them, gentlemen, if
you would be so good, and give them a few wrinkles.

DUPONT-DUFORT SENIOR. Certainly! Certainly!

Aside to his son.

Let us be pleasant.

DUPONT-DUFORT JUNIOR. Very, very pleasant.

They bow themselves out.

Exit.

JULIETTE *crosses furtively.*

EVA. Why, you're not dressed!

JULIETTE. I'm going up now.

EVA. You'll make us late.

JULIETTE. Go on ahead. I'll take the two-seater.

EVA, *unexpectedly.* Are you in love with this boy?

JULIETTE. Why do you ask me?

EVA. Yes indeed, why does one ask people if they're in love, when one can tell at a glance, always.

JULIETTE. Can you tell?

EVA. Yes.

JULIETTE. Well, you're wrong. I'm not in love with anyone.

She turns to go, when EVA *calls her back.*

EVA. Juliette! Why do you look upon me as your enemy?

JULIETTE. You are my enemy.

EVA. No, I love you very much. Sit down.

JULIETTE, *turning on her.* You're in love with him too, that's it, isn't it? You're going to take him away from me, and you want to warn me first so that I won't be hurt too much? Why, you've even agreed on that between you, probably. You have, haven't you? Haven't you? For heaven's sake say something! Why do you smile like that?

EVA. How lucky you are to be in love as much as that.

JULIETTE. You're prettier than I am; you can get any man you want.

EVA. Oh, if I could only bring myself to want one.

JULIETTE. Don't you want him then?

EVA. No, little silly.

JULIETTE. Have you never spoken to him when I wasn't looking?

EVA. Had I ever wanted to I should have found it very difficult. He only has to come near me by accident and you can't take your eyes off us.

JULIETTE. I'm wary. I love him, you see.

EVA. Little gambler!

JULIETTE. You swear you've never set out to attract him?

EVA. I swear.

JULIETTE. Even the day you danced with him twice running?

EVA. The orchestra had struck up a second tango.

JULIETTE. Even the day you went out on the river while the Dupont-Duforts tried to teach me roulette?

EVA. Even then. He looked so sad that I suggested he should row straight back, but we couldn't find you anywhere.

JULIETTE. That day I'm not so sure. He had a strange look in his eyes that evening.

EVA. Because he'd asked me if I thought you cared for him, and I said you were an unpredictable little girl and there was no knowing what went on inside your heart.

JULIETTE. Was that truly why?

A little pause.

All the same, I do think you might have told him something else.

EVA. Are you satisfied now?

JULIETTE. Did you never try to attract him, not even at the beginning, not even the very first day?

EVA. Not even the first day.

JULIETTE. Yes, then, I'm satisfied.

EVA. Why will you never trust me? I feel like an old woman beside you sometimes.

JULIETTE. You're so much better-looking than I am, so much more poised, more feminine.

EVA. Do you think so?

JULIETTE. It surprises me, you know, in spite of what you say. You must admit that he's a good deal more attractive than Hector, and you don't mind *his* attentions.

EVA. Do you think I couldn't have denied myself a mere flirtation, when I could see you were so much in love?

JULIETTE. That's grand of you.

EVA. Oh no. I wish I could have wanted him so much that I'd have sacrificed you without giving you a moment's thought.

JULIETTE. When you chew your pearls, I know there's something wrong.

EVA. Yes, there's something wrong.

JULIETTE. Yet you look so lovely tonight. You'll have all the men around you at the Ball.

EVA. All of them.

JULIETTE. I'm not joking.

EVA. Nor am I. I'll have them all. And yet it's very sad.

JULIETTE. Aren't you happy?

EVA. No.

JULIETTE. Yet it's so easy. You only need to let yourself go. Why, hardly a moment goes by that one isn't unhappy, yet I think that must be what it means, to be happy.

EVA. You've always thought me cleverer, stronger, more beautiful, than you because the men flocked round me. And yet you see, there's only you who is alive, in this house—you're the only one perhaps in Vichy, perhaps in the whole world.

JULIETTE, *smiling, lost in her dream.* Yes, I am alive.

EVA. And untouched, and eager to believe . . .

JULIETTE. To believe everything.

EVA. You've never had, as I have, a man without love in your bed. You haven't even a jewel at your throat, not a ring on your finger. You're wearing nothing but this simple linen dress, and you're twenty years old, and you are in love.

JULIETTE *sits motionless, yielding to the unseen with a faint smile.*

Looking sharply at her.

Juliette, why are you not in thieves' dress like the rest of us?

JULIETTE, *bursting with sudden joy.* Oh, I'm too happy! I haven't the courage to stay beside you who are sad. When I'm a little less happy, I'll think of you, I swear I will! *She kisses her and runs off.*

Ssh!

EVA. All this mystery! What are you trying to say?

Enter LADY HURF *with the* DUPONT-DUFORTS.

LADY HURF. We will make a truly magnificent entrance.

DUPONT-DUFORT SENIOR. The Spanish gentlemen are ready.

LADY HURF. Do they look all right?

DUPONT-DUFORT SENIOR. That's a matter of taste.

DUPONT-DUPORT JUNIOR. Anyway, here they come.

Enter PETERBONO *and* HECTOR. *They have contrived to disguise themselves as absolutely ludicrous comic opera bandits. They are greeted with shrieks of laughter.*

HECTOR. What are they laughing at?

PETERBONO. What do they *think* thieves look like? Don't they ever go to the theatre?

LADY HURF. But, my dear Duke, what are you supposed to be?

PETERBONO. A thief.

HECTOR, *to* EVA. It wasn't like this, I suppose?

EVA. Heavens, no!

PETERBONO, *to* LADY HURF. Don't you like us?

LADY HURF. Enormously!

PETERBONO. Admit there's something wrong.

LADY HURF. My dear friend, one really can't expect a Spanish grandee to make much of a showing as a common thief.

PETERBONO. Well said, eh, Hector?

Enormous nudgings.

LADY HURF. Come along, all of you. The car's waiting. Where is Lord Edgard? Still glued to the mirror I suppose. Edgard!

He appears, still in his own suit, and wearing his police helmet, but he has shaved off his moustache.

LORD EDGARD. Do you think I did well to shave off my moustache?

LADY HURF, *without looking at him.* I don't know! Come along! To the Carnival!

The music immediately strikes up a lively quadrille, which the thieves dance with the ladies, without the DUPONT-DUFORTS *getting a look in. Then follows a piece of extremely vulgar jive, and the* DUPONT-DUFORTS, *making the best of a bad job, finish up by dancing together with tremendous spirit. All the characters dance their way out.*

DUPONT-DUFORT SENIOR, *bringing up the rear with his son.* Things are getting better and better and better.

DUPONT-DUFORT JUNIOR. Let's be as witty as the very devil!

DUPONT-DUFORT SENIOR. And, remember, Didier, twice as nice.

The room remains empty for an instant. A servant comes in to close the windows and turn out the lights. Another moment of silence, and GUSTAVE *appears, and listens. The car is heard driving off. He goes right round the room, examining its contents one by one. All of a sudden he flattens himself against the wall.*

JULIETTE *enters, dressed for a journey.* Here I am.

GUSTAVE. What are you doing here? Why didn't you go with the others?

JULIETTE. I've come to find you.

GUSTAVE. Get out of here, will you?

JULIETTE. Why are you so harsh with me?

GUSTAVE. Go on, get out!

JULIETTE. I'll go, of course, if you don't want me, only I thought you would want me. What's the matter?

GUSTAVE. I've got a headache. I want to stay here.

JULIETTE. Why this yarn, to me?

GUSTAVE. It isn't a yarn. Get out, will you? Go on, quick march!

JULIETTE. But—you've never spoken to me like this!

GUSTAVE. There's a first time for everything.

JULIETTE. What have I done?

GUSTAVE. Nothing in particular. It's too difficult to explain, and anyway you wouldn't understand.

JULIETTE. But, Señor Pedro . . .

GUSTAVE. There isn't any Señor Pedro, for a start. My name is Gustave. And secondly, will you please go away?

JULIETTE. And there was I thinking that you loved me——

GUSTAVE. We all make mistakes, don't we?

JULIETTE. But you used to tell me so.

GUSTAVE. I was lying.

JULIETTE. Oh, no! I don't believe it!

GUSTAVE, *going to her purposefully*. Listen, my little pet, I'm telling you to get out of here, double quick.

JULIETTE. Why?

GUSTAVE. You'll see why later on. In the meantime go up to your room and weep over your lost illusions.

He takes her arm to lead her to the door.

What are you dressed up in this coat for? What kind of a costume is that meant to be?

JULIETTE. Travelling costume.

GUSTAVE. Travelling costume? You're mad.

JULIETTE. Please don't be angry. I came to find you so we could go away. You told me once we'd go away together.

GUSTAVE. I was joking. Anyway, how do you know I mean to go away?

JULIETTE. I know.

GUSTAVE. You look as though you know a lot of things. Come along with me.

JULIETTE. We might meet one of the servants in the passage.

He looks at her.

We'd better not move from here. We'll be quite safe in this room.

GUSTAVE. The Dupont-Duforts must be waiting for you. Go and dress up as a pickpocket like the rest of them.

JULIETTE. Don't pickpockets ever wear travelling clothes?

GUSTAVE. You're not going to travel. You're going to a carnival.

JULIETTE. Once they've stolen thieves go away as a rule. Why won't you let me come with you, since you're going away?

GUSTAVE *seizes her*. You know too much, my girl!

JULIETTE. Oh, please, don't hurt me!

GUSTAVE. Don't be afraid. Just a precaution.

He ties her to a chair, and searches in her handbag.

JULIETTE. Oh, don't rob my bag. There's nothing in it. Anyway, I give it to you.

GUSTAVE. Thank you. All I want is a handkerchief.

JULIETTE. What for?

GUSTAVE. To gag you with.

He finds her handkerchief, which is microscopic.

I ask you, what's the point of a handkerchief that size? Never mind, mine's clean.

JULIETTE. I'm not going to scream—I swear I won't scream—Señor Pedro! Gustave—Gusta . . .

He gags her.

GUSTAVE. There. If you think this a Thieves' Carnival, my lass, you'll have to think again. I'm a real thief, I am. So is Hector, and so is the Duke of Miraflores. Except that those two, they're imbeciles as well. You've built yourself a castle in the air, that's all, and your aunt, who's got bats in her belfry, has built herself a dozen. But let me tell you *I* came to do a job, and I intend to do it.

She struggles.

All right. All right. It's no good trying to soften me. I'm used to girls.

He begins to fill his sacks with the most unlikely objects in the room. After a while he looks at her with misgiving.

It's not too tight, is it?

She shakes her head.

That's a good girl. You see, old girl, I did a bit of billing and cooing, I know, but to be frank I didn't mean a word of it. I had to do it for the job.

She struggles again.

Does that upset you? Yes, I know, it isn't very pretty. But then in every trade there's always a little bit like that which isn't very pretty. Apart from that, I'm an honest sort of chap in my own way. I follow my trade, simply, without frills and fancies. Not like Hector and Peterbono. Peterbono has to be the Duke of Miraflores. One must be honest in one's own particular line. Life's not worth living otherwise.

He takes a furtive look at her.

You sure it's not too tight?

He gives her a smile.

It worries me a bit, playing a trick like that on you, because you know, I lied just now. I am fond of you really.

He goes back to his work.

After all, when God invented thieves He had to deprive them of a thing or two, so He took away from them the esteem of honest folk. When you come to think of it, it's not so terrible. It could have been much worse.

He shrugs, and laughs, without daring to meet her eyes.

In a little while, you'll see, we'll have forgotten all about it.

He goes on collecting objects. She struggles again, and he looks at her.

If there's anything you care for specially, you must tell me. I'll leave it for you, as a souvenir. I mean, I'd *like* to give you a little present.

She looks at him and he stops in embarrassment.

Please, don't look at me like that! You're breaking my heart! Can't you see I've got to do this? So just let me get quietly on with my job.

She moves.

Are you uncomfortable? You're not choking, are you? Look, Juliette, if you swear not to call out, I'll take the gag off. Do you swear?

She nods.

All right then, I trust you.

He removes the handkerchief.

What are you going to say to me, now that you know I'm a real thief?

He sits down, resigned.

JULIETTE, *the moment she is ungagged.* This is absurd! Absolutely absurd! Untie me at once!

GUSTAVE. Oh, no! I'm a good sort, but business is business.

JULIETTE. At least listen to me!

GUSTAVE. What do you want to say?

JULIETTE. You don't imagine I came to find you, wearing my travelling coat, merely in order to sit here like a nincompoop bound and gagged in a chair? Of course I know you're a thief. If you weren't a real thief, I wouldn't have thought you were planning to leave in the middle of the night, would I, seeing you're a guest of my aunt's?

GUSTAVE. What are you talking about?

JULIETTE. I've been telling you over and over again for the last hour. I love you. I saw you take a car out of the garage, I guessed you really were a thief, and that tonight was the night. As I supposed you'd go the moment the job was done, I dressed and got ready to go with you. You don't intend to stay, do you?

GUSTAVE. That's no question to ask a thief.

JULIETTE. Well then, take me with you.

GUSTAVE. But I'm a thief.

JULIETTE, *crying out in exasperation.* I tell you I know you're a thief! There's no need to go on and on about it. I wonder you don't draw attention to yourself. Come along, untie my hands.

GUSTAVE. But, Juliette——

JULIETTE. Untie my hands. They're terribly painful.

GUSTAVE. Do you swear not to run away and raise the alarm?

JULIETTE. Yes, yes, I swear. Oh, how stupid you are!

GUSTAVE. I trust you of course, but I just don't understand. *He unties her. She immediately powders her face, and then gets up with determination.*

JULIETTE. We've wasted at least a quarter of an hour. Make haste. It wouldn't do to get caught now. Have you enough with this lot?

She indicates the sacks with her foot.

GUSTAVE. What are you doing?

JULIETTE. Really, I shall begin to wonder if you're all there soon. Yes, or no, do I appeal to you?

GUSTAVE. Oh yes, but——

JULIETTE. Good. That's the main thing. Now, listen to me. Gustave, if you like me, I love you and I want to be your wife—oh, don't worry, if you're afraid of awkward questions at the Registry Office, we won't get properly married. There. Now then——

She picks up one of the sacks.

Is this all we're taking with us?

GUSTAVE, *snatching the sack from her.* Juliette, no! You don't know what you're doing! You mustn't come with me. What would become of you?

JULIETTE. I'd help you. I'd keep a look-out, and I'd whistle when I saw someone coming. I can whistle beautifully. Listen——

She gives an earsplitting whistle.

GUSTAVE, *terrified.* Ssssh! For heaven's sake!

They listen for a moment.

JULIETTE, *humbly.* I'm sorry. What a fool I am. Take me away. I'll whistle very quietly, I promise you, and then only when it's absolutely necessary.

GUSTAVE. Juliette, this is only a whim. You're playing with me. It's unkind of you.

JULIETTE. Oh no, you mustn't think that! Never think that! I love you.

GUSTAVE. But do you know the dangers of this kind of life?

JULIETTE. Yes. Kiss me.

GUSTAVE. Juliette, it's good-bye to your tranquillity.

JULIETTE. It was on the way to killing me, my tranquillity. Kiss me.

GUSTAVE. But you're happy here, Juliette. You don't know what it means to be on the run, to be afraid. You're used to luxury.

JULIETTE. Why, we're rich! Look at this! If it worries you, we won't steal so long as the police are out looking for me.

GUSTAVE. Thieves aren't wealthy folk. You get precious little for what you sell.

JULIETTE. Well, we'll be poor then. Kiss me.

They join in a long kiss.

Radiantly.

I am so happy. Now, hurry.

She stops.

Why, you haven't taken the little Fragonards. You're mad, my darling, they're the most valuable things in the house.

She runs to take them down.

And the little enamels.

She rummages in the sack.

Leave the candlesticks. They're imitation bronze. You see how useful I am to you. I shall be such a help, you'll see. Kiss me.

GUSTAVE, *taking her in his arms again.* My little robber girl.

They go.

ACT FOUR

In the conservatory, an hour later. The clarinet, which has begun by playing the Carnival theme, takes it up again in a nostalgic manner. The characters wander in in single file, heads hanging, and sit down, vexed and dejected.

LADY HURF. It's positively absurd.

HECTOR. I do think they might have let us in.

LADY HURF. Too absurd. Fancy writing the title of the Carnival in microscopic lettering. Economy is an absolute obsession with the French.

LORD EDGARD. We were turned away in the most humiliating fashion.

EVA. What do you expect, Uncle? I can quite see that our attire alarmed them.

LADY HURF. A Carnival of Leaves! The idiocy of it!! A Carnival of Leaves!

DUPONT-DUFORT SENIOR. What puzzles me is how you could confuse a Carnival of Leaves with a Carnival of Thieves.

LADY HURF. You should have consulted the notices yourself then, my good friend, if your eyesight is so sharp.

DUPONT-DUFORT SENIOR. But dammit . . .

DUPONT-DUFORT JUNIOR. Don't be rash, Dad.

LADY HURF. To begin with, it's thanks to your disguises that our party was shown the door.

PETERBONO. I should definitely have got in, for one. It's a funny thing. They quite thought I was going as a palm tree.

LADY HURF. Of course, but for them we should all have been admitted. What abominable taste! Look at them, will you? They might be a couple of pantomime buccaneers.

DUPONT-DUFORT SENIOR. I should have thought for a Carnival of Thieves . . .

LADY HURF. Leaves! Leaves! Leaves! Are you going to spend the rest of the evening calling it a Carnival of Thieves?

DUPONT-DUFORT JUNIOR. Keep calm, Father.

To LADY HURF.

We are dreadfully sorry.

DUPONT-DUFORT SENIOR, *abjectly*. We'll never do it again.

LADY HURF. A fine time to say so!

LORD EDGARD. Could we not perhaps spend the evening as we are, among ourselves, so as not to waste our efforts altogether?

LADY HURF. Edgard, what an insane idea. Let us go up and change. We'll play yet one more stupefying game of bridge.

She sighs and the guests sigh with her.

LORD EDGARD. If I'd known we were going to play bridge I would have preferred to keep my moustache.

LADY HURF, *distractedly*. So would I!

To PETERBONO, *on her way out*.

My dear Duke, can you forgive me for this wasted evening?

PETERBONO, *nudging* HECTOR. No evening is ever really wasted.

LADY HURF. Another time I'll be more careful when I read the posters, and more discriminating in my choice of company.

She goes with EVA *and* LORD EDGARD.

PETERBONO. Ring. Pearls.

HECTOR. Pocket-book.

PETERBONO. Perfect.

The DUPONT-DUFORTS *find themselves alone.*

DUPONT-DUFORT SENIOR. Things are going badly.

DUPONT-DUFORT JUNIOR. Very badly.

DUPONT-DUFORT SENIOR. These gay dogs are here on the same errand as we are, that's quite obvious, but everything is going their way and nothing is coming ours.

DUPONT-DUFORT JUNIOR, *looking in a mirror.* Yet we achieved a really lovely make-up.

DUPONT-DUFORT SENIOR. Not for a Carnival of Leaves.

DUPONT-DUFORT JUNIOR. Fancy organizing a Carnival of Leaves!

DUPONT-DUFORT SENIOR. Fancy, what's more, reading "Carnival of Thieves" when it's down in black and white on all the posters "Carnival of Leaves." The old goose!

DUPONT-DUFORT JUNIOR, *catching sight of the drawing-room through the open window.* Daddy!

DUPONT-DUFORT SENIOR. What is it?

DUPONT-DUFORT JUNIOR. Look at the wall!

DUPONT-DUFORT SENIOR. What about the wall?

DUPONT-DUFORT JUNIOR. The Fragonards!

DUPONT-DUFORT SENIOR. If you think at a time like this I feel like going into ecstasies over a lot of paintings!

DUPONT-DUFORT JUNIOR. Daddy, the Fragonards aren't on the wall.

He rushes into the room.

DUPONT-DUFORT SENIOR. Well?

DUPONT-DUFORT JUNIOR, *from the room.* Nor are the enamels!
The bronze candlesticks are missing! And the snuff-boxes!
All the drawers are open!

Rushing out again.

Daddy, there's been a burglary!

DUPONT-DUFORT SENIOR. Let's go. They'll think we did it.

DUPONT-DUFORT JUNIOR. Don't be ridiculous! We were at the
Carnival with everybody else! Daddy! There's been a robbery here!

DUPONT-DUFORT SENIOR, *who has been to make sure.* You're
absolutely right. There's been a robbery. But what are you
so pleased about? That won't set our affairs to rights.

DUPONT-DUFORT JUNIOR. Don't you understand? There's been
a robbery while we were at the Casino. Don't you see suspicion can only fall on the one person who made himself
conspicuous by his absence? Now then, who, I ask you,
made himself conspicuous by his absence?

DUPONT-DUFORT SENIOR. Young Pedro?

DUPONT-DUFORT JUNIOR. Of course! Young Pedro.

DUPONT-DUFORT SENIOR. In that case, surely the others would
be his accomplices.

DUPONT-DUFORT JUNIOR. They are his accomplices. They came
with us to allay suspicion, that's quite clear. But now you
may be sure they're gone, or will have before very long.

DUPONT-DUFORT SENIOR. Didier, you're magnificent! You do
my old heart good. Kiss me, son! At last they are un-
masked. They're done for, laddie, and our affairs have
never looked so promising.

DUPONT-DUFORT JUNIOR. We must clinch matters. There's to
be no escape and no denial. We must telephone the police
at once.

He picks up the receiver.

Give me the police please. And hurry!

DUPONT-DUFORT SENIOR, *trundling round the drawing-room
and bellowing.* The Fragonards! The enamels! The candle-

sticks! The snuff-boxes! Two drawers burst open! Magnificent!

DUPONT-DUFORT JUNIOR. Hallo? Is that the police station? This is the Villa des Boyards. A serious robbery has just taken place. Yes, the thieves are still on the premises. You'll catch them red-handed if you hurry. Hurry!

DUPONT-DUFORT SENIOR, *coming back radiant.* Come to your father, laddie!

They embrace.

DUPONT-DUFORT JUNIOR. Let's call the company and confront the rascals! Hey there! Come quickly, everybody!

DUPONT-DUFORT SENIOR. Hey there! Hey!

LORD EDGARD, *entering. He, and likewise the others when they come down, have all changed back into their usual clothes.* What's the matter?

DUPONT-DUFORT JUNIOR. There's been a burglary!

LORD EDGARD. That's no surprise to anybody in these troubled times. Where?

DUPONT-DUFORT JUNIOR. Here!

LORD EDGARD. Here!

DUPONT-DUFORT SENIOR, *breathless with excitement.* Here! Here in this very room!

LORD EDGARD. In the drawing-room? What did they take?

DUPONT-DUFORT SENIOR, *like a street hawker.* Fragonards! Enamels! Snuff-boxes! Candlesticks! Drawers! Come in and see! Come and see!

LORD EDGARD *goes into the room, comes back and staggers into an armchair.*

LORD EDGARD. Terrible! Terrible! I had an idea this would happen.

DUPONT-DUFORT SENIOR ⎱ So had we!
DUPONT-DUFORT JUNIOR ⎰

LORD EDGARD. Do you know who did it?

DUPONT-DUFORT SENIOR. We have an idea!

LORD EDGARD. So have I!

Enter EVA.

My child, we've just been burgled!

EVA. What?

DUPONT-DUFORT SENIOR, *off again.* The Fragonards! The enamels! The candlesticks! The snuff-boxes!

EVA. I'm glad about the candlesticks, they were appalling. But it's a shame about the Fragonards.

HECTOR *enters triumphantly in a new make-up.*

HECTOR. Eva, this time I've got it!

EVA. No.

LORD EDGARD, *leaping on him.* At last! The detective! My dear fellow, you're in the nick of time. A serious robbery has just been committed. We suspect some impostors whom we are entertaining at the moment, owing to a curious fancy of my cousin's. Kindly arrest them at once, my dear fellow.

EVA. What's come over you, Uncle? That's Prince Hector. Hector, do take off that beard.

HECTOR, *modestly, as he reveals himself.* Yes sir, it's me.

LORD EDGARD, *in a sudden rage.* How much longer do you intend to make a fool of me, young man?

HECTOR, *backing imperceptibly towards the door.* But, your lordship, I'm not making a fool of you, really.

LORD EDGARD. I can take a joke, in doubtful taste though it is with a man of my years, but don't repeat it a dozen times a day!

HECTOR, *nearing the door.* But I'm not making a fool . . .

He bumps into the DUPONT-DUFORTS, *who have cut off his retreat.*

DUPONT-DUFORT JUNIOR. Oh no.

DUPONT-DUFORT SENIOR. Of course you're not making a fool of him. Don't go. Everything will be all right.

HECTOR. Look here, what's going on? Am I under suspicion?

EVA. Gentlemen, will you please leave His Highness alone?

HECTOR. I should think so. Why it's absurd, isn't it, Eva?

LADY HURF, *entering with* PETERBONO. What is all this shouting? I've never heard such a commotion!

PETERBONO. We simply can't hear ourselves speak!

LORD EDGARD. It's terrible! There's been a dreadful robbery!
I had my suspicions all along. I told you he died in 1904!
I told you they were all impostors!

DUPONT-DUFORT SENIOR, *at the same time*. The Fragonards!
The enamels! The snuff-boxes! The candlesticks! The
drawers!

LADY HURF. One at a time, please! I don't know what you're
talking about. First of all I must sit down. I'm worn out.
*During the ejaculations of the others, and the silence which
follows,* HECTOR *is desperately indicating to* PETERBONO
that they must be off. PETERBONO *thinks his cuff-links are
undone, his tie crooked or that something is hanging down.
He brushes himself, looks in the mirror, still fails to understand, and finally shrugs his shoulders and gives up.*

Now. Tell me all about it.

PETERBONO, *engagingly*. Splendid idea. Tell us all about it.

LORD EDGARD, *before they stop him*. Didn't I tell you he died
in——

DUPONT-DUFORT SENIOR, *at the same time*. Everything! Everything! The Fragonards! The . . .
They look at each other and stop dead.

EVA. There's been a burglary.

LADY HURF. A burglary?

EVA. Yes. While we were out the enamels were stolen, and
the Fragonards, and believe it or not, the candlesticks.

LADY HURF. Oh good. They were imitation.

LORD EDGARD. I told you so! I told you so!

LADY HURF. One of the servants, I expect. Are they all here?

EVA. I don't know.

DUPONT-DUFORT SENIOR. We must inform the police.

LADY HURF. No.

DUPONT-DUFORT SENIOR. What do you mean, no?

LADY HURF. No, I tell you. I will not have policemen in my
house.

DUPONT-DUFORT JUNIOR. But we've already telephoned, your
ladyship.

LADY HURF. My good sirs, have you completely forgotten your
manners? I beg you to remember that this is my house.
You appear to have abandoned every vestige of constraint
these last few days.

DUPONT-DUFORT JUNIOR. But we——

DUPONT-DUFORT SENIOR. You see, we——

LADY HURF. Eva, ring through at once and tell them not to
come.

DUPONT-DUFORT SENIOR. Too late. They're bound to be on
the way.

All this time PETERBONO *and* HECTOR *have been quietly
edging towards the door. When* LADY HURF *tells* EVA *to call
off the police, they stop, still hopeful. At these last words,
they make a frenzied dash for it.*

Look! They're getting away!

DUPONT-DUFORT JUNIOR. This is too much! We'll save you,
whether you like it or not! Hands up!

DUPONT-DUFORT SENIOR. Hands up!

They cover the thieves with their revolvers.

LADY HURF. Gentlemen, I am mistress in this house! I order
you to put away those firearms!

DUPONT-DUFORT JUNIOR. No!

DUPONT-DUFORT SENIOR. No. You'll thank us for it later on.

LADY HURF. Eva, I'm going to have hysterics! Call the servants! Emile! Here, quickly! Joseph! Help!

Enter police, during her cries.

POLICEMAN. Here we are! Horace, you take the fat one!

*They have seen these two horrible bandits pointing their
guns at the gentry. Without a moment's indecision, they
hurl themselves on the* DUPONT-DUFORTS.

Aha, me beauties! We've got you!

DUPONT-DUFORT SENIOR *and* JUNIOR, *backing away.* But—
but—— We didn't do anything! No, no, not us! Not us!
Quite the reverse! We're the ones who telephoned! This is
preposterous! It's they!

*They collide as they retreat, try to escape the other way
and collide again, in the course of a droll little ballet which
culminates in their capture.*

POLICEMEN, *hoisting them on to their shoulders with the show-
manship of circus acrobats.* Upsadaisy!

To HECTOR.

If you'd like to give us a hand, sir, by taking the trouble
to open the door, sir, it'd be much appreciated.

HECTOR. No trouble. Absolutely no trouble at all.

The POLICEMEN *carry off the* DUPONT-DUFORTS *despite their
agonizing protestations.*

LORD EDGARD, *wildly.* But, my dear . . .

LADY HURF, *sternly.* Edgard! Be quiet.

DUPONT-DUFORT SENIOR, *yelling in vain as he is borne away.*
For God's sake say something! Tell them! Tell them!

DUPONT-DUFORT JUNIOR, *as he whirls past her.* Mademoiselle
Eva!

They have gone, played out by their own little melody.

LADY HURF, *calmly.* There! That's a relief. Three whole weeks
those folks have been here, and I hadn't a notion how to
get rid of them.

LORD EDGARD, *overcome by so many emotions, falls semi-
conscious into an armchair.* When I think I came here to
cure my liver trouble!

LADY HURF. Eva dear, run up and get your uncle his smelling-
salts.

EVA goes. LADY HURF *looks at* PETERBONO, *who ever since
the arrest of the* DUPONT-DUFORTS *has been choking in the
grip of irrepressible hysteria.*

My dear man, save your laughter. I know perfectly well
you are the real thief.

He stops dead. She feels in his pocket.

Give me back my pearls. You haven't been very clever.

PETERBONO. What do you mean?

LADY HURF. Have you a lot of luggage? How long will it take you to pack?

PETERBONO, *piteously*. Not long.

LADY HURF. Then I advise you to make the greatest possible haste upstairs.

PETERBONO. Yes.

Enter HECTOR.

HECTOR, *superbly*. There. The rascals are in good hands, your Ladyship.

PETERBONO *coughs*.

Father dear, are you not feeling well?

LADY HURF. No, he's not feeling at all well. I think you had better both go up to your rooms.

HECTOR. Really, Father? Where's the trouble exactly?

LORD EDGARD, *himself once more*. I told you the Duke of Miraflores died in 1904!

LADY HURF. I knew it long ago, my dear.

HECTOR, *still not understanding* PETERBONO's *desperate dumb-show, says waggishly*. Ha! Ha! Ha! Still the same old joke, eh?

LADY HURF. The duke died in my arms, or near enough. So that I knew quite well whom we were dealing with. Only you see, my poor old Edgard, I was so very, very bored.

HECTOR, *finally going to* PETERBONO. What's the matter, for heaven's sake?

PETERBONO. Idiot! I've been trying to tell you for the last half-hour. The game's up, but she's letting us go free.

HECTOR. Uh? Don't be silly, they've arrested the others.

LADY HURF, *going to them with a smile*. You don't, I'm sure, want to await the visit of the inspector of police, gentle-men.

HECTOR. This is unthinkable! What are we accused of? We were with you the whole evening!

PETERBONO. Don't be canny. Come on.

HECTOR. My dear father, I don't know what you're talking about. Madam, we are here as your guests, and this robbery is no reason to treat us, the Miraflores y Grandes, in this cavalier fashion.

PETERBONO, *unable to suppress a giggle, despite the tragic situation.* Miraflores y Grandes! Oh, my Lord! You're off your head, old chap. Come on.

LADY HURF. Go along, sir, do, as everyone advises you.

HECTOR. I will not tolerate this attitude.

To PETERBONO.

Play up, will you?

EVA, *coming back.* Here are the salts.

HECTOR. I will not tolerate this attitude. Because if you consider our presence undesirable, I laugh to scorn—do you hear, to scorn, your utterly unfounded and insulting allegations. There's someone here, I know, who will think my presence far from undesirable. Eva, Eva my darling, I've found my face at last!

He turns away and rapidly re-creates the appearance he had in the first scene.

PETERBONO. Hector, stop playing about. The police are on their way.

HECTOR, *making up.* Let me alone. We're saved, I tell you!

LADY HURF *sits down dispirited.* Edgard, if this headstrong child falls in love with him again, the situation is absolutely hopeless.

LORD EDGARD. I have not the faintest idea of what is going on. What is he doing? Is this another piece of comicality? He goes very much too far, that boy.

HECTOR, *turning round triumphantly.* Eva beloved! It *was* like this, wasn't it?

A silence. EVA *looks at him. The others hold their breath.*

EVA, *calmly breaking the tension.* Yes, that's how you were. Only I must have looked at you too hastily, I think, because now you don't appeal to me at all.

LADY HURF, *leaping up.* Heaven be praised! Now, off with you! Quickly, off with you!

HECTOR. But, Eva, listen! Eva, I can't believe . . .

PETERBONO, *in a whisper.* Hurry, idiot, hurry! She's taken back the necklace, but I've still got the ring.

They go with great dignity. A gay little tune signals their departure.

LADY HURF, *watching them go with a tender little smile.* Poor old fellow. I let him keep the ring. They stayed here a full fortnight after all, because of me. We haven't any right to make them waste their time. I imagine it's a trade which can't bring in all that much.

LORD EDGARD. What I don't fathom is where the boy comes in.

The two women look at him in sudden anguish.

The boy, the young one, who was so pleasant, you remember?

EVA. Juliette! Where's Juliette?

LADY HURF. Juliette! She didn't come to the Carnival. Isn't she upstairs? Perhaps in the morning-room? Or in the garden?

EVA. I'll run and see. Oh, it's inconceivable.

LORD EDGARD. What is inconceivable? I don't understand, quite.

LADY HURF drops on to the sofa, and plays nervously with her pearls.

Why do you look so tragic? It's all over now, isn't it?

LADY HURF. No, stupid, it is not all over. This boy has carried off Juliette along with the pictures in the drawing-room. How many times did I tell you to bestir yourself and take precautions if we didn't want disaster?

EVA, *coming back.* She's not upstairs. The servants are combing the grounds.

LADY HURF. It's horrible!

LORD EDGARD. Juliette, our little Juliette. Is it possible? Can she have been stolen?

EVA. Yes.

LORD EDGARD. But she's a big girl now. She could have defended herself. Or called for help. The house is overrun with staff.

LADY HURF. Can't you understand? She's in his power! He's bewitched her. He'll make her steal for him, or walk the streets!

LORD EDGARD. The streets.

It dawns on him.

The Streets!

He staggers under the blow. The clarinet plays an air heavy with tragedy. The three of them lapse into pensive and painful silence. The clarinet resumes its tragic theme with an overtone of mockery, and then leads into the romance which is indeed altogether fitting at this moment, for GUSTAVE *enters on tiptoe, laden with so many things that he cannot see where he is going. He is carrying* JULIETTE, *who is asleep, and his various sacks. He crosses the drawing-room, unseen by anybody; suddenly he bumps into an armchair. He drops his sacks with a clatter, and startles the others, who see him and cry out.*

He's killed her!

GUSTAVE, *terrified, makes to put* JULIETTE *down on the sofa, but at the cries she wakens and clings to him.*

JULIETTE. No, no, no! Why did you bring me back? No, he's not to go! If he goes I'm going with him!

LADY HURF. Juliette!

LORD EDGARD. My child.

JULIETTE, *screaming through a flood of tears.* Yes, you despise him, I know, but I love him. Don't try to tell me anything —I want to go with him because I love him. Don't say a word, I'd only hate you for it. Gustave, Gustave, why did you bring me back?

He struggles and tries to run away but she clutches him.

No. Stay here, or let me come with you. Why did you bring me back? Was I too stupid for you? Too naïve? Is it

because I fell asleep beside you in the car that you don't
want me? It's true one doesn't as a rule doze off the night
of one's elopement, but I was tired, my darling. I'm not
used to staying up so late.

She hides her head in his arms.

LORD EDGARD. What is she saying?

LADY HURF, *moved.* Do be quiet! It's very lovely what she is
saying.

JULIETTE, *turning to them like a little fury, without letting
go of* GUSTAVE. No, no, I'm not ashamed! I'm not ashamed!
You can say anything you like, I'll never be ashamed! I
love him. I want him for my lover, since you will never let
him be my husband. Look. I'm going to kiss him now in
front of you.

*She throws her arms round his neck. He holds back for a
second, then as he sees her tousled hair and her radiant
tear-stained face, he too forgets the others.*

GUSTAVE. I love you, Juliette.

JULIETTE. You see, we're kissing here, in front of them.

They kiss.

LORD EDGARD, *adjusting his pince-nez.* Why, they're kissing.

LADY HURF. That's right. They're kissing. What about it? Did
you never do as much?

She contemplates them, entranced.

How enchanting they are!

LORD EDGARD. Aren't they? Do you remember, Emily?

LADY HURF. They make a delightful couple, don't they?

LORD EDGARD, *lost in his memories.* Delightful. Do you remember? The Crystal Palace?

LADY HURF. She's nearly as tall as he is. He is adorable. Look
at the breeding in that profile. The exquisite shyness and
yet the strength of it. He will make a fairy-tale husband
for our terrible, gentle little Juliette.

She stops.

Edgard, what are you talking me into? He's a thief!

LORD EDGARD, *smiling.* Ah yes, a thief.

LADY HURF. Well then, it's out of the question. He must go at once.

The clarinet stops from shock.

LORD EDGARD, *crestfallen.* But—but they love each other.

LADY HURF. I know they love each other. But it's the only thing to do. Absolutely the only thing. She simply cannot marry a boy who has neither a father nor a mother.

LORD EDGARD. Ah!

He thinks furiously for a moment, then cries suddenly.

Wait a minute! Wait a minute!

GUSTAVE *and* JULIETTE, *startled by his cry, come out of their embrace.* LORD EDGARD *runs out like one demented.*

LADY HURF. Where do you suppose he's going?

JULIETTE. I'll never leave him, never, never, never.

GUSTAVE, *holding her to him, says by way of explanation.* We love each other.

The clarinet plays a little supplication.

LADY HURF. I gather so. But there it is. You're nothing but a nobody, if not worse. I'm afraid you'll have to go.

Another entreaty from the clarinet.

JULIETTE. If he goes I go with him.

LADY HURF. This time we will be here to stop you.

The clarinet screams in heart-rending imploration. LADY HURF *turns furiously on the musician.*

As for you, my good sir, you're beginning to get on my nerves! Go away!

The clarinet attempts a musical protest.

Get out of here this instant!

She drives him out. Pathetically the musician goes, expressing his despair on his instrument. LORD EDGARD *returns like a meteor, carrying ribbons, medals and a photograph. He marches threateningly over to* GUSTAVE.

LORD EDGARD. You are twenty years old, are you not?

GUSTAVE. Yes.

LORD EDGARD. Right.

He looks at the photograph, looks at it a second time, backs, screwing up his eyes in the manner of a painter scrutinizing a picture.

Hold your head up. Fine. Open your shirt. Fine. Now for the mark behind the ear.

He turns back his ear.

Fine.

He shows him the medal.

Do you recognize this medal?

GUSTAVE. No.

LORD EDGARD, *throwing it away*. Never mind. You are my son! My son who was stolen from me at a tender age.

He falls into his arms.

LADY HURF. Edgard, have you taken leave of your senses?

GUSTAVE, *furiously*. Let me go, sir. I don't know what you're talking about.

To JULIETTE.

What's the matter with him?

LORD EDGARD, *to* LADY HURF. Do you deny that a son was stolen from me at a tender age?

To GUSTAVE.

Do you deny that you are uncertain of your paternal origins? Yes, yes, you are my son, my own son, my beloved son!

He falls on his neck again.

JULIETTE. Isn't that lucky! Gustave, isn't that lucky!

GUSTAVE, *freeing himself roughly*. No, it won't work.

LORD EDGARD. What won't work?

GUSTAVE. I'm quite sure I'm not your son.

LORD EDGARD. So I shall have waited twenty years for Heaven to give me back my child, and now when Heaven at last sees fit to give him back to me, it is this very child who refuses to acknowledge his own father!

GUSTAVE. No. It's all a scheme because you can see your little girl is in love with me, but I'm sorry, I can't accept.

LADY HURF. That's very honourable of him.

LORD EDGARD. This is horrible! Horrible! My son denies me!

He prances with rage.

GUSTAVE. No, I can't accept. It's nice of you to do it, very nice of you. But I can't. I'm not one of your sort.

LADY HURF. It is really unfortunate that this boy should be the only one amongst us to suffer from class-consciousness.

LORD EDGARD. I am abominably humiliated. Such contempt from my own son! I shall crumple up with sorrow.

He does in fact crumple up with sorrow on the nearest sofa.

Here I am, crumpled up. How much longer do I have to stay crumpled?

LADY HURF. Couldn't you see your way to accepting? You're making your father very unhappy.

GUSTAVE. How can I! I haven't any reason——

JULIETTE. Oh, but you have! Come into the garden as you did before. I'm going to explain all your reasons to you. Do come, please. Come anyway. You haven't anything to lose after all, by coming into the garden.

She drags him out.

LADY HURF, *as soon as they're gone.* Edgard, it's not true! You never had a son stolen from you at a tender age!

LORD EDGARD. No, it isn't true. It's a picture I cut out of a magazine.

LADY HURF. So you've acted like an imbecile for over fifty years and yet you had it in you to think of that all by yourself.

EVA. How happy they are going to be.

LADY HURF, *dreamily.* Yes.

EVA. And I shall continue to play the young and charming widow who is always such a great success.

LADY HURF. My poor Eva, faith is a gift, alas, and there's no learning it. It's over, our fine escapade. Here we are alone again, like bobbing corks. It's only for those who have played it with all the zest of youth that the comedy is a success, and only then because they were playing their youth, a thing which succeeds always. They were not even conscious of the comedy.

Enter a bearded gentleman.

BEARDED GENTLEMAN. I am from Scotland Yard.

LORD EDGARD *lets out a roar, leaps on to him and pulls his beard.* Oh no, it won't work this time!

DETECTIVE. Stop it! You're hurting me!

LORD EDGARD, *greatly astonished.* What! Do you mean it's your own?

DETECTIVE. Of course it's my own!

LORD EDGARD. Then you really are the detective I sent for?

DETECTIVE. I've just said so, haven't I?

LORD EDGARD. Well we don't need you any more. The entertainment is over.

DETECTIVE, *blithely.* In that case . . .

He pulls his clarinet out of his pocket—for it is none other than the musician—and strikes up a quick-step which does duty as a finale. The characters come in through all the doors, dancing and exchanging beards.

NOTES

NOTES

GAMBLERS. The first draft of the play was written before Gogol left Russia, that is, before June 1836; he revised the draft in the summer of 1842 for the four-volume edition of his collected works; the play was first performed in February 1843 at the Maly Theatre in Moscow. Two literal translations have been published in English: Constance Garnett's in *The Government Inspector and Other Plays*, 1926, and Alexander Berkman's in *The Gamblers* and *Marriage*, 1927. Mr. Berkman made a few cuts, and, indeed, so much of Gogol's satire is obscure or uninteresting to non-Russians that it seems justifiable, if not downright necessary, to cut even more of it—in fact to cut the play down to that hard bone of farce which underlies the fleshy tissue of local allusions. The changes which automatically result from this process exact from the translator-adaptor some further, non-automatic changes, for, in its new and admittedly attenuated form, the dialogue must at all costs have the pace of farce, the tone of frivolity; hence the presence, in this new version, of many lines that Gogol did not write. He referred to no civil war or higher mystery; could scarcely have brought up liberty, equality, and fraternity; and did not attribute to Hussars a white uniform and giant epaulets. Producers who feel that these inventions are too extravagant can omit them. Some will feel, too, that the tone cannot shuttle between "Much Obliged I'm Sure" on the one hand and "Okay Pal" on the other; however, just such shuttling is familiar to old vaudeville fans, and it is easy to imagine Groucho Marx delivering himself of either phrase.

In the original, Ootesh is called Uteshitelny; a director who felt that the full name was manageable could reinstate it. There is also the possibility of translating the name: it means Mr. Comforting or Reassuring. But such a title suggests *The Pilgrim's Progress* rather than low comedy; it is recorded here only as a hint to the actor: Ootesh is a Soapy Sam. If the form Ootesh seems outlandish, not to say zany, that is the intention.

The first American production of this version, and perhaps of the play in any form, took place under the direction of Eric Bentley at the Herbert Berghof Studio, New York City, in 1955. Further liberties were taken with the text. Some of Ootesh's lines were given to Shonev and Krugel, who otherwise would too often have been left out in the cold. And further "echoing" sequences were included on the lines of:

OOTESH. It's a small world.

SHONEV. Tiny.

KRUGEL. Infinitesimal.

The latest edition of Gogol's plays in Russian is useful even to those who cannot read it, because of its many superb pictures of Russian actors in Gogol parts. This is *Gogol i teatr*, Moscow, 1952.

ITALIAN STRAW HAT was an immediate success at its Paris première in 1851 and, except that Labiche inevitably had to be debunked by the generation immediately junior to his own, may be said to have been a success ever since. A great revival was staged by Gaston Baty at the Comédie Française in 1938 and was reanimated by the same director nine years later. Two very free adaptations of the play were made by the leading English "comedian" of the day, W. S. Gilbert; they were entitled, respectively, *The Wedding March* and *Haste to the Wedding;* and one of the curiosities of cultural history is that Franklin D. Roosevelt played Vézinet (Uncle Bopaddy) in the former while a student at Groton. In the face of all this it is extremely odd that no English text of the play itself has ever been widely available. A translation by Clair Vincent Chesley appeared in the periodical *Poet Lore* in 1917. In 1926 an adaptation by Paul Tulane and Agnes Hamilton James was performed by the American Laboratory Theatre; and in 1936 an adaptation by Orson Welles and Edwin Denby was produced by the Federal Theatre Project. No script at all seems to have survived from the 1926 production, while the 1936 text survives in a single MS copy at the New York Public Library. And so the Hoffmans may feel that they are here presenting their readers with an established classic which is also a brand-new play.

It remains to add a remark on the songs. Obviously they do not correspond to the set "numbers" of musical comedy. They belong to the tradition of a quite different genre, the French *vaudeville*, which again has nothing to do with *vaudeville* in our sense. What should be done about them in an American production is a matter of opinion. Gilbert's adaptations were personal: he naturally inserted songs of the type he made famous. It is reported that musical "numbers" of the familiar American sort were inserted in both the 1926 and 1936 productions. The Hoffmans have stayed close to the French text in order not to change, for our readers, the character and texture of Labiche's method. Producers are recommended to use the André Cadou score, which is made up to a fair extent of French tunes of the mid-nineteenth century; copies may be obtained, complete with the Hoffman lyrics, from Theodore Hoffman, c/o Epstein, Doubleday & Company, New York City. Permission to use it must, however, come from M. Cadou, c/o Eric Bentley, Doubleday & Company.

One last oddity should also be mentioned: the best edition of the play in French is an American textbook, edited by Alexander Y. Kroff and Karl G. Bottke for Appleton-Century-Crofts, Inc., 1952. Most of the facts reported in this note are taken from the admirable introduction.

ONE DAY MORE (1905). In his introduction to Conrad's three plays, published alongside the fictional fragment *The Nature of a Crime* in 1926, John Galsworthy wrote:

"The process of adaptation is, generally, fatal to the achievement of a stage masterpiece; yet in *One Day More* Conrad so nearly achieved a little masterpiece as to show natural aptitude of the highest order.

"He wrote from Capri in May, 1905: 'Another piece of news is that (would you believe it?) the Stage Society wishes to perform *Tomorrow* [as it was then called*] next June. . . . Several men, and amongst them G. B. Shaw, profess themselves very much struck.' They were right to be struck—the little play has a strange and haunting quality. Old Hagberd, Harry, and Bessie are very remarkable creations."

The Stage Society did perform the play, and Max Beerbohm reviewed it enthusiastically in *The Saturday Review*, July 8, 1905: the review is reprinted in *Around Theatres*.

*And as the story is called from which the play is adapted. It first appeared in *Typhoon and Other Stories* in 1903.

Beerbohm's remark "Miss Collier, as the central figure, played admirably in just that minor key which was needed . . ." sent the present editor to the typewriter to write a letter to Miss Constance Collier, now a resident of New York, who replied with characteristic charm (and a very natural error in the first sentence): "I played in the only play Conrad ever wrote. He directed it himself. I had the script with his own markings and corrections until a few years ago, when I lent it to Mr. Burgess Meredith and he unfortunately lost it. I have just returned from Italy where I visited Sir Max Beerbohm." (November 9, 1954)

JUDITH had its première at the Théâtre Pigalle in Paris in 1931. Mr. Savacool's English version—apparently the first one to be made—was performed at Williams College, Massachusetts, in 1954. It is here first published. Mr. Savacool writes: "This is a fable of sex and God. It is written with a smile of tolerance for those creatures of imagination who cannot accept God's indifference to the world He created." Mr. Savacool adds that the best further pointers to the meaning of the play are supplied by two remarks in the play itself. First: "God made little girls to be devoured by monsters, but somehow the little girls find a way of giving themselves to some man" (HOLOFERNES). Second: "Hasn't the sight of a sleeping body next to yours ever made you feel that perhaps murder is the tenderest and most lasting embrace of all?" (JUDITH). The play has been expertly discussed by Bert M-P. Leefmans under the title "Giraudoux's Other Muse" in *The Kenyon Review*, Autumn, 1954.

THIEVES' CARNIVAL, though not performed even in France till the late thirties, had been completed in 1932 when the author, like Büchner when he wrote *Danton's Death*, was in his twenty-second year (though it is his fourth, not his first, play according to the list provided in Marcel Doisy's *Le Théâtre Français Contemporain*). Produced both in Washington, D.C. and in Greenwich Village, it has not yet reached Broadway. Miss Hill's English version was first published in England in 1952, and appears here for the first time in America. There is an unpublished American version by E. G. Marshall and Emy St. Just.

ANCHOR BOOKS

for the permanent library of the serious reader

These ANCHOR BOOKS are available at your bookseller's at prices ranging from 65¢ to $1.25.

A 1 THE CHARTERHOUSE OF PARMA. Stendhal. A novel.

A 2 THE ROMANCE OF TRISTAN AND ISEULT. Bédier.

A 3 AN ESSAY ON MAN. Cassirer. An introduction to the philosophy of human culture.

A 4 THE IDEA OF A THEATER. Fergusson. The art of drama in changing perspective.

A 5 STUDIES IN CLASSIC AMERICAN LITERATURE. D. H. Lawrence. A dispassionate and searching critique.

A 6 TO THE FINLAND STATION. Wilson. A study of the socialist movement and the men and ideas behind it.

A 7 LAFCADIO'S ADVENTURES. Gide. A novel.

A 8 THE SECRET AGENT. Conrad. A great modern novel of espionage in London.

A 9 SOCRATES. Taylor. The best short study of the life and thought of the great philosopher.

A10 MODERN SCIENCE AND MODERN MAN. Conant. A perceptive study of the influence of science on contemporary life.

A11 SHAKESPEARE. Van Doren. A major critic considers Shakespeare's plays and poems.

A12 AMERICAN HUMOR. Rourke. A study of the national character.

A13 THE LIBERAL IMAGINATION. Trilling. Essays on literature and society by one of America's great critics.

A14 THE WANDERER. Alain-Fournier. A novel.

A15 MAN ON HIS NATURE. Sherrington. A revolutionary new theory of human life.

A16 THE LONELY CROWD (abridged). Riesman. One of the best books about American culture ever written.

A17 THREE PHILOSOPHICAL POETS. Santayana. An important examination of three dominant modes of Western philosophy as found in Lucretius, Dante, and Goethe.

A18 LOVING. Green. W. H. Auden calls the author "the best English novelist alive."

A19 THE SEVENTEENTH CENTURY BACKGROUND. Willey. A contribution to the history of ideas.

A20 THE AENEID OF VIRGIL. A new translation by C. Day Lewis.